Closing Children's Homes:
An End to Residential Childcare?
David Cliffe with David Berridge

For my Mum and in memory of my Dad

The National Children's Bureau was established as a registered charity in 1963. Our purpose is to identify and promote the interests of all children and young people and to improve their status in a diverse and multiracial society.

We work closely with professionals and policy makers to improve the lives of all children but especially children under five, those affected by family instability and children with special needs or disabilities.

We collect and disseminate information about children and promote good practice in children's services through research, policy and practice development, publications, seminars, training and an extensive library and information service.

ISBN 0 902 817 80 9

Published by the National Children's Bureau, 8 Wakley Street, London EC1V 7QE. Telephone 071 278 9441

Typeset, printed and bound by Saxon Printing Ltd, Derby.

Contents

List of figures

List of tables

Acknowledgements

Without the help and support of a number of organisations and many individuals, the research which is reported here would not have taken place and this book would not have been produced.

The first people to thank must be the officers of Warwickshire Social Services Department and members of the County Council, who were not only far-sighted enough to open up their childcare services to independent scrutiny but also provided the funding to make the research possible. The Department also made available an office-base in Shire Hall, Warwick and gave us unrestricted access to records and to staff, all of which helped make our research an enjoyable and, hopefully, productive task. We are also very grateful to other staff at Social Services Headquarters in Warwick, and especially to staff in the Research Section, for the welcome and constant support they provided. In addition, thanks must go to all the other staff of the Department who were so generous with the time they gave to the research in interviews and during our survey. Their commitment was tangible in their remarkable response to our survey – over 98 per cent of questionnaires returned, which is much better than we could ever have expected.

Also in Warwickshire we would like to thank 'Angela', 'Becky' and 'Chris' and their carers and social workers. Their honest and detailed personal accounts of being in care in Warwickshire provided us with material which hopefully brings our findings to life.

The project's advisory group consisted of: Tom Kirkbride, Mike Ransom, Tim Smith and Gill Hill of Warwickshire Social Services Department; Jim Fitzgibbon and Glyn Essex of the Education Department; and Roger Bullock of the Dartington Social Research Unit. To all of the members of the group we would like to express our gratitude for the guidance and support provided throughout the three years of the research.

A number of people read early drafts of this book and provided helpful and sometimes very detailed comments and suggestions. We are particularly grateful to: Roger Bullock, Roy Parker, Jane Rowe, Ruth Sinclair and Peter Smith.

Finally, to our colleagues at the National Children's Bureau. Val Ball, Janine Glaser and Sarah Dudley provided secretarial support and typed and retyped the drafts of this book very quickly and accurately. Nicola Hilliard and her colleagues in the Library and Information Service provided not only information but other help too. Anjana Nathwani organised our successful conference at the National Exhibition Centre and Fiona Blakemore patiently and effectively coordinated the production of this book. To all of these and our other unnamed colleagues, thank you for all your support, advice and friendship.

1. Introduction

The early 1990s witnessed a crisis of confidence in residential childcare. This was largely prompted by a series of revelations of malpractice – including the sexual abuse of some children – in residential institutions of various types. There were also recorded instances of major problems of control of young people's behaviour. On the one hand, residents were felt to be beyond control and the residential facility seemed to be offering few boundaries; on the other, inappropriate coercive regimes and techniques of control were found to have been used in specific settings.

One series of events that caused particular public, political and professional outcry was that occurring under the 'Pindown' regime in parts of Staffordshire throughout the 1980s. The report arising from the detailed inquiry undertaken by Allan Levy and Barbara Kahan (1991) revealed an alarming catalogue of inhuman and degrading treatment of children, some as young as nine-years-old. Under a particularly oppressive regime, the liberty of children was restricted by long-term confinement to bedrooms, and a deliberately harsh and negative experience of care was offered in a naive but brutal attempt to encourage children to stay with their families.

The Pindown report, in a way similar to the Cleveland revelations four years earlier, rocked public opinion and dominated media coverage for several days. It played a major part in revealing the degree of maltreatment in Staffordshire and carefully documented its nature. In response to these events and other reported scandals, many quite properly turned the spotlight on residential childcare. Indeed, a number of commentators questioned whether we would be better off without children's homes completely. In this context, the research reported here, undertaken by the National Children's Bureau, was particularly timely. One local authority in England – Warwickshire – had, in 1986, taken the unprecedented and radical step of closing the last of its children's homes. It was thus left with no residential childcare facilities of its own whatsoever.

This book examines the background to these developments in Warwickshire, the reasons for them and their consequences. The headlines in the social work press reported starkly, 'County closes all its children's homes'. Our aim was to investigate the facts behind these headlines. The first step was to identify the key questions which the investigation should address and the second was to find the methods which would help provide the answers. In relation to the changes in childcare policy made by Warwickshire County Council there were two key questions:

- what exactly happened; and
- what were the consequences of the changes?

What happened?

Answering this question required not only getting behind the headlines to identify what was actually involved in the decision to close the children's homes but also necessitated taking a longer-term view. This was so that this final decision could be seen in the context of both the development of childcare placement policies in the County over a long period and national changes in policy on a similar time-scale. The changes since the early 1970s when the Social Services Department was created will be examined particularly closely. Also, the 'starting position' for the newly created Department will be identified, that is, the residential childcare stock it inherited, and the relative use of residential and foster care.

How the County managed to support an unusually large proportion of children in foster care, and the resource implications this had, will also be investigated. The issue of cost was an important element in the national trend towards increased use of foster care. What were the cost implications of the policy changes in Warwickshire? Furthermore, the organisational issues will be important. How was the County able to overcome the deep divide between residential childcare and fieldwork which has been typical of the national picture for the whole of the post-war period? Nationally, the existence of large numbers of unqualified staff has proved to be a restraint on the move away from residential care. These issues must somehow have been resolved in Warwickshire.

What were the consequences of the changes?

The specific focus for this, the second of the two main questions the research addressed, was the effect of the changes on the clients of the Social Services Department and, most particularly, the children and young people concerned.

The first of the consequences we needed to explore was the effect of the changes on placement patterns: where, after the closures, was Warwickshire placing children in care? It was the County's stated aim to find 'family' placements for most children in care. To what extent were they successful and what proportion of children were in 'home on trial' or lodgings placements? Furthermore, given the Department's aim of limiting the use of residential care, what proportion of residential placements was actually being made?

We were not only interested in the County's pattern of placements, however, we were also naturally interested in whether the placements which were made met the needs of the children and young people in care. Did social workers consider that objectives for placements were being met? Were the foster carers sufficiently skilled? Did the location of placements mean that the experience of admission to care or change of placement was as undisruptive to the child as possible; were parental contacts, continuities of schooling and contacts with friends affected by the placements which were made? Moreover, what was the impact on children from minority ethnic groups in Warwickshire?

We also needed to know whether children moved from placement to placement without good reason; how many placements children had in total; and, conversely, whether placements lasted longer than was desirable. In relation to placement endings, we investigated how and why the endings happened – for instance, whether or not they ended in a planned way.

The national context

We now begin by placing these profound changes in the context of long-term national trends in childcare and by exploring the explanations for them.

Changes take place in different authorities at differing speeds, although the movements have been in the same general direction as far as the increasing use of foster care and the decline in residential care are concerned. By the late 1980s Warwickshire had fewer than two per cent of children in care placed residentially, a very low number for the County. At the same time the average for all English authorities was about 20 per cent, which was itself an all time low figure. But in some authorities as many as 40 per cent of children were in residential care; a comparatively high proportion, but historically a low figure all the same.

Childcare practice in Warwickshire has been subject to the same forces and influences as that in other authorities, but what makes the County particularly interesting is that in some ways it has been at the leading edge of childcare placement trends. Twenty or even ten years ago Warwickshire was not in a position to close all of its children's homes, nor was such a possibility a part of even the long-term plans of its social services' managers. But a few years later the changing patterns of provision in the County had reached the point where the policy makers had the opportunity to take such a radical step – and the opportunity was grasped.

The trends we are interested in, however, concern more than just the shift from residential care to foster care. Nationally, the in-care population has changed significantly; for instance it has, on average, become considerably older. Local authority care is also used in different ways, with a trend towards increasing preventative work and shorter periods in care for those children who are admitted, and the Children Act 1989 will encourage moves in this direction. The nature of residential care and foster care have adapted too. Residential establishments have changed in size and, after a period when 'family group homes' were the norm, the move has been to more specialist provisions. The 1970s and 1980s saw foster care increasingly change from providing substitute families towards a provision which was more complementary to children's own families.

The changing roles of residential and foster care

The last four decades, looked at overall, have seen residential care in retreat. In the early nineties the general impression is that the post-war period has seen residential provision for children (and other groups) under constant assault from a series of official inquiries, from child care researchers and from the academic disciplines of psychology and sociology.

Figure 1.1 shows how the number of children in care, in foster placements and in residential placements have changed since the early 1950s. The trends identified in Figure 1.1 fall into three main phases. First, from 1951 to the mid-sixties the number of children fostered increased from about 25,000 to about 32,000 (nearly 30 per cent increase in 14 years). The number of children in

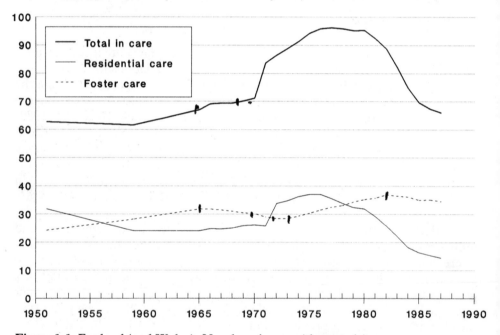

Figure 1.1 England (and Wales): Numbers in care (thousands)

Notes
* Because of the ways in which the data have been presented in official publications, the figures up to 1970 are for England and Wales; since 1971, for England only.
* In 1971 young people in approved schools, on supervision after release from approved schools and in remand homes were deemed to be subject to care orders.

Sources: Department of Health, *Health and Personal Social Services Statistics*, various years.
Department of Health, *Children in the Care of Local Authorities – England*, various years.

residential care fell from 32,000 to about 24,000 (a 25 per cent fall), although this lower figure was not reached until the end of the 1950s. By the mid 1950s the number of children who were fostered exceeded those in residential care for the first time.

The trends in the period from 1965 to the mid 1970s were very different. In 1971, discontinuities were introduced by the change in the statistical base from England plus Wales to England-only and the incorporation into the care system of the approved school population. However, despite these changes, it is clear that the number of children in foster placements fell slightly (by over 3000, approximately 10 per cent) and that there was an underlying increase of over 20 per cent in the number of children in residential care. The fall in foster placements is more surprising when we note that there was also an underlying increase of nearly 20 per cent in the total number of children in care. During this period the number of children in residential care once again overtook the number with foster carers, partly because of changes in the law regarding young offenders but also because of the underlying trends we have identified.

The final period we examine is that since the mid 1970s. The peak for the total number of children in care occurred during the latter half of the seventies, when around 95,000 children in England were in care at any one time. From 1981 this number fell very rapidly, to just 66,000 in 1987 – a fall of over 30 per cent. This rapid change was largely a result of demographic changes – the general population contained over a million fewer 0–17 year-olds in 1987 than in 1980. But the change also resulted, in part, from a lower proportion of children from the total population being in care – an issue we will discuss later on.

How were the different types of placements being used during the period from the mid-seventies onwards? The number of children in residential care fell dramatically, by over 60 per cent, from 37,000 to just over 14,000. On the other hand, the numbers of children in foster care did not fall at all but actually increased from 30,000 to nearly 35,000 (about 15 per cent). In 1987, 20,000 more children were placed with foster carers than were in residential care; that is, at any one time, more than twice as many children were with foster carers than were in residential care.

The fall in the in-care population between 1977 and 1987 is reflected almost totally by the reductions in the residential sector. The average age of the 0–17 population fell during this period and it is likely that this demographic change provides a part of the explanation for the fall in residential numbers, since residential care in the 1980s was mainly used for older children and young people. However, we need to look for other, and probably more significant, factors to provide a complete picture.

To summarise, the post-war period has not seen a slow and steady decline in the use of residential care; nor has there been a corresponding uniform increase in the use of foster care. Residential care numbers fell slightly during the first part of this period, recovered slightly in the middle and then plunged to a post-war low by the late 1980s. The fortunes of foster care were quite different. A steady increase to the mid 1960s was followed by a slight decline, even during a period of increasing numbers in care, in the late 1960s and early 1970s. From then on numbers rose slightly, even though the total number in care fell dramatically. However, it is pertinent to remind ourselves that since the mid-sixties the overall numbers of foster placements have changed remarkably little. Nationally, there were only about 3000 more foster placements in 1987 compared with 1965. In this latter period, the change in the balance of care between the residential and the fostering sectors was facilitated by demographic changes.

In-care rates

Figure 1.2 shows the rate of children in care per 1000 of the 0–17 year-old population. The most striking features are the rapid upturn in the proportion of children in care in the period 1971 to 1980 (from 6.5 to 7.8 per thousand) and even more rapid decline in the 1980s (to 6 per thousand in 1987).

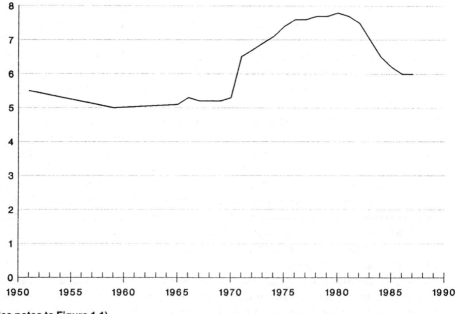

(See notes to Figure 1.1)

Figure 1.2 England (and Wales): In-care rate (per 1000 of 0–17s)

The upturn coincided with the first few years of the newly created, unified social services departments, but it was also associated with what Dingwall and others (1983) described as a 'Growing conservatism about discharge'. Throughout the 1970s there were more children admitted to care each year than were discharged. This period was also associated with a decline in the proportion of children in voluntary care. In Packman's words, 'Departments appear to be taking long-term responsibility for a greater proportion of the children in their care and to be risking rehabilitation rather less frequently' (1981).

The downturn in the rate of children in care, from 1980 onwards, was associated with a reversal in this trend of more admissions to care than discharges. The key to understanding this turnaround was the widespread adoption of 'permanency planning' as a central philosophy by social services departments. Proponents of permanency planning, including Maluccio and others (1980) and Thoburn and others (1986), emphasised the importance of permanent family life for children: if it is not possible for children to live with their own parents, substitute parents should be found and the permanency of this arrangement made clear to all parties – especially the child. The effects of such policies were increased efforts aimed at the rehabilitation of children in care or, for those in long-term care who could not return home, greater use of fostering as an alternative to residential care. Where possible, admissions to care were prevented but this mostly affected voluntary admissions (Parton, 1983).

In Britain and the USA permanency policies were influenced by Rowe and Lambert's seminal research of 1973, which identified that a large number of children in care were drifting with no clear plans for a return home or a move to a permanent placement. These were the 'children who wait'.

The lack of planning for children in care was also one of the main themes running through a series of research projects which reported in the mid 1980s. A summary of this research was produced (DHSS, 1985) and, admirably, considerable effort was put into dissemination. As a result, this programme of research, and its implications for policy and for practice, became more widely discussed in social services departments than much previous research. It has played an important role in the buildup to the Children Act 1989.

There were other key pieces of research which appeared in the 1980s which demonstrated that children admitted to care who remained for more than six weeks were very likely to remain in care for a relatively long period (see Millham and others, 1986; Thorpe and Bilson, 1987). Thorpe and his colleague recommended identifying potential long-stayers so that intensive work could be undertaken with them to bring about moves out of care. Some authorities, such as Leicestershire (see Bunyon and Sinclair, 1987), developed monitoring systems which incorporated this type of analysis.

To summarise, the proportion of children in care rose in the 1970s as authorities increased their use of compulsory admissions to care and maintained children in care for longer periods. In the eighties, tighter planning, largely associated with the 'permanency' movement, meant shorter stays in care, more discharges from care than admissions and a falling rate of children in care. Shorter stays were also associated with budgetary constraints within social services departments, as we will see later.

The 'stock' and 'flow' of childcare placements

To continue to set the context for the examination of Warwickshire's radical policies, Figure 1.3 shows the proportion of children in care who were living with foster carers and those living in residential care on a national scale.

The trend for residential care placements, nationally, was for a fall from over

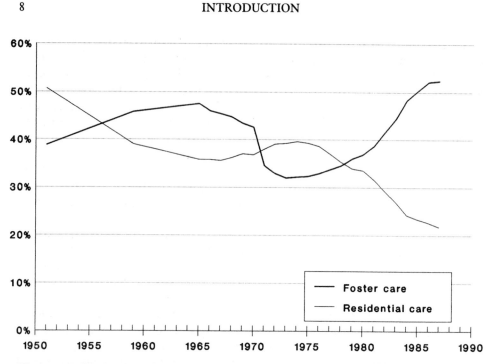

Figure 1.3 England (and Wales): Residential and foster placements (%)

NOTES

* Because of the ways in which the data have been presented in official publications, the figures up to 1970 are for England and Wales; since 1971, for England only.

* In 1971 young people in approved schools, on supervision after release from approved schools and in remand homes were deemed to be subject to care orders.

50 per cent of children in residence in 1951 to about 36 per cent in 1965. This fall then changed to a slightly rising trend for the decade to the mid-seventies, during which period, as we have seen, the actual numbers of children in care rose rapidly. In the period since 1976, the proportion in residential care fell steadily and steeply until, in 1987, a figure of just over 20 per cent was reached. Warwickshire, in comparison, had only *two per cent* of children in residential care in 1987.

Nationally, the proportion of children in foster care (the boarding-out rate) changed in ways which complemented the developments in the use of residential care. As the proportion in residential care fell, the percentage in foster care rose. From 1965 to 1975, however, the boarding-out rate fell sharply from over 47 per cent to 32 per cent. This fall was exaggerated by changes to the law concerning young offenders in 1971, but the underlying trend was still equivalent to a fall of over seven per cent. As we saw earlier, the actual number of foster placements fell slightly, even as the number in care rose. As a result, for much of the 1970s there was a smaller proportion of children in foster care than in residential care.

So far the main conclusions to be drawn are that the proportion of children in care and placed residentially fell from over 50 per cent in 1951 to just over 20 per cent in 1987. However, this fall was not steady. The number of residential placements fell by about a quarter in the 1950s but actually saw an underlying increase in the period between 1960 and 1976. The most dramatic fall in residential numbers took place in the period 1976 to 1987 when placements fell from 36,000 to 14,000, a drop of 60 per cent. This decline was made possible by a rapid fall in the total number of children in care. The changes in the proportion of children in foster placements look equally dramatic: from 25 per cent in 1951 it doubled to 52 per cent in 1987. However, the actual numbers of foster placements grew only slightly, from 32,000 in 1965 to less than 35,000 in 1987 – an increase of less than 10 per cent.

We must beware of drawing too many conclusions from these figures without being aware of what they are actually measuring. The figures are based on returns from social services departments to the Department of Health on 31 March each year. So Figures 1.1 to 1.3 represent trends in an annual census of the placements of children in care: we might call this the childcare *stock*. The disadvantage of this measure is that it presents a *static* picture of a very *dynamic* process. In a typical authority well over half of the children admitted to care will have left within the year. This stock of placements gives no idea of this turnover, nor does it reflect the fact that many of the children in care will move from one placement to another.

Another distortion inherent in this measure, and one which is significant for this research, is exemplified by the fact that a child in long-term care (more than a year) is over 50 times more likely to appear in the census (the stock figure) than a child admitted to care who leaves again within a week. We saw earlier that, partly because of the impact of *Children Who Wait* (Rowe and Lambert, 1973) and the permanency movement, it became increasingly likely that children in long-term care would be placed in 'family' rather than residential placements. Therefore, it might be anticipated that the Department of Health's figures would overestimate the importance of 'family' placements including foster care and 'home on trial', and the use of those types of placement used more often as comparatively short-term resources.

Rowe, Hundleby and Garnett (1989), in their invaluable large-scale study of care placements, addressed this issue. They collected details of nearly 10,000 care placements made in six different local authorities. Figure 1.4 shows the details of placements made in each of these authorities together with the average (mean) results for all six.

The first column in each group shows the figure provided by the Department of Health's annual census, which represents the proportion of all the children in care who were in foster placements on one day of the year – the stock of foster placements. The figures for the six authorities ranged from 48 per cent to 68 per cent, with an overall average of 56 per cent.

The second column in each group, represents what we might call the 'foster placement flow'. So in Authority A, 45 per cent of all the placements made in the year were with foster carers and the average (mean) foster placement flow for the six authorities was 37 per cent.

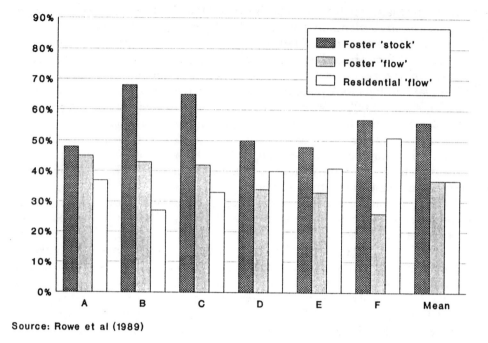

Source: Rowe et al (1989)

Figure 1.4 Placements made by representative English authorities

The third column is the 'residential placement flow', which is measured in the same way as the foster placement flow figures. For Authority A, for example, the 'residential placement flow' stood at 37 per cent. This means that in one year in this authority, over a third of all the placements made were in residential settings. The average 'residential placement flow' figure for the six authorities was also 38 per cent. We will see later that using foster placement flow and residential placement flow measures makes placement practice in War-wickshire even more markedly different from other authorities than might previously have been anticipated.

There are a number of important issues which Figure 1.4 highlights.

● In each of the six authorities the 'foster placement flow' (over the whole of the year) was lower, in most cases considerably lower, than the 'foster placement stock' (measured on the one particular day). High foster placement stock figures were associated with higher than average proportions of children in care placed in long-term foster placements. Rowe commented:

The boarding-out rate...is not a very satisfactory basis for making comparisons between authorities especially if a high boarding out rate is considered meritorious. Well developed preventive services, the use of residential family centres and emphasis on time-limited foster placements instead of long-term fostering can all have the effect of lowering the boarding-out rate. (Rowe and others, 1989, p. 51)

● Measuring placements over a period of time to produce 'flow' figures more accurately reflects the intensity of social work input in childcare work. A child in a long-term foster placement will typically be visited by a social worker much less frequently than a child newly placed, but, as we have seen, it is these long-term placements which are most likely to appear in the 'stock' figures. On the other hand, the placement flow figures pick up both new admissions to care and changes of placement, and will thus reflect the social work tasks of placement finding and support; the preparation of children, parents and carers for the placement; and the intensive work which can go on to minimise the stay of new admissions to care. Over one third of new admissions leave care within six weeks and social work input falls off rapidly if an early return home is not achieved (Millham and others, 1986).

- If we compare the foster placement flow and the residential placement flow for each authority, we are comparing like with like. What we find is surprising. In half the authorities, *more* residential placements than foster placements were actually made – overall, 37 per cent of placements were made with foster carers while 38 per cent were in residential care. This is a very different picture from the one seen earlier in this chapter, which was based on the annual census report provided by the Department of Health. For England in 1987, the proportion of children placed residentially was just over one in five. If Rowe's figures are representative then we are looking at a figure of nearer two in five of all placements being made in residential establishments.
- The final point which Figure 1.4 illustrates clearly is the wide variations in childcare practice in these six authorities. The foster placement stock varied from 48 per cent to 68 per cent, foster placement flows from 26 per cent to 45 per cent, and residential placement flows from 28 per cent to 52 per cent. We will see later how Warwickshire compares, but the important point to note is that these wide variations exist and can only be understood through a close examination of local circumstances, and, if we are interested in trends, in the historical processes in each authority.

Rowe and her colleagues identified that policy factors accounted for some of the differences between their six authorities, but issues such as the different levels of availability of residential places were also important. The way in which local policies develop is a complex process in which local actors (mainly the professionals and politicians) respond both to local circumstances but also to the prevailing national – or even international – orthodoxies.

From residential to foster care

What are the broader reasons for the move away from residential towards foster care? One of the main reasons is the historical legacy. Current childcare institutions have descended from the workhouses of the Poor Law and continue to be stigmatising for that reason. The experience of the workhouse was designed to be deliberately harsh in order to discourage dependence on the Parish. This is one ideological underpinning of current social work services, including residential services, which continues to influence perceptions and practice, implicitly if not explicitly.

A second factor to have affected the shift from residential to foster services is the influence of research. This is despite the fact that our understanding of how childcare services operate and their effects is actually very patchy (Berridge, 1985; Triseliotis, 1988; Parker, 1987). Goffman (1961), every undergraduate sociologist's companion, identified a series of 'ideal types' of institutions and then proceeded to describe their negative consequences for inmates. Barton (1959) also produced a general critique of institutional care based on studies of patients in psychiatric hospitals. Elsewhere in the field of psychiatry the notion of mental illness and the purpose of psychiatric institutions was being questioned. The works of Foucault, Szasz, Laing, Esterson, Cooper and others sold well (whether or not they were actually read), which reflected and strengthened a widespread antipathy towards institutional care. But the most significant contribution was probably the work of Bowlby (1951; 1953), who concluded from his own clinical work and from studies by others that prolonged separation of young children from their mother (or mother-substitute) tended to lead to developmental problems and delinquency. Though Bowlby's ideas have received much subsequent critical comment (for example, Rutter, 1981; Frost and Stein, 1989), his work was certainly favourably received and was of considerable influence on the promotion of substitute family-based rather than residential care.

Another factor which contributed to the unpopularity of residential childcare services was its perceived expense. In whatever way costs are measured, from 1948 to date residential care has consistently cost more than foster care and this differential has been a constant, if infrequently acknowledged, factor in the changing balance of provision. Parker (1966), restricting himself to an examination of direct costs only, identified that in 1953 residential care cost 2.9 times as much as foster care but by 1962 the difference had increased to 3.7 times. Knapp and Fenyo (1989) produced a more sophisticated analysis of costs and showed that the *direct cost* differential in the early 1980s had widened to almost sixfold. However, when *indirect* costs are included (such as fieldworker time, recruitment and training costs) the difference is much less than has previously been thought. Nonetheless, evidence consistently shows that greater cost-consciousness, especially in the 1980s, helped push policy towards greater use of foster care and less residential care.

There are no doubt other explanations for the shift from residential to foster care. These would include the fieldwork/residential divide, and, more controversially, the unionisation of residential work and possibly also the residential workers' strike of the early 1980s. But we feel the above are the major factors.

In order to set the scene for what happened in Warwickshire, this overview of how placement patterns have changed will be completed, not just in terms of numbers but also in terms of the *use* of different types of placement for different groups of children and young people.

Residential care: the changing population

In his 1985 study of children's homes, Berridge demonstrated that most residents in children's homes nowadays are adolescents. Over 70 per cent of the residents in the 20 homes he looked at were aged 12 or over; just eight per cent were under six. In 1984 the Social Services Inspectorate surveyed nearly 150 community homes and found an even higher proportion of adolescent residents: about 80 per cent being 13 or over (DHSS, 1986).

One of the reasons for this ageing of the residential care population is the fact that the proportion of younger children in care has fallen, while the proportion of adolescents in care, especially those aged 16 and over, has increased significantly. Table 1.1 shows this clearly. In 1987 five times as many 16–17 year-olds were in care compared with 0–4 year-olds.

Table 1.1 In-care rates by age

| | In-care rate (per thousand of age group in population) | | |
	0–4	*5–15*	*16–17*
1951	3.5	6	9.7
1973	3.4	7	15.7
1987	3.1	6	16.9

Source: Department of Health, *Children in the Care of Local Authorities* – England and Wales (up to 1971), England (since 1971), various years.

There were other factors which accounted for the increasing average age of children in residential care, but by the mid 1980s it was technically inappropriate to describe these residential institutions as 'children's homes' since most of the residents were in fact adolescents.

The size of residential establishments

The criticisms of the Curtis Committee in 1946 were in part directed at the large size of some of the residential childcare establishments. In 1954, only one in ten children in residential care were in homes with less than 12 children; in 1984, the proportion was one in four. Packman (1975) identified how the larger and more isolated institutions were closed and replaced with a limited range of more specialist provisions plus a much larger group of comparatively small, 'ordinary' children's homes.

Table 1.2 shows how the numbers and proportions of children in different types of residential establishments changed through the 1970s and 1980s. (Note: these are the residential 'stock' figures not the 'flow' figures.)

Table 1.2 Residential care placements

	1972 No.(000s) (%)	1977 No. (000s) (%)	1982 No. (000s) (%)	1987 No. (000s) (%)
Children's homes	15.9 (47)	19.9 (56)	15.1 (58)	8.5 (59)
Community homes with education	6.3 (19)	6 (17)	3.9 (15)	1.8 (12)
Observation and assessment centres	4 (12)	4.7 (13)	4.4 (17)	2.8 (19)
Residential nurseries	2.1 (6)	1.4 (4)	0.3 (1)	– (0)
Voluntary homes	5.5 (16)	3.6 (10)	2.2 (8)	1.3 (9)
Total residential	33.8 (100)	35.6 (100)	25.9 (100)	14.4 (100)

Source: Department of Health, *Health and Personal Social Services Statistics for England*, various years.

Community homes with education (CHEs) along with residential nurseries saw the biggest decline both in absolute numbers and in their share of residential placements. The term observation and assessment (O and A) centres was not in general use until the mid 1970s, so comparisons before then are difficult, but since then they have maintained their share despite probably being the most expensive types of residential childcare provision.

The functions of residential care

Specialist residential provisions have always existed. These have included secure units, approved schools (later CHEs), residential nurseries and O and A centres. The majority of children have, however, been placed in so called 'ordinary' community homes, that is children's homes. With the closure of the larger, isolated units in the 1950s, the trend was towards small, local homes staffed by 'houseparents' plus assistants. The aim was to replicate, as far as possible, family life, but as Fuller and Stevenson (1983) pointed out, this aim could not really be achieved.

There were age restrictions, not all took children under five and few children were allowed to stay beyond school leaving age. The mixture of children ... often emotionally disturbed and frequently clustering in age, did not look like a family.

The failed attempt at 'family group homes' led to a move towards provisions more adequately and professionally staffed, in which the functions of the homes were more clearly identified. In 1985, Berridge identified three broad types of children's homes:

- the small family group homes;
- medium sized adolescents' hostels, essentially for those aged 15 or over, and undertaking more specialist functions such as preparation for leaving care;
- multi-purpose homes, most of which accommodated residents in two or three small groups. Functions included reception units, leaving care units and emergency and short-stay provisions. Staffing reflected these more specialist functions.

The trend towards specialisation of functions in different homes does of course depend on having sufficient establishments to allow specialisation, especially when, as in geographically large county authorities, the aim of providing local facilities is also taken into consideration. We will see later how this was an issue in Warwickshire when the long-term closure programme resulted in only a small number of establishments being left in operation.

Time spent in residential care

With the publication of *Children Who Wait* (Rowe and Lambert, 1973) and the influence of various other factors which we will identify in the next section, the length of time which children typically spent in residential care began to fall. Berridge (1985) identified a group of children in children's homes who had spent a large part of their lives in care and in residential care, but certainly, of the children admitted more recently, the periods of time they spent in the homes were comparatively short. In fact, among the main functions of the homes were short-term receptions into care, preparation for leaving care and preparation of children for foster placements.

Many commentators (Parker, 1980; Barclay, 1982; House of Commons, 1984; King, 1988 and many of those, including the National Association of Young People in Care [NAYPIC] and the British Agencies for Adoption and Fostering [BAAF], who made submissions to the Wagner Inquiry into residential care) have argued that residential care is an essential element in an integrated childcare service and is the element which can most effectively undertake many of these shorter-term, task-centred roles. This was in fact the policy adopted by a number of local authorities in the 1970s and 1980s. (*See* for example Strathclyde Regional Council, 1979). Sir William Utting's review came to a similar conclusion (1991).

We will now examine parallel developments in foster care and see to what extent foster care has taken over certain roles previously carried out by residential care. This will enable us subsequently to make better sense of what happened in Warwickshire.

Foster care: changing functions

The age of children in foster placements

Much of the published information about fostering in the 1980s has focused on what are usually called 'specialist' fostering schemes. According to reports by Shaw and Hipgrave based on surveys of such schemes (1983 and 1989) 'specialist' usually means 'adolescent' and less often applies to children who have a physical or mental handicap. We might assume, on the weight of published information, that large proportions of adolescents in care, as well as children with special needs, are being fostered. This is not the case, certainly as far as adolescents are concerned. Shaw and Hipgrave identified a large number of schemes but those run by most local authorities were relatively small in scale and found placements for only a minority of the children in care. Many of them also focused on finding longer-term placements. Aldgate and her colleagues commenting on specialist fostering schemes, which they called treatment schemes, said:

While treatment foster schemes can be successful, they serve only a minority of the foster adolescent population... Since the time of Shaw and Hipgrave's [1983] review, the rapid expansion [of specialist foster schemes] has slowed down and consolidated. (Aldgate and others, 1989)

Rowe's large scale placement study in the second half of the 1980s enables us to identify the extent to which adolescents were found foster placements. Over three-quarters of the placements for 0–4 year-olds in her study were in foster homes; for the 5–10 age group, it was 65 per cent; but for the 11–17 group only 15 per cent of placements were in foster homes and over a half were residential placements. There were wide variations between the six authorities in Rowe's study. In one authority only one in ten foster placements were made for the over-10s, whereas in another the proportion was closer to four in ten (Rowe and others, 1989).

It was not until the late 1970s that fostering came to be thought of as suitable for more than a very small minority of older children. The general attitude towards fostering adolescents in earlier decades is summed up by Packman:

The committal and reception of a greater number of adolescents – many of them delinquent – produced a demand, not for foster homes, but for more residential accommodation. The high failure rate of older children and children with persistent behaviour difficulties who were placed in foster homes, suggested that this was rarely an appropriate method of care. (Packman, 1975)

As we shall see later, the developments in Warwickshire were quite unique in this respect.

Length of stay in foster care

The Children Act 1948 stated that fostering was the preferred method of care and, with the implementation of the Act, boarding-out officers (later called children's officers) were appointed in local authorities. The main function of these workers was to find placements for children expected to be in long-term care. Short-term admissions (except for some very young children) were usually accommodated in residential homes. It was not until the late 1960s and early 1970s that foster care came to be used more widely for what was 'temporary' fostering, although this included placements lasting up to several months (Packman, 1975, p.139).

The early studies of fostering in the post-war period all focused on long-term fostering (see Trasler, 1960; Parker, 1966; George, 1970). Each of these studies identified problems in fostering, the scale of which had not before been apparent. Success rates of less than 50 per cent (assessed in terms of continuity) were found and such results accounted, in part, for the declining proportion of foster placements in the late-sixties and early-seventies.

In 1987, Berridge and Cleaver found considerably more variety in the use of foster placements. They classified placements by duration into:

- long-term, which is planned to last for at least three years;
- short-term, with a maximum intended duration of eight weeks; and
- intermediate, envisaged as lasting between 18 months and three years.

At the time they undertook their fieldwork Berridge and Cleaver estimated that upwards of 10,000 children a year in England and Wales experienced a stay in a short-term foster placement. Clearly in the 1980s foster care had a significant part to play in the provision of short-term placements.

Meeting children's needs

From the late 1970s a number of demonstration projects showed that with sufficient preparation, planning and support, foster placements for 'special needs' children could be made to work. One of these was the pioneering Kent Family Placement Scheme (Hazel, 1981) which placed 'delinquent' adolescents. Others showed that foster placements for children with a disability could be successful if well planned and supported. Here, however, it should be noted that the Health Service has a major role in the provision of support for handicapped children and that schemes such as respite care facilities for children with disabilities are usually provided in this sector (see Russell, 1989).

There was also growing interest in the situation of Black children in the care system. The available evidence suggests that Black and mixed parentage children have not only been disproportionately represented in their entrance to care but also that the care system has met their needs less well than those of White children.

In *Children Who Wait* Rowe and Lambert (1973) reported that social workers identified racial background as one of the obstacles to finding long-term placements for some children: Black children were disproportionately represented among the children who wait. The exception to this in the 1960s and 1970s was possibly the placement of Black babies for adoption but, as Stubbs (1987) has argued, this practice met the needs of the predominantly White adopters better than it met the needs of the Black children.

In the early 1980s, the traditional 'colour blind' placement practices of social services departments came under criticism from Black organisations such as the Association of Black Social Workers and Allied Professionals and Black and In Care. 'Colour blind' placement practices usually meant that Black children were placed with White carers. The argument about the importance of same-race placements had yet to be won. Some writers (for example, Cheetham, 1981 and Ahmed, Cheetham and Small, 1986) argued for these and other changes in relation to social work policy and practice as it affected Black people. On the other hand, Tizard and Phoenix (1989) concluded from their research that transracial placements could work well and that the objections to such placements were more political than based on sound research findings.

By the end of the 1980s, most social services departments had acknowledged that transracial placements were not in children's best interests and their (usually explicit) aim was to make same-race placements. Following this development of policy in the field, the Department of Health (Social Services Inspectorate, 1988) issued a document recommending such a practice but not making it an absolute rule.

The role of foster carers

The *Boarding Out Regulations* (1955) required local authorities to pay special regard to the structure of a foster family so that the ages of the children in the household should give the appearance of a natural family. The fostered child should feel as though he or she was living in a substitute family and the foster carers that they were taking over the role of parents; the natural parents, and to some extent 'outsiders', even social workers, should be kept at a distance. This is what Holman (1973) called 'exclusive' fostering. He found that nearly two-thirds of local authority foster parents regarded the foster child 'as their own' and would have liked to adopt him or her. Holman's alternative to 'exclusive' was 'inclusive' fostering in which foster parents do not regard themselves as substitutes for the 'real' parents, but encourage contact between the parents and their child, and include them in decisions. Social workers are also seen as a more positive resource (Holman, 1980).

In 1980 a National Children's Bureau working party proposed a distinction between alternative temporary care and prolonged *substitute* care. The role of substitute parent would only be appropriate where the child was not at all likely to return to his or her family. Alternative care involved the carers in the role of caretaker, friend or even 'therapist' – but not as 'parent'.

In some of the specialist foster care schemes, which we have already described, the roles of 'alternative' care became well developed. Adolescents who cannot return to their families present perhaps the greatest demands on childcare placements. Able to make their own decisions, wanting to maintain existing ties and relationships and not wanting to be disloyal to their parents, such adolescents do not want an 'exclusive' placement. The response of this care group will be an important litmus test of whether or not Warwickshire's policies are successful.

The problem for the foster carers lies in balancing the different roles – to demonstrate commitment without threatening the bonds between parent and child; and to provide the framework for a secure and caring relationship without imposing demands and expectations which the child will find difficult to meet. The role of alternative carer is clearly a difficult one to fill and two factors made it possible in many of the specialist fostering schemes. The first was the careful preparation of placements so that carers, child and parents were clear about roles and relationships, and the second was the availability of continuing social work support for foster carers, usually independent of input from the child's social worker.

To what extent were the issues raised in relation to 'special' fostering schemes common currency in 'ordinary' fostering situations? Berridge and Cleaver (1987) found that:

Many of the planned, long-term arrangements that we studied were clearly of a 'quasi-adoptive' nature... children who retained strong parental allegiance... often found this 'role ambiguity' difficult to bear.

The same authors were also surprised and dismayed that many foster carers still encouraged foster children to call them Mum and Dad.

Foster carers: training, support and payment

Berridge and Cleaver (1987) were critical of the lack of experience and training of many of the foster carers in their study. Recruitment practices traditionally focused on ensuring that people approved as foster parents were suitable to be 'substitute' parents. But as the authors concluded:

The assumption that damaged children can be accommodated in an 'ordinary' family environment ... is frequently over-optimistic, if not naive.

Those carers approved for intermediate placements were identified as being better prepared. Berridge and Cleaver's 'intermediate' placements included what other writers have called 'specialist' placements. These specialist foster carers would appear to be comparatively well prepared, trained and supported (Shaw and Hipgrave, 1983 and 1989) unlike the majority of foster carers. For local authorities operating under resource constraints, the dilemma, described by Rowe and others (1989), is between having well resourced and supported specialist schemes or dispersing skills and knowledge as widely as possible, and thereby running the risk of inadequate skills and support being available for the most demanding placements. Again, we are short of reliable evidence, but that which is available suggests many foster carers are asked to undertake their role with only minimal training and support.

In the period we have been considering, the roles undertaken by foster carers underwent changes in response to the different demands placed on them; in particular the placing of increasing proportions of damaged and difficult children, coupled with increasing numbers of adolescents. Many of these changes were most explicit in the specialist fostering schemes we have described and one specific change concerned the introduction of payments as reward rather than just to cover expenses. This element of payment played a part in the changing relationship between carers and social workers. Social workers became more able to require a different role of the carers, and carers felt that their commitment and effort was recognised.

Summary

The aim of this opening chapter is to provide a context within which the Warwickshire experience can be evaluated. The use of residential care and foster care has changed considerably in the post-war period: in terms of numbers and proportions of children in the different types of placement; in the characteristics of the children; and in the roles and functions of residential workers and foster carers. The key changes are summarised below.

- The numbers of children in residential care decreased substantially in the 1950s and again in the 1980s. The fall in the eighties took advantage of a very sharp fall in the *total* number of children in care.
- The numbers of foster placements grew in the period up to 1965 and again from 1975 on. However, the later changes in foster placement numbers were much less dramatic than the change in residential placement numbers: a 15 per cent rise in foster placements compared with a fall of over 60 per cent in residential numbers.
- During the ten years or so from 1965, the trends were different. The numbers in foster care fell slightly, despite overall increasing numbers in care, and the numbers in residential care rose.
- The changes look very different in terms of proportions. In 1951 over 50 per cent of children in care were placed residentially compared with less than 40 per cent in foster homes. In 1987, over 50 per cent were fostered and only just over 20 per cent were in residential settings. However, this means of assessing placement use by measuring the *stock* of placements on one day gives a very misleading impression of the relative importance of residential care and foster care. If instead we examine all placements made over a period to produce a figure for the *flow* of placements, we find that although the use of residential care has declined, in the late 1980s residential care and foster care each accounted for about 38 per cent of all placements made. Looked at in this way, residential care remained equal in importance with foster care.
- In recent years residential care has mainly been used for adolescents and for short-term placements. Residential units are now smaller, more professionally staffed (though still to an inadequate degree) and more are specialised.
- Foster care has also changed with the development of specialist foster carers. These carers are usually better trained and supported, and often receive what amounts to a small wage. They do not see their role as that of substitute parents but more as alternative carers. They are often much more actively involved with the social worker and in the case planning. Children in specialist foster placements are usually older and often present quite severe difficulties.
- It is difficult to know how large the specialist foster care sector has become, but from available evidence we can conclude that a more traditional style of fostering is still widespread. Such foster carers act as substitute parents, mainly for younger children and often on a long-term basis, with limited social work support and usually for expenses payments only.

2. Design of the research

The research in Warwickshire was approached in several ways and policy and practice were examined from differing angles. The main sources of historical data were the records kept by the Social Services Department in Warwickshire. Annual childcare statistical records were kept for returns to the Department of Health and these were also available. In addition, the minutes of the Social Services Committee recorded major decisions, such as the closure of particular residential facilities and the allocation of additional resources to fostering. Equally important were the background papers presented to the Committee in the reports of the Director of Social Services.

Equally valuable sources of contemporary data were the staff of the Department who had been in post before, during and after the changes. The key senior managers were interviewed but discussions were also held with both qualified and unqualified social work staff who had been in the residential and fieldwork sectors prior to the closures. Some of these staff moved from the residential sector to the newly created specialist children's teams in the reorganisation which resulted from the policy changes. Others had left the authority. The access to both senior management and to staff elsewhere in the hierarchy meant that it was possible to construct a balanced picture of the changes.

Although resources were not available to enable us to undertake a large-scale, multi-authority study, we did conclude that there were important reasons for adopting the elements of a comparative approach as one of the central features of the research. Our solution to this problem was to draw on recent research published in the 1980s, and to make our comparisons with the findings from that research which related to those aspects of childcare practice and outcomes in which we were interested. These other research projects covered, in total, quite a large number of local authorities of different types and with different patterns of childcare placements. As far as the outcomes of care placements were concerned, some consistent messages emerged from these projects and it was the comparisons with these messages which proved most revealing about the consequences of Warwickshire's original childcare policies.

Overall, the research projects with which we drew comparisons used a wide variety of measures to assess whether the placements met children's needs and whether the outcomes could be judged successful or not. These measures included:

- comparative 'breakdown rates' of placements;
- the location of placements and whether this affected parental visiting;
- whether the type of placement was encouraging or discouraging to visits by parents;
- the effect of the placement on schooling;
- the quality of the care offered;
- whether the placement lasted as long as the child needed it to, which is a separate question from whether it lasted as long as was planned.

Each of these measures looks at different aspects of the placement, but taken together they provide a broad view of the overall effectiveness or appropriateness of a placement. It was our decision to use a range of indices in the research since our focus was not on a narrow aspect of placement outcomes, such as breakdown rates, but on the overall impact of a set of policies on placement practice and outcomes. By using a range of indices it was possible, as we will see later, to assess the extent to which the different measures were presenting similar messages about the effects of policy. In order to ensure that the data to be collected in Warwickshire could be most validly compared with the results from other research, we endeavoured, when designing our research instruments, to ask similar questions to those posed by other researchers.

There were some issues in which we were interested where comparative data from other studies were not available: for example, there is little information on child-related 'outcomes' according to different placement experiences. Therefore, one of the approaches we adopted in dealing with these issues was to ask social workers not only for factual information but also for their personal assessment of how satisfactorily they were able to meet children's particular needs. Social workers were also asked, in relation to each placement, whether a residential placement would have been a better option than the one which was made.

Survey and questionnaire design

One of the central features of our research was a survey of childcare cases in Warwickshire. The survey involved the prospective monitoring of 215 cases over a period of 15 months. The sample was drawn from those childcare cases which involved children aged five or over. The under fives were excluded for several reasons. First, in Warwickshire separate family centres provided specialist social work input for this young group. For older children the specialist involvement came from Children's Services Teams (CSTs), which will be discussed in detail later. Second, the under fives age group were relatively unaffected by the policies concerning the closure of children's homes. Warwickshire's residential facilities – as is the case with a number of other areas – had not been used in any significant way for placements of children aged under five for many years before the final closures. Nor had any children in this age group been placed in other residential care facilities for some time. Finally, the issues surrounding the care of young children were somewhat different. In particular, in relation to the placement of very young children in long-term care, permanency policies with the aim of adoption were pursued more rigorously.

The survey sample was constructed from three separate groups:

- children in long-term care, that is over one year;
- children newly admitted to care;
- children with whom the Department had a substantial involvement but who were not in care.

The two in-care groups were identified separately so that the effects of the policy changes, and associated organisational implications, could be assessed in relation to both groups. The 'not admitted' group was included so that the role of the specialist Children's Services Teams in relation to children in this situation could also be examined – the CSTs were given a central role in the prevention of admission to care. A number of the not admitted group were subsequently admitted to care and placements made for this group were then considered along with placements for the original in-care groups.

The long-term, in-care group was randomly sampled from all the children aged five or over who had been in care for a year or more. A total of 55 cases were identified for this sub-group. Details of the sample of long-term in-care cases were compared with details of the long-term in-care population from which the sample was drawn. In terms of age, gender, racial background, type of placement, time in care and legal status, the sample was found to be highly representative.

The new admissions cohort was identified over a monitoring period of almost six months. All admissions to care and Place of Safety Orders involving children over four were included with one exception: when admissions or Orders involved groups of siblings, only one of the siblings was included in the sample, this sibling being selected at random. The decision not to include all siblings was made because in most cases the background data would have been largely similar and also because there was a need to limit the demands made on social workers who would be required to complete detailed, periodic questionnaires on each case. However, the important issue of whether it was possible to place siblings together was followed up. In fact more than a third of the new admissions to care were accompanied by one or more siblings and, as other research has pointed out, this considerably restricts social workers' placement options.

The third and final group was the not admitted to care group. Again this cohort was identified over a monitoring period of approximately six months and was selected from the over-four age group. Sibling groups were treated in the same way as those in the new admissions group. Establishing criteria for the identification of this sub-group required careful thought and the criterion which was finally established was that, at referral, it was anticipated that the case would involve substantial input from the Department. The cases in the sub-group were identified in meetings between the researcher and Community

Team Managers at which newly referred and allocated cases were assessed in relation to the qualifying criterion.

Table 2.1 breaks down the survey group into sub-groups, with the not admitted group being further sub-divided into the cases where the child was not subsequently admitted to care and those where the child did later enter care during the course of the monitoring period.

Table 2.1 The survey group

Group	No.	(%)
Long-term in care	55	(26)
New admission to care	72	(33)
Not admitted	74	(34)
Not admitted/later admitted	14	(7)
Total	215	(100)

We will see in a later chapter that the 141 children who were at some time in care provided information on well over 200 placement episodes, excluding the initial placements of the long-term in-care group.

Four types of questionnaires were used in the survey. The initial questionnaire which gathered detailed background information on the cases; a second which asked a series of questions about the making of new placements; a third one which was used when placements had ended; and a fourth which asked about any involvement by the Children's Services Team Direct Work Teams. Only one initial questionnaire was completed in relation to each case but a 'new placement' questionnaire was completed as a child was admitted to care or when he or she moved from one placement to another while remaining in care. Each time a child left a placement, either to leave care or to move to another care placement, the third questionnaire was completed. A copy of the fourth questionnaire was completed at the end of the monitoring period and covered CST Direct Work Team input over the 15 months.

There were three versions of the initial questionnaire, one for each of the sub-groups in the survey. All of the versions shared large parts in common but included only those questions which were applicable to the group.

All of the questionnaires were designed to be completed by the case worker, that is the social worker to whom the case was allocated. The format used for the questionnaires was mostly multiple choice. This format was chosen because to have used a more open-ended format would, first, have demanded too much time of the social workers completing the questionnaire; second, it would have resulted in inconsistent responses; and, finally, would have introduced coding and analysis problems.

Considerable groundwork was undertaken with team managers and social workers to introduce the research to them and to describe the methods which would be used. This preparation, together with the time spent designing, revising and piloting the questionnaires, paid dividends. Feedback from social workers indicated that the forms were straightforward and did not take too long to complete. Response rates were 100 per cent for the initial questionnaires and nearly 98 per cent for others. Most of the two per cent non-responses were not returned because the social workers concerned had left the Department. This remarkably high rate of return reflects the commitment demonstrated throughout the research by the County overall and by its individual employees.

Analysis of the data was undertaken using SPSS (Statistical Package for the Social Sciences). When reporting on our analysis, details of the tests used to establish statistical significance have not been included since we assumed that the general reader would not be sufficiently interested. The convention used throughout the following chapters is that the associations we describe are all statistically significant unless specifically stated otherwise. Further details of the tests used can be obtained by writing to the authors at the National Children's Bureau.

In addition to the large-scale survey, additional research methods were used. These were:

- case studies;
- a detailed examination of all residential placements made over a period of two and a-half years; and
- a study of the effects of the Social Services Department's childcare policies on the use of residential special schools by Warwickshire Education Department.

First, the case study approach was adopted because it would provide material which would be complementary to that emerging from the survey. The survey produced large-scale, quantitative data most of which was factual (for instance where children were placed and how long they stayed), and some of which was attitudinal (such as social workers' assessments of the suitability of the placements which were made). The survey data enabled us to reach conclusions about placement patterns and outcomes which were statistically valid because of the size of the data base. The case studies, in contrast, provided information from a wider range of sources, including children themselves, foster carers and social workers in both the generic teams and in the specialist children's teams.

After the closure of its children's homes, Warwickshire continued to place a small number of children and young people in residential placements but these placements were bought in and were mostly in the voluntary sector. We decided that it would be important to examine the County's use of residential placements in some detail, but the survey approach proved unsuitable for this task. The low numbers of residential placements made by the Department meant that very few cases involving residence were picked up in the process of identifying the sample.

To overcome this problem, a decision was made to study *all* of the cases which involved one or more residential placements made during a period of two and a-half years following the closure of the last of the in-County children's homes. Details were gathered from case files and from interviews with social workers. *See* Chapter 11 for an analysis of the results of this study.

When the research was being discussed by the National Children's Bureau and representatives of Warwickshire County Council, one of the issues raised was the possibility that the successive decisions made by the Social Services Committee to close children's homes might have had an impact on the numbers of children, not in care, placed in residential special schools by the Education Department.

Particular concern was expressed about children with special educational needs which were identified as 'emotional and behavioural difficulties' (EBD) and who, prior to the implementation of the Education Act 1981, would have been designated 'maladjusted'. In Chapter 12 this issue is explored in detail, by examining placement trends in the Education and Social Services Departments and by placing these trends in a broader historical and theoretical context. To provide some comparative data a survey, albeit modest, of local education authorities was undertaken. The intention was to gather recent comparative data on EBD placements from other authorities relating to the period since 1984. Prior to that date the Department of Education and Science collated and published data on the placement of children with different types of 'handicap' or special educational need. Collation of that data ceased with the implementation of the Education Act, 1981.

Childcare placements: key issues and comparative data

In order to evaluate Warwickshire's radical childcare policy, we decided to focus on a number of key childcare practice issues. Fortunately, the mid and late 1980s saw the publication of results from a number of valuable research projects into childcare, most of which were funded by the Department of Health, and the Economic and Social Research Council. The results from these projects were summarised in a Department of Health publication (HMSO, 1985). Perhaps most significantly for our research, Rowe, Hundleby and Garnett reported on their large-scale study of childcare placements in 1989 – *Child Care Now.* We had access to early drafts of their results, which were invaluable in providing us with accurate comparative data which previously had been unavailable.

Children's characteristics and circumstances

If we look at the experiences of thousands of children using the evidence available in Department of Health statistics and from research projects, it is evident that some characteristics and some circumstances are associated with certain other factors: such as the type of placement children are more likely to experience, as well as the likelihood that those placements will be more or less successful. For example, age has been identified not only as a key factor in the types of placement which are made but also in how those placements develop. Studies over three decades have identified that foster placements tend to have less successful outcomes when children are older (Trasler, 1960; Parker, 1966; George, 1970; and Berridge and Cleaver, 1987). There is clear evidence that age is associated with much greater use of residential care but is also linked with less successful outcomes, whatever the type of placement. The age of children when placed will, therefore, be a key factor to analyse when we are examining provision in Warwickshire. In the County, as we will see, the main placement resource nationally for older children – that is residential provision – is not available.

The experiences of siblings coming into contact with social services in Warwickshire are also examined. Certainly, it is often whole families who are of concern to social services departments (*see* Packman, 1986) and finding substitute care placements for sibling groups is a common problem. But is it important to keep brothers and sisters together? By and large, research which has looked at this question would say that it is if we consider the long-term effects on the children involved (Trasler, 1976; Triseliotis, 1980; and Hill and others, 1989). Indeed, the Children Act 1989 emphasises the significance of this. Other research has identified siblings as an important source of continuity for children in care when so many other links are broken (Berridge and Cleaver, 1987; Rowe and others, 1984; and Whittaker and others, 1985 [quoted by Parker, 1988]).

For Warwickshire, the important questions to ask in relation to this issue become, first, was there a recognition of the importance of keeping siblings in care together in most circumstances? Second, given the more limited range of placement possibilities open to them, was it actually possible to keep siblings united?

The situation of children from minority ethnic groups is also scrutinised. In the late 1970s the routine placement of Black children with White carers began to be questioned (ABSWAP, 1983; Rowe and others, 1984; Weise, 1986; Ahmed and others, 1986; and Stubbs, 1987) and policies of same-race placements began to be adopted by local authorities and other agencies. What success these agencies had in applying these policies is unclear but at least the argument appeared to have been won that Black children's interests were best served by placements which recognised and reinforced their racial identity. Indeed Government policy, while acknowledging that children's *individual* needs must always be considered, now supports this view, and the Children Act 1989 provides further reinforcement. We shall, therefore, examine the extent to which Warwickshire was able to provide continuity in racial and cultural background for children in its care from minority ethnic groups.

How and why children and their families come to the notice of social services departments and why decisions are made to admit children to care appear to have a significant influence on the experience of care, including:

- the types of placement made for those who are admitted;
- the duration in care; and
- the extent to which the experience is likely to be satisfactory.

Packman (1986) identified three broad groups of children who were admitted to care:

- **The victims** – children admitted because of concern about their emotional or physical safety.
- **The villains** – children who are admitted because their behaviour is causing problems outside the home.
- **The volunteered** – who are admitted as part of a service to families unable to provide for the child.

It is the second group, the so-called villains, which could be expected to pose the greatest problems for Warwickshire: an older group, predominantly adolescents, admitted to care often as a last resort and displaying behavioural problems (Millham, 1986; Vernon and Fruin, 1986; Packman, 1986; Rowe, 1989). The admission of older children to care is also strongly associated with long stays in care (Millham, 1986; Vernon and Fruin, 1986; Packman, 1986; Rowe, 1989) and with residential placements (see the authors referred to above plus Berridge, 1985). Wolkind and Rutter (1973) also found that more children who were placed residentially were emotionally disturbed at placement. How would Warwickshire provide care for this difficult group who in other authorities would mostly be placed residentially? If they were placed in foster homes, how would these be maintained? Triseliotis (1989) reviewing the research, identifies the scale of the problem:

Behaviour problems are responsible for most [foster placement] breakdowns... The relationship between increased disturbance and breakdown holds true also for specialist fostering.

Finding and making placements for children in care

The second group of issues on which our research focusses can be summarised as follows: what are the key issues to examine when we look at the process of finding a placement for a child admitted to care or moving from one placement to another? In relation to this research project, the *type* of placement is clearly a central factor, but prior to that there are issues about the extent to which placements are planned and moves prepared. Lack of planning in making placements is associated with worse outcomes – a lesson some of the specialist fostering schemes are aware of (Hazel, 1981). It will be important to examine whether Warwickshire's policies, and the resources put into implementing the policies, have made it possible for this lesson to be learned.

It is also important to know if the placement made was the most *appropriate* one. Warwickshire's decision to close its children's homes and to restrict the use of the residential option represents a clear limitation on the type of placement available. One of the issues addressed will be whether the County introduced alternative choices which would meet the needs of children for whom, in other areas, residential care would be the placement of choice. The second question about choice asks whether there is any choice at all – not just choice between placements of different types but even between alternative foster placements, for instance. Recent research presents a depressing picture when addressing this question.

Social workers experienced greater disquiet about the placement decisions they have to make than they did about the admission of the child to care or the choice of legislation...

In only half of the 450 cases was the social worker able to place the child in the specific [setting that they deemed most suitable. (Millham and others, 1986)

Good practice and the care experience

Far less attention is given to what is to happen after admission than to whether or not to admit and if children stay long in care, social work attention fades. (DHSS, 1985)

This remark is taken from the DHSS summary of research into childcare decision making and gives a good introduction to the third group of questions our research poses. The questions which can be asked under this heading of good practice are many. Here we have attempted, first, to identify those areas which could have been affected by the changes made in Warwickshire in recent years; and second, those about which good quality comparative data exist so that conclusions may be reached about practice in Warwickshire.

One of the requirements of any placement for children in the care of a local authority is that it should meet standards of physical care and emotional warmth. Work put into maintaining the child-parent relationship is also extremely important and is strongly associated with leaving care early (Fanshel, 1975; Aldgate, 1980; and Millham and others, 1986). Regular visits are associated with fewer placement disruptions (Millham, 1986; and Berridge and Cleaver, 1987). The importance of maintaining links seems now to be becoming recognised by social workers and is, indeed, formally constituted in the Children Act 1989.

In relation to Warwickshire the first question to ask is, has the increased dependence on foster care resulted overall in more 'exclusive' care with the effects this can have on parent-child links; on resulting longer stays in care; and also on more placement disruptions? Moreover, has the County learned the lessons of specialist foster schemes and found the resources for training, support and planning to enable 'ordinary' foster carers to become more inclusive carers?

Indeed, the skills and experience of foster carers in the County will be important issues. Certainly we needed to ask about the degree of experience of the foster carers who are providing the majority of placements but in addition to this we needed to examine the extent to which the County is able to *retain* its experienced carers. What training, preparation and support is provided so that foster carers can successfully meet the needs of children, especially older children and those with behavioural problems, who in other areas could more often be placed in a residential establishment?

Measuring outcomes in childcare placements

This final section on the questions our research addresses focuses on the measures which can be used to assess whether a particular childcare placement can be judged to have been successful or not. This is a complex issue. The success or failure of childcare placements has frequently been approached by examining *breakdown rates* – that is the proportion of placements ending before it was planned that they should. One of the problems with using breakdown rates as a measure of outcome is that results are sensitive to the definitions used (as pointed out by Parker, 1988b and Rowe, 1987) and to the context. A study focusing on long-term foster placements cannot really be compared with one which considered all types of placement and included some which were both short- and long-term. Our response to these methodological problems was to identify the studies with which comparisons would be most useful and then to ensure that we used definitions and methods which would make comparisons valid.

Study after study has shown that a large proportion of children in care experience considerable instability of placement. The distress of admission to care is often compounded by frequent movements from one care placement to another (Millham, 1986; Marsh and Fisher, 1986; Packman, 1986; Vernon and Fruin, 1986; Rowe and others, 1989). In fact Stein and Carey (1986) identify change and instability as one of the most common factors in the way in which care is experienced. It was necessary to examine whether children in care in Warwickshire experienced more or fewer placement changes than children in other authorities, and then to try to identify the causes for any differences found. Obvious issues to consider included the comparative lack of availability of residential placements and differences in resources put into supporting placements.

One of the problems with outcome measures which focus on breakdown rates or on the number of placement changes is that these issues 'come to be viewed by parents as a demonstration of their child's difficulty and problematic state' (Millham and others, 1986). It is quite likely that the fault may lie with the social services department for failing to find a placement which was suitable for the child (perhaps because there was little or no choice between placements); or perhaps for failing to do the necessary groundwork in preparing the child, parents and carers for the placement; or even for failing to provide adequate support for the placement once it was made.

To shift the focus away from the child, we developed a series of questions which looked at the aims of the placement (for example, short-term care, assessment, 'treatment') and at the extent to which these aims were or were not achieved. Similarly we asked social workers to identify particular needs which the child had at the time the placement was made (for example, the extent to which the child needed a placement where his or her behaviour could be managed in a constructive way) and then asked the social worker to assess how well each of these particular needs were met in the placement. Finally, social workers were asked to assess how well adapted the child was to the placement. Clearly a placement is less likely to be successful if a child is not settled and whether or not he or she is settled will be as much a measure of social work practice as anything else.

These measures of outcome, depending as they do on assessments made by individual social workers, are less precise than some of the other factors we have described. But used in conjunction with these other measures, and given that they provide a different perspective on outcomes, it was important that they should have been included to give some overall insight.

Let us now look in detail at exactly what happened in Warwickshire.

3. A history of recent developments in childcare in Warwickshire

The general picture is very encouraging ... Warwickshire had fewer than average children in care per 1,000 population under 18. At the same time the population in residential care was about ten per cent less than average. There is every reason to suppose that the population boarded-out will continue to increase during 1976/77 as considerable efforts are being devoted to achieving this desirable objective. (Warwickshire Director of Social Services, 1976)

The Department operates upon a series of beliefs about practices and about services, for want of a better word-values. The basic belief is that EVERY CHILD DESERVES THE RIGHT TO A FAMILY LIFE (sic), in their own or in a substitute family. (Smallridge, 1988)

From the time Warwickshire Social Services Department was established in 1974, one of its main aims in relation to children in care was to reduce the proportion of children who were placed in residential children's homes and to increase the proportion who were fostered This policy was pursued consistently over many years by the Social Services Committee on the advice of two successive directors (Bob Bessell and Peter Smallridge).

In 1986 Warwickshire closed the last of its residential children's centres. This decision to close the centres was not, however, inevitable. As was discussed in Chapter 1, there was a substantial shift nationally away from residential childcare towards fostering but, in 1986, no other social services department had withdrawn all of its residential childcare facilities. In fact, the first Director of Social Services in Warwickshire has remarked that, while he was in post (up to 1983), it was never envisaged that the County would reach the point where the final closures of the homes would be made.

How did Warwickshire reach the point in 1986 where the final closure decision could be taken? This is the question which this chapter will address by providing details of the policy decisions in their historical context; the facts and figures about where children in care were actually placed; and details about the organisation and structure of services, which enabled Warwickshire to undertake the closures with confidence.

Childcare numbers and placements in Warwickshire

What happened, precisely, to the patterns of placements made for children in Warwickshire since the creation of the Social Services Department in 1974? We know, broadly, that residential placements decreased and foster placements increased, but at what rates? And how did any changes compare with what we described in Chapter 1 as happening nationally? The detail of these changes will be established in this section before moving on to look at why the changes occurred.

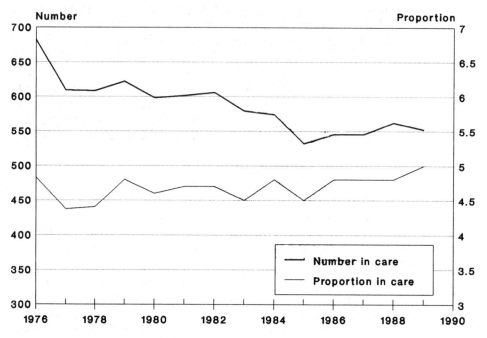

Figure 3.1 Warwickshire: Numbers and proportions per 1000 of 0–17s in care

Figure 3.1 covers the period 1976 to 1989. The top line shows the numbers of children in care in Warwickshire at 31 March each year. Between 1976 and 1977 the in-care numbers fell by over ten per cent but then, for the next five years, the number in care remained fairly steady. Between 1982 and 1986 there was another fall of about ten per cent. These trends are more or less consistent with the national trends shown in Figure 1.1, with the exception that the fall in the early 1980s taken nationally was greater. (These are all figures for the *stock* of placements and not the *flow* of placements.) This difference is also reflected in the line in Figure 3.1 which represents the proportion of 0–17 year-olds in care in Warwickshire. During the period 1976 to 1986 the proportion in care remained in a very narrow band between 4.3 and 4.8 per 1000. Nationally (*see* Figure 1.2) the rate varied much more widely – the late 1970s peak figure was 7.8 per 1000 but this had fallen to as low as 5.0 per 1000 in 1986.

In Chapter 1 we argued that the influence of *Children Who Wait* (Rowe and Lambert, 1973) and of the developing permanency movement could be used to account, at least in part, for falls in the proportion of children in care. However, in Warwickshire, as can be seen in Figure 3.1, the total number of children in care and the proportion per 1000 in care did not fall significantly in the early

1980s. Why the experience in Warwickshire was so different from the national trend is not at all clear.

What was happening to the types of placement made for children in care? In Chapter 1 (Figure 1.3) we identified dramatic changes in the placement patterns of children in care in England and Wales. The proportion of children boarded out increased from 33 per cent to 52 per cent in a decade, and the proportion in residential care fell from 40 per cent to 22 per cent during the same period.

Let us see what was happening in Warwickshire in the years up to 1986, the year in which the County closed its last children's homes. Figure 3.2 shows the trends for Warwickshire alongside the national trends. From having a boarding-out rate ten per cent higher than the national rate in 1976 the differential between the County and the national figure jumped to 28 per cent in 1980. Similarly, with residential placements, Warwickshire had nine per cent fewer children in residential care in 1976, but in 1980 the difference was 23 per cent.

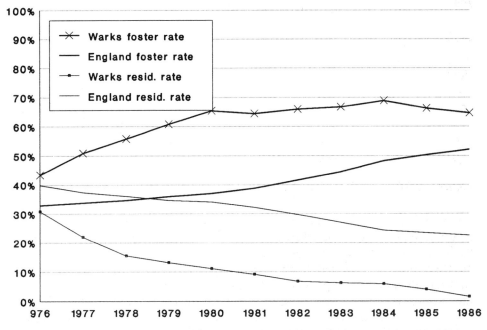

Figure 3.2 Warwickshire and England: Foster and residential rates compared

We will try to provide explanations for these changes later in this chapter. But if we move on to look at the period 1980 to 1986, we see that Warwickshire experienced a rate of decline in the use of residential care, which was similar to the national rate of decline. However – and this is a very important point – *starting from a lower point*, by 1986 the County had fewer than two per cent of children in care placed residentially and was, therefore, in a position to close its last children's homes. Nationally, over 22 per cent of children were placed residentially, which meant that places for over 15,000 children were needed. In England and Wales from 1980 to 1986, the proportion of children boarded out increased steadily from 37 to 52 per cent. In Warwickshire a ceiling appears to have been reached in the number of children in foster care; the figures in these years ranged from about 65 to 69 per cent. So although there was no substantial increase after 1980, a much higher proportion of children were still boarded out in Warwickshire.

In Chapter 1 we converted the proportions of children in foster and residential care into the actual *numbers* of placements required, and we found that the *number* of foster placements grew only slightly (about 10 per cent) over a long period, but that the numbers of residential placements fell dramatically (by 60 per cent). In Warwickshire we find a similar pattern. As Figure 3.3 shows, between 1976 and the mid to late 1980s the number of residential placements fell from over 200 to around ten, with the most dramatic falls occurring in the late 1970s whereas the County increased the number of foster placements in use by nearly a third. However, in the 1980s Warwickshire did not have to find extra foster carers, it had only to maintain the number reached during the growth period of the late-seventies.

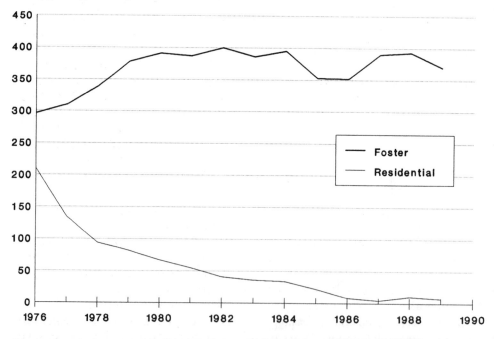

Figure 3.3 Warwickshire: Numbers of foster and residential placements

Taking these two trends together, we can summarise what appears to have been happening both in Warwickshire and nationally:

● From 1976 to 1980 residential placement numbers fell sharply and foster placements increased almost as rapidly. There appears to have been positive action to shift the balance of care further away from residential care and towards foster care.

- From 1980 to 1987 foster care numbers did not increase. Residential numbers fell but this was paralleled by a similar fall in the total number of children in care.

We will see later in this chapter how these changes related to policies implemented by Warwickshire Social Services Department.

In Chapter 1 we went beyond using childcare stock figures, which are essentially a static measure, and drew instead on the research by Rowe and colleagues (1989) to consider the process of making placements over a period. This more dynamic picture demonstrated that in all six authorities Rowe studied, residential care was used *more often* than foster care when placements were made, even in the mid 1980s when their research was carried out. Residential care continues to be a crucial resource for most social services departments, especially for new, and unplanned, admissions to care and very often remains the placement of choice when an existing care arrangement has broken down. In later chapters the results from our research, when we followed the care careers of over 200 children, will be compared directly with Rowe's figures and detailed answers will be given to questions such as, what does Warwickshire do with emergency admissions and placement breakdowns when it has no emergency residential facilities of its own?

There are two outstanding issues to be addressed which relate to patterns of placements in Warwickshire. The first concerns the placement of children in care in residential schools. At a conference held in 1987 to discuss Warwickshire's radical policies, one external observer commented on the fact that between 1984 and 1987 (which covered the closure of the last of Warwickshire's children's homes) there had been an increase in the number of children placed in residential special schools by Warwickshire's Education Department. 'You haven't got rid of residential care at all,' he said, 'You've shoved it somewhere else.' (quoted in Hardingham, 1987). The relationship between the care system and the provision of residential special education proved, on investigation, to be a complex one and the issue is covered in detail in Chapter 12.

The other outstanding issue concerns a similar accusation made against Warwickshire to the effect that, as the children's homes were closed, increasing numbers of children in care were being placed home on trial (that is, with their parents – now termed, somewhat brusquely, charge and control) and in placements other than fostering, residential or even home on trial.

Figure 3.4 compares the County's home on trial placements with the national figures. Since the trend for Warwickshire was downwards during the period of home closures and since the County's figures were also either at or below the national figures, it would appear reasonable to conclude that children in care were not diverted from residential care to home on trial placements.

Figure 3.5 compares the County's 'other' category of placements with the national figures and at first sight there would appear to be some evidence for the allegations made. While the national figure for other placements remains constant at around 10 to 11 per cent, Warwickshire's figures have increased steadily since 1980, until 1986 when the County's figure is 18 per cent compared with a national figure of 10 per cent. The response of Warwickshire's Social

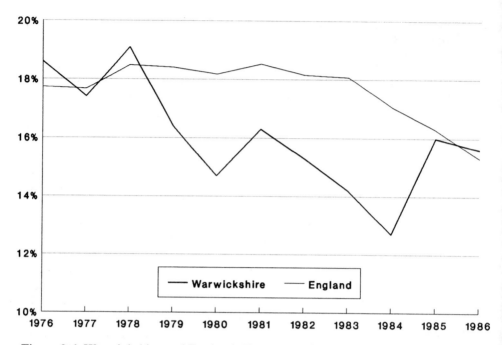

Figure 3.4 Warwickshire and England: Home on trial rates compared

Services Department when this issue was raised was to point to rapid and marked increases, since 1982, in the numbers of children in care and placed for adoption. Annual returns required by the Department of Health included a separate category of placed for adoption only from 1987, and so comparative data for earlier periods are not available. However, Warwickshire did collect this category of data from 1982 and these figures are also shown in Figure 3.5. If the line representing Warwickshire's other placements and the category of placed for adoption are compared, it would seem that the latter category may account for the majority of the differences between the national and Warwickshire figures from 1982 to 1989.

Policy and provision 1974 to 1986

The figures in the previous section tell us what happened in Warwickshire in terms of where children in care were placed. This section will now identify the key policy decisions and practice developments which made possible the final step to close the last of the County's residential childcare facilities. For the sake of brevity, we are unable to go into great detail about these decisions and developments but it is worth noting that three features stand out.

First, residential care in Warwickshire was consistently seen as the inevitable placement for some children but certainly not a desirable option. The refrain was 'Every child deserves the right to a family life' and, throughout this period, this view of residential care as second best ran counter to attempts to create a positive role for residential care. The second key feature was that there were few initiatives in the area of foster care provision, at least until 1985. The third

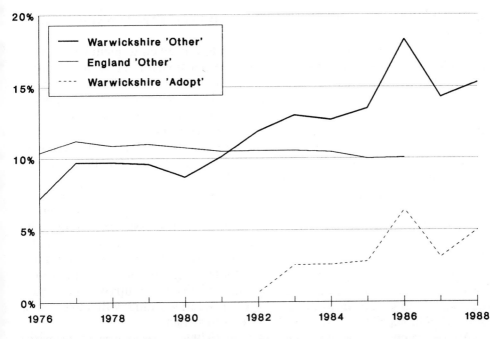

Figure 3.5 Warwickshire and England: 'Other' placement rates compared

notable feature was that none of the changes prior to 1986 (in residential care, intermediate treatment, juvenile bureaux and so on) had, as their aim, the elimination of residential care from the County. The key point is, however, that without each of these changes, and some others, it is very unlikely that Warwickshire would have had the option in 1986 of making the final closures. Policies implemented and practices developed over a decade opened up unintended and largely unimagined possibilities.

From 1974 to 1979

During this period childcare policy in Warwickshire focused on, 'A vigorous programme ... to prevent children being received into residential care or to provide substitute family care where care was appropriate' (Warwickshire SSD, 1987). The rationale for this programme was an overriding belief in 'the family'. As the then Director of Social Services put it to the Short Committee:

It was from within ourselves, both officers and members, where this fundamental belief in the importance of family life came and if anything characterises the philosophy of the department here it is that family life matters and that good social policy is based on family life. (House of Commons, Social Services Committee, 1984)

This is very much in tune with espoused Conservative ideology of the 1980s. Indeed, in his evidence to the Short Committee, the Director of Social Services went on to describe the small family group home type of residential childcare provision as, 'the most disastrous social experiment in childcare since the Second World War'.

Warwickshire concentrated on getting young children out of existing residential placements and preventing new children entering. Thus, between

1975 and 1978 residential numbers fell by more than half and foster placements increased by about 30 per cent, or 80 places.

Responsibility for finding foster placements was given to members of staff called Homefinders. Each Homefinder was responsible for one of the County's five divisions and was employed on unqualified scales. Homefinders were not social work trained and they were not expected to provide any expert support to foster carers; their job was recruitment of carers and the finding of placements. In fact any support which was provided came from the child's social worker. But in Warwickshire, as in other areas at this time, the majority of children who were fostered were young and the carers were expected, essentially, to act as their substitute family.

Meanwhile, the reduction in the numbers of children in residential care homes meant that it was possible to close a number of homes and to redeploy some residential staff, usually after secondment for professional training. The changes up to this point had happened in a somewhat piecemeal fashion, but by 1979 two problems required a more substantial rethink. First, some buildings were unsuitable; having been appropriate for larger groups of young children in care, they were obviously impractical premises for small groups of adolescents. Second, many of the staff were not experienced in working with adolescents, and new and experienced staff were difficult to attract.

An agreement reached with the unions in 1979 left a residential sector with:

- staff paid on qualified social work scales;
- secondments for training for unqualified staff;
- a policy of recruiting only CQSW (Certificate of Qualification in Social Work) qualified staff to work in the homes; and
- four, 12-bedded children's homes spread across the County.

The name of the homes was changed to Children's Centres. Staff in the Centres were to undertake assessments of children newly admitted to care and to work with 'families, foster parents, schools and other agencies in an attempt to assess and meet the child's real needs' (Warwickshire SSD, 1987).

What was to prove problematic over the next few years was the differentiation between the roles of those qualified staff based in the Children's Centres and the social workers in the field teams. However, looking forward a few years, not the least significant of the decisions reached in 1979 was that of employing only CQSW-qualified staff in residential childcare. As we shall see, without this policy further closures of children's centres in the 1980s, culminating in the final closure in 1986, would have been difficult and perhaps impossible to achieve.

From 1979 to 1986

With four new Children's Centres across the County providing just 48 places, the all-qualified residential staff policy and a brief for these staff to work with the broader community, further substantial changes in the residential childcare sector in Warwickshire were not anticipated. However, as we have seen, the numbers of children placed residentially declined steadily so that, by the end of

1985, there remained only two Children's Centres (one serving the north of the County and one the south). By the end of 1986 these two had also closed.

One way of understanding these developments would be as a continuation of the 1970s policy of deliberately diverting children and young people away from residential care. However, this was not the explicit policy of the department in the 1980s. Managers did, however, continue to espouse the philosophy that 'every child deserves a right to a family life' and it is likely, as Payne has pointed out (1978 and 1987), that negative messages about the value of residential care as the second-best or residual alternative are unlikely to encourage a positive view of residential provision among staff. In a letter to a social services journal a former officer-in-charge of one of Warwickshire's Children's Centres wrote:

The (then) management of the department [was given] too much credit. If the truth be known, it was the work of the social workers (residential workers in particular) that created the pace for the run-down of residential care for children. (Knox, 1987)

The author then went on to criticise Warwickshire's management for arranging for limited access to residential care in the voluntary sector after the last of the Children's Centres was closed.

The philosophy of a significant number of residential workers was not simply the concept that every child deserves the right to a family life, which was undoubtedly supported. It was also the belief that children should never have to spend even a short part of their lives in an institution. (Ibid.)

From someone who had the responsibility for managing one of the four remaining residential facilities in the County these comments are to say the least surprising, but they do tie in with what we have already mentioned: that is, there was some lack of clarity about the role of the Children's Centres as distinct from fieldwork teams and, as they were developed, Intermediate Treatment Centres.

What assessment role did Children's Centre staff have and how was this to be differentiated from the role of the case-accountable workers in the field teams? Who took on responsibility for preventing admissions to care, the Children's Centre or IT Centre? If Children's Centres were to, 'work in the community with families, foster parents and schools', where were other staff with childcare responsibilities supposed to work?

There was evidence of confusion of roles emerging from our own interviews with former staff who had worked in the Department in the early 1980s. This was confirmed in a report by Baldwin (1986); a dissertation by Bowen (1986); and in internal departmental documents – notably a report prepared by a working party in 1983 for the Divisional Director with responsibility for services for children.

The Group looked at the nature of interaction between Area Teams, IT Projects and Residential Centres in relation to referral, assessment and treatment of adolescent clients. It is obvious that even where a close relationship exists the absence of a coherent strategy can result in a response that is at best patchy and at worse inappropriate. (Warwickshire Social Services Department, 1983)

The membership of this Working Party was principally operational managers from area teams, IT projects and Children's Centres, together with some social workers and a Homefinder. Their report went on:

The key issue is the absence of a Departmental strategy that would enable individual supervisors, be they strategic or operational, to manage the services coherently. The services for adolescents have developed in a somewhat piecemeal fashion over the County – sometimes responding adequately to the needs of the Areas, sometimes not. Generally there is a tension between the three groups of staff which has great creative potential, but in the main has been a rather negative phenomenon. (Ibid.)

We will suggest later that this 'creative potential' was perhaps achieved in 1986 with the culmination of a largely non-residential childcare provision in Warwickshire. First, however, it will be worthwhile spending a little more time explaining the negative aspects of the tension between the different groups involved in childcare provision – and we are really talking about provision for adolescents since for younger children residential care had ceased to be an option by the end of the 1970s.

Baldwin (1986) undertook an 'action research' project in the early 1980s with staff from all the Children's Centres in Warwickshire. The aim of the project was to try to clarify the role of residential staff within the opportunities and constraints of the local authority. In writing about her experience of the project Baldwin reflected that:

It is only by taking a broad view of the part which residential care currently plays in affecting children's lives, and the part it *should* play, and its relationship to other services which claim to provide for their needs, that residential establishments can have a constructive role and residential staff can be supported in achieving manageable objectives. (Baldwin, 1986)

However, it is clear from her report that the clarity of role for residential services did not emerge at a County level, and that aspects of departmental structures and organisation acted against such a clarification.

Some staff groups had clearly worked out aims, others expressed confusion about what they should – or could – be doing... There was a large measure of frustration, anger and resentment that they were not in *control* of the aims of their establishment... The tasks which they were expected to undertake sometimes conflicted with each other. (Ibid.)

Not the least of the frustrations was the fact that the Children's Centres were used as a 'dumping ground ... when other parts of the system cannot cope'. Admission to Children's Centres was decided at divisional management level.

Baldwin interviewed and worked with staff while they were still based in the Children's Centres. These staff described their work using different methods of residential care, which were not necessarily compatible and which were not all implemented. One of these models was that of the 'therapeutic community' but the Director of Social Services was explicitly opposed to the Children's Centres operating on this model (Baldwin, 1986). He saw the development of residential care as being:

To provide: asylum from damaging experiences and a period of tranquility; opportunities for good nurturing; opportunities to relate to their families; opportunities to develop social skills, to take part in group work discussions, to be kept active and happy. (Ibid.)

Most of the staff involved in Baldwin's study agreed with these aims but placed much greater stress on the role of Children's Centres in outreach work and preventive work.

Very importantly both Baldwin and Bowen (1986) found that residential staff had difficulty in providing the basic residential services described in the above quotation, attributed to the Director. Their difficulties were based in part on having no control over admissions but also because a typical residential group consisted of 'the most damaged children from everywhere', 'the worst delinquents' (Bowen, 1986, quotes from interviews with residential social workers).

Bowen's central argument is that, in at least some of the Children's Centres, group dynamics were given secondary consideration while staff tried to work with individual young people. She argues that:

The group dynamics in any residential setting is a powerful force which should be given *primary* consideration... If it is not, the unintended consequences of group living will inevitably manifest themselves. (Bowen, 1986)

The Head of one Children's Centre commented that:

60 per cent of effort tackled problems of institutional living and only 40 per cent tackled the reasons why they (the residents) were there. (Ibid.)

All the residential workers in this Centre:

started to see residential care as inhibiting good social work practice as the containment and control of behaviour constantly undermined any development and progress in the child... The social processes in the Centres came to be seen as working *against* the central social work requirement for casework plans to be followed. (Ibid.)

According to these accounts, therefore,

the residential staff had become so involved in the individual casework approach that the essential importance of group work in a residential setting appears to have been lost. (Ibid.)

The contemporary interviews and analyses provided in the reports of Bowen and Baldwin, and in the Departmental Working Party Report are invaluable documents in this attempt to analyse the developments of this period. Our own interviews with staff were undertaken after the Children's Centres were closed and, even with the interviewees having the advantage of hindsight, their comments were consistent with the descriptions and analysis already provided.

One specialist team manager interviewed in 1987 reflected on the period of the Children's Centres.

By 1984 there was a strong staff group at (Children's Centre) who were fundamentally opposed to the use of residential care. The area staff weren't anything like so opposed.

An Area Team Manager from the same division also commented:

I made my support clear for some level of local residential provision... Falling numbers (of children placed residentially)? It wasn't possible to get young people into the

(Children's) Centre by this time (1984/5)... I didn't think the provision was very good anyway.

The lack of a clear County strategy for residential care appears to have been compounded by the development of strategies at a divisional level or sometimes at the level of a Children's Centre, which were inimical to good residential care practice. These local developments were clearly only possible in the vacuum created by the lack of a broader policy, but other factors were at play.

- There was an assumption by management that a shift from children's homes with resident houseparents to Children's Centres with qualified, non-resident staff would provide a more professional service. But it was not clear what this new provision would consist of.
- There was considerable turnover of staff and subsequent disruption during the years following the 1979 decisions. Experienced staff left to undertake training but often, once qualified, these staff members did not choose to return to the residential sector.
- New, qualified staff were recruited to the Children's Centres, attracted by salaries on qualified social worker scales and by what were described and seen as progressive policies in residential childcare. However, what is not clear is how much experience of residential work these new staff members had. Certainly some of the ones interviewed had limited experience at best.

At this point it is appropriate to comment on the explanation given by Warwickshire Social Services managers for closures of Children's Centres in 1985. It was, it was claimed, possible to make these closures because the numbers of children placed in the Centres fell and it became unviable to continue to operate all of the Centres. That the closures were demand-led is undeniable. However, what is less clear is whether demand would have remained at a higher level if the County had developed a clearer role for residential childcare and if the staff groups working in some of the Children's Centres had been more committed to residential care as an essential service rather than an unavoidable one.

There were other developments in the period 1979 to 1986 which it is important to mention before moving on to the circumstances surrounding the final Children's Centres' closures. The first of these was in the field of juvenile justice.

In 1977 Warwickshire set up its first Intermediate Treatment (IT) Centre in its Rugby Division. The aim of this Centre was to work with 'at risk' adolescents to prevent admission to care and to work with young people in care to facilitate their return home. The Criminal Justice Act 1982 gave courts the power to make intermediate treatment orders as an alternative to custodial sentences and, in response, Warwickshire invested further in IT Centres. By 1984 there was a Centre in each of the five divisions.

The County's investment in IT was much higher than that of many other authorities and indeed, in 1985, was at a level about five times the national average. By 1985 only 13 juveniles were given custodial sentences which was one of the lowest, if not the lowest figure in the country – an admirable achievement. In 1984 Warwickshire SSD and the Probation Service agreed a joint policy in relation to juveniles, with an agreement that care and custody should be prevented where possible. This cooperation was extended in 1985 to include the police, and a Juvenile Bureau was established in Warwick and staffed by an officer from each service. The aim of the Bureau was to divert juvenile offenders from both the court system and care. In 1986 two further Juvenile Bureaux were established to cover the rest of the County. The success of the IT Centres and the Juvenile Bureaux is demonstrated in the figures given in Table 3.1.

Table 3.1 Number of juveniles given custodial sentences in Warwickshire

Year	1984	1985	1986	1987
Number	28	13	5	10

These developments in the juvenile justice field and their success, together with low numbers of children committed to care for reasons of offending, remanded in care or subject to residential care orders, played their part in allowing Warwickshire to close their Children's Centres. Berridge (1985), in his study of children's homes identified the 'control of adolescents', some of whom had committed offences, as one of the main roles of the residential sector.

In 1984 and 1985 there were developments in different parts of the County which deserve mention, because they acted as forerunners for the organisation of services post-1986. In 1984 the smallest of the Children's Centres (in Stratford-upon-Avon) closed and the staffing establishment freed by this closure was used to set up a Community Resources Team (CRT) in Warwick, which served the south of the County.

This CRT proved itself to be essential in enabling the community placements of children to take place and to support the children and the foster families within those placements. (Warwickshire Director of Social Services, 1986)

In 1985 the Children's Centre in Rugby was also closed, although this was against the advice of the Head of the Rugby Children's Centre and the other two Heads of Children's Centres. Their worries were, first, that the community alternatives to residential placements, particularly foster care, were not sufficiently well developed; and, second, that demand for residential placements would exceed those available. These objections were not accepted and the Rugby Children's Centre closed.

The majority of the staff from that unit joined a new team with the (Rugby) intermediate treatment team staff and the new combined team was called the Children's Services Team (CST). The CST took the concept of the CRT a stage further in that it incorporated within it the very successful skills demonstrated by the IT staff... To enable the Rugby CST to operate effectively, three contract foster homes were created. Contract foster care is a new initiative designed to provide a short-term assessment resource for young people being received into care. It is designed ... to be always available for the placement of some of the most difficult children coming into the Council's care. (Ibid.)

The Children's Services Team, combining juvenile justice work, direct work with families and the recruitment and support of foster carers was to become a key plank in provision in the County after 1986, as was the recruitment of contract foster carers.

The final Children's Centre closures – 1986

By 1985, as we have seen, residential provision in Warwickshire was reduced to just two Children's Centres. In a paper to the County Management Team, the Divisional Director with responsibility for childcare services identified three options for August 1986 (the Director having made the commitment that no more Children's Centres would close before then). The first option was to close both units but this would not address the need for a residential respite facility, nor enable time for other resources to be established. The second option involved closing just one Centre. However, it was anticipated that staff in the remaining unit would see that Centre as being used as something of a 'dustbin'. The third and recommended option was to take staff committed to residential care into one unit and leave one Children's Centre on one site.

All these options were of course based on an acceptance of the inevitability of falling numbers of residential placements. However, as we have shown, there was really nothing inevitable about falling demand for residential placements. It was more an unintended consequence of a series of policy decisions combined with the lack of a clear role for the staff in the residential sector.

Before deciding on what recommendation it should make to the Social Services Committee, the Department's managers held a consultation meeting with staff from the remaining two Children's Centres, the IT Teams, the Community Resources Team from Warwick and the Children's Services Team from Rugby.

During a half-day meeting between the Director and ... 90 or so staff ... there was an almost unanimous decision by staff to close both Centres. With only one or two exceptions they felt that it would be a mistake to keep one Centre open. That Centre would be dealing with one or two (sic) very difficult children and perhaps in a way not best suited to their needs, since such children are more likely to benefit from more specialised care. (Warwickshire SSD, 1987)

This summary again begs the question about numbers, but certainly in interviews undertaken during the research, no one wanted to work in a lone Children's Centre. Staff feared that they would have no control over admissions and that the Centre would become a last resort and dumping ground. Inevitably, staff in the Centre would be able to undertake very little work with the children's families, schools and so on. In a single resource in a geographically disparate County, most children would also be placed at a distance from their homes.

Warwickshire had come a long way since 1979, when the five Children's Centres were set up to offer a local resource tied in to Divisional departmental structures and reaching out into the child's community.

Residential home closures and financial savings

Nothing has been said so far about the costs of the move away from residential childcare provision to community-based provisions. Certainly good quality residential care is not a cheap option, although neither is good quality foster care. Did Warwickshire save money by closing children's homes? The Short Committee asked this question when it visited Warwickshire in 1982. The Chair of the Social Services Committee responded:

We developed plans that could eventually lead us not only to getting children from out of residential care but ... being able to reallocate the money in what we thought was a more appropriate manner for the development of foster services. (House of Commons, 1984)

The Short Committee noted that figures had not been available for them to examine. During this research, with commendable openness, access was provided to *all* the relevant papers, including those from the Social Services Committee meetings at which closures of children's homes were decided. On each occasion from 1979 to 1986, savings in revenue expenditure made when homes were closed were channelled back into services for children. The 1979 closures led to savings, which were spent on improved staffing ratios, qualified pay scales and the costs of secondments to training courses for unqualified staff. The 1984 and 1985 closures resulted in savings, which were used to set up the Community Resources Team and the Children's Services Team, and to pay contract foster carers. The final closures in 1986 also freed revenue and this was spent on the new provisions which will be outlined in the next section.

The organisation of childcare services in Warwickshire since 1986

After its consultations with staff, Warwickshire's management decided early in 1986 to recommend to the Social Services Committee that the last two Children's Centres should be closed down with effect from 31 July 1986. The Committee accepted this recommendation at its meeting held in April of that year. In his report to the Committee, the Director was not only making the recommendation for the closures but was proposing alternative structures and services which would achieve the Committee's objectives in relation to services to children and their families. Prime among these objectives was keeping children with their families – and to that end preventing admission to care or custody wherever possible. If children needed to be admitted to care, they should be placed in substitute family placements rather than residential care and their stay in care should be as short as possible. As will be clear by now, those were the objectives which had been pursued consistently by the Department for a decade or more.

Managers had only a matter of months from their decision to recommend closure of the remaining Children's Centres to the Committee meeting at which this recommendation and the proposals for alternative structures would be considered. This being the case, these alternatives were based on what had been tested out in practice in parts of the County in the previous years. In particular, the proposals drew on the experiences of the Community Resources Team, set up when the Stratford Children's Centre closed in 1984, and the Children's Services Team, set up after the closure of the Rugby Children's Centre in 1985. The remainder of the chapter will outline the central features of services for children implemented in August 1986.

Children's Services Teams (CST)

The Rugby CST was formed as a result of combining the staff from the Children's Centre and the IT Centre and its brief was:

- to prevent admission of children and young people to care or custody;
- to find non-residential placements for children admitted to care; and
- to support children in these placements.

As the Director reported to the Committee in April 1986:

There are already very clear indications from Rugby that the concept of a Children's Services Team is being successful in achieving its objectives. (Warwickshire Director of Social Services, 1986)

Five CSTs were created, one in each of the Department's divisions. Each CST had a manager on the same grade as the Community Team (area fieldwork team)

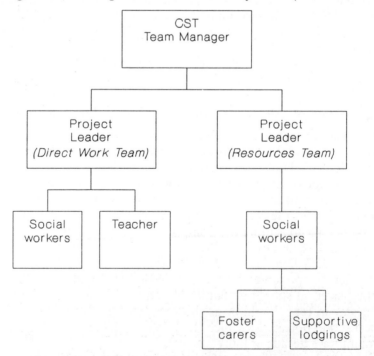

Figure 3.6 Organisation of Warwickshire CSTs

managers, and the CST managers and Community Team managers all reported directly to the Divisional Fieldwork Services Manager. Figure 3.6 shows the structure of a typical Children's Services Team.

The CST manager supervised two project leaders, one of whom headed the Direct Work Team and the other the Resources Team. The Direct Work Team provided:

- intermediate treatment;
- group work for young people in care or at risk of admission to care;
- intensive work with individual young people including education for those excluded from school;
- co-working with Community Team social workers.

The Resources Team, in contrast, was responsible for:

- recruiting and assessing foster carers and providers of supportive lodgings;
- providing a link social worker for each foster carer;
- maintaining a foster care register;
- ensuring that a foster placement was available when required;
- supporting local foster carer support groups.

More detail of the services of the CSTs and an analysis of their effectiveness will be found in Chapters 9 and 10, but one important point to make here concerns the relative size of the CSTs. In a typical division between 25 per cent and 30 per cent of the total social work staff were employed in the CST. This was clearly a very substantial commitment. The work of the CSTs was all child-focused. Most of the remaining social workers were based in the generic Community Teams and there they had responsibility for other client groups, as well as for work with children and their families.

It should also be noted that CST Direct Work Teams were responsible only for providing services for children aged five or over. Separate Divisional Family Centres worked with children under five and their families.

Foster care

With the closure of the Children's Centres, foster carers in Warwickshire would be required to provide services including:

- emergency placements;
- assessment placements;
- accommodation for adolescents; and
- accommodation for 'difficult' children.

As we have seen, by 1985 the number of children and young people accommodated in the Children's Centres was very low, and so their closure did not require large numbers of additional foster placements to be found to accommodate young people being transferred from residential care. However, it was clear that the Department would have to increase its pool of foster carers to ensure the availability of placements when there was no fall-back of a Children's Centre placement. Other priorities were also identified:

- improving the training and support for carers;

- reducing the high wastage rates;
- providing for emergency admissions to care; and
- ensuring the availability of placements suitable for assessment purposes.

The CST Resources Teams were given the responsibilities for improving recruitment and training. And, as mentioned above, each foster carer was to have their own social worker – link worker – in the Resources Team, who would be their point of contact, whether they had a child placed with them or not.

The Department also introduced a banded payment system to foster carers as a way of rewarding them for the difficulty of the tasks they were expected to undertake, and to address the problems of recruitment and retention. The payment system, based on one developed by Derbyshire Social Services Department, had six bands, and foster carers in the top band were paid at a rate of £125 a week (1986 price levels) in addition to the standard boarding out payment. The band was assessed according to the perceived difficulty of caring for the child placed. An assessment form was used to identify 'difficulty'.

Most foster carers received a small payment (one-third of the lowest point on the banding scale) for up to 12 weeks when they had no child placed with them. However, there was a separate category of carer called *contract foster parents*, who were paid on the top band for all children and received a 50 per cent payment when not being used. The contract to which these foster carers agreed involved accepting any child or young person for placement, even at short notice. The contract foster carers were used as a time-limited resource, primarily for assessment purposes when a child was newly admitted to care or when a previous placement ended in an unplanned way. Financial provision was made for the recruitment of 11 sets of contract foster carers across the County but the Director reported to the Social Services Sub-Committee in March 1988 that the Service had only five contract foster parents.

It has proved to be difficult to recruit these very skilled and flexible foster parents...[They] find it difficult to maintain the high level of commitment required over an extended period. (Warwickshire Director of Social Services, 1988)

The case studies in Chapters 5 and 7 look in detail at the placement of some children with contract foster carers, and in Chapter 9 the whole issue of recruiting, retaining and using foster carers in Warwickshire is examined in detail.

Residential care

Warwickshire did *not* adopt a non-residential policy in 1986.

We needed to ensure that residential placement was retained as an option for children in care. It was clear that for some children substitute family care did not always provide an appropriate response and for these very few children residential care would always be required as an alternative. The system which was already in existence for the allocation of placements in medium- to long-term settings was working well... It was clear that we would continue to need to provide a small amount of short-term residential care for children. This factor had to be taken into account with the reorganisation. (Warwickshire SSD, 1987)

Medium- and long-term residential placements required an evaluation of available options and a justification to be presented to, and approved by, the Director of Social Services.

For short-term use, Warwickshire negotiated an arrangement with National Children's Home for it to provide four retained places at a residential unit just over the border in the north of the County. Warwickshire made full use of these retained places, access to which was also subject to very tight gatekeeping procedures (see Chapter 11).

Coordination of services for children

Earlier in this chapter we noted the County's recognition that in the early 1980s, services for children and their families would have benefited from improved, County-wide, practice guidance. In particular, there was uncertainty about the distinct roles of staff in the Community Teams, the Children's Centres and the Intermediate Treatment Centres. The opportunity was taken in 1986 to clarify the basic ground rules and to establish procedures to ensure their application.

We have already outlined the role given to the new CSTs. An issue we have not yet clarified, however, is that of case-accountability. In all circumstances, for children in care, the case-accountable worker would be a member of a Community Team. Staff in the CST would be accountable for the provision of a service. In modern parlance, Community Teams would be purchasers and the CSTs providers of services.

Two structures coordinated provision of services. First, Divisional Monitoring Groups, chaired by the CST Managers and made up of representatives from the Community Teams and other agencies where appropriate, were established. Each Monitoring Group considered all referrals involving children and their families, and decided on whether work should be undertaken. If work was needed a key worker would be identified, usually to come from a Community Team (but not from a CST) and the services required would be identified (often from the CST Direct Work Team but not necessarily).

The second coordinating structure, a Community Based Assessment (CBA) system, was implemented for urgent referrals. A CBA would take place if:

- a child's living situation (with parents or substitute carers) was under threat;
- there was a risk of a custodial sentence being imposed on the child; or
- there was a demand for substantial resources from a CST Direct Work Team.

The CBA procedure involved an initial meeting with all involved professional staff, together with the child and his or her parents. At this meeting a short-term plan would be made, which might involve identifying a care placement for the child but would also specify those responsible for undertaking an assessment of the child's longer-term needs. These would be reported back to a second CBA meeting, which would be held six to eight weeks later.

It will become clear in later sections of this book the extent to which the Divisional Monitoring Groups and the Community Based Assessment procedure were effective in clarifying the role of different teams, and in achieving the objective of more effective planning of children's admission to, and careers in, care.

Summary

This chapter had provided an overview of developments in Warwickshire in the decade preceding the closure of the County's last residential childcare facilities.

- The County has had a long-term commitment to a belief that 'Every child deserves the right to a family life' and that residential care should be avoided wherever possible.
- Warwickshire's use of residential placements declined at about the same rate as other authorities in England and Wales but starting from a lower point they reached such a low base in 1986 that the final residential closures became feasible.
- The fall in residential placements was only possible because the numbers in care fell, not because additional foster carers were recruited.
- From 1974 to 1979 Warwickshire pursued a policy of closing 'family group homes' and concentrating provision on a limited number of specialist, divisional residential facilities.
- In 1979 Warwickshire had only five Children's Centres and a policy to staff them with CQSW-qualified social work staff.
- The closures of Children's Centres between 1979 and 1986 were possible because the numbers of young people placed in residential care fell. But the explanation for these falling numbers involved opposition to residential care from some Children's Centre staff themselves and a lack of clarity in the role of the Centres.
- In 1986 the last of the Children's Centres closed. A Children's Services Team was established in each division. Each CST accounted for over a quarter of each division's qualified social worker establishment.
- Each CST had a Resources Team, which focused on the recruitment, training and support of foster carers, and on the provision of foster placements; and a Direct Work Team which provided group work and intensive individual work for children in care or at risk of care or custody.

---

4. Finding and making placements

The actual decision that a child should be admitted to care is only one part, and in many ways a small part, of a process which may well have begun much earlier and which will often continue long into the future. Many other decisions also have to be made, not the least important of which concerns where the child should live. Will he or she remain with parents or does an alternative placement need to be found? There are a whole range of issues which will need to be considered when deciding where the child should stay.

This chapter will focus on the process of making placements for children in care and on the issues which are central to this process. However, the focus will not just be on children newly admitted to care; once in care, many children move from one placement to another. Sometimes such moves are made for good reasons, for instance a move from a short-term placement where the child's requirements have been assessed, to a longer term placement which will begin to meet these needs. And sometimes the move will be unplanned and may have happened because the relationship between child and carers has broken down. Whatever the reasons for the move, finding suitable placements for children is both complex and time-consuming for social workers but fundamentally important in determining the young person's future.

We will look first at the pattern of placements made for the children in our study. To what extent is the County succeeding in its stated aim of providing foster homes for the majority of children and making use of residential care for only a small minority? This is followed by an examination of the degree of success which social workers had in making the types of placement they thought most suitable for the children and young people in this study. We then go on to look at how much choice was actually available to social workers about where the children were placed – were there a number of, say, foster homes available which had different things to offer, or was there only one placement which was at all suitable?

The social worker who is looking for a placement for a child in care has many issues to consider, not all of which may point towards the same conclusion. She or he needs to be clear about the reason why the child is in care and about what the aims are when she or he is trying to identify a placement. The social worker may want somewhere which would be suitable as a short-term base for a child whose mother is in hospital for a few weeks, or may be looking for a long-term placement for a child who is not expected to return home. Similarly, what would be the best location for the placement must also be considered – one near to the child's home so that regular visiting is possible or one at more distance because contact between the child and parents has to be carefully managed. If a more distant location is preferred, the social worker also needs to consider what effect such a placement would have on the child's education.

If a child comes into care along with brothers and sisters, one of the social worker's priorities should be to find a placement which will enable these siblings to continue to live together. If a child has particular special needs or poses specific problems, then carers will be required who have the skills and experience to provide the child with a positive experience.

All of these issues are discussed in this chapter. We take the aims and priorities which social workers identified and begin to assess how well these aims were achieved and priorities met. But throughout, the main focus is on the extent to which appropriate and beneficial placements are available.

How do we go about evaluating the results of our research on the making of placements for children in care? Recent research has given us a much clearer picture of what amounts to good practice. One of those researchers, Jean Packman, commented on the results of her research,

A crucial area of practice concerns the admission process itself. Too often this was conducted in a way calculated to reinforce rather than reduce the shock and damage of separation for the children and young people involved. Long established lessons of good child care practice ... were honoured more in the breach than the observance... But improvements do not solely depend on statutes, or on the efforts of social workers alone. They rely heavily upon providing placements that are actually in excess of demand ... to make it possible to reserve placements in advance and to make choices between them; and they require methods of allocation which do not merely respond to last minute crises. (Packman, 1986)

This is the approach which rightly says that we must compare what we do with what we know to be the best. But in the real world no one achieves what is the best, they fall short of the best to a greater or lesser extent. The Dartington Social Research Unit made this point in the conclusion to their study of the links between children in care and their parents.

While the placements that children in care experience may be suitable in theory, we have seen that in practice many of them leave much to be desired. Social workers find it extremely difficult to find suitable placements... There are too few short-term foster situations and many residential homes are both insufficiently flexible and distant. (Millham and others, 1986)

We fully accept that social work practice in the real world, as with any other occupation, falls short of perfection. For this research the implication is that we need to identify a *realistic and achievable* set of targets for good practice against which we can assess our findings for Warwickshire. These targets derive from research which has been carried out in other authorities. Therefore, throughout this chapter and the whole book, the results from our research in Warwickshire will be compared not only with what we know to be the *best practice* but also with what *actually happens* in other areas.

Patterns of placement in Warwickshire

One way of providing an overview of the placements of children in care is that adopted by the Department of Health. Their reports on children in care present figures for the stock of childcare placements on one specific day in each year (31 March). These details were used to produce the historical data in Chapter 3, which showed how placements made by Warwickshire compared with the figures for all English Social Services Departments (SSDs). We saw that from the mid 1970s, Warwickshire, in comparison to other authorities, placed considerably more children with foster carers and considerably fewer in residential establishments.

One of the aims of this research has been to provide a more detailed view than is reflected in official figures for the stock of placements. Following our cohort, which included children in long-term care and children newly admitted, has given us a dynamic picture of the use of care placements in Warwickshire over a period of time. (For details of how these figures were calculated, *see* Chapter 1.) How do the static and the dynamic pictures compare? Table 4.1 compares the in-care figures for Warwickshire as a whole for March 1988 with the results for our cohort.

Table 4.1 Stock and flow placement figures for Warwickshire

	In care at March 1988 (%)	*Cohort* (*No.*=256) (%)
With parents (home on trial)	14	7
Foster care	68	81
Residential care	2	2
Residential school	4	3
Other	12	8
Total	100	100

Totals in this and subsequent tables may not equal 100 per cent due to rounding.

The differences between these two sets of figures are clearly noticeable, especially the differences between the stock of foster placements in the left hand column (68 per cent) and our figure for the flow of foster placements (81 per cent). The home on trial figures are also markedly different. How are we to understand these differences?

The foster placement stock figure significantly underestimates the extent to which foster placements are used by Warwickshire. The foster placement flow is a higher figure because foster care is used, to a greater extent than the stock figure suggests, as a short-term resource. Many of the movements between placements, therefore, are excluded from the official statistics. The difference between the two sets of figures for home on trial placements results from the fact that these types of placement tend to be relatively long-term and are, therefore, more likely to appear in the stock figures. They are, however, less significant when considered alongside all of the placements made in a particular period.

As we saw in Chapter 3, Warwickshire has historically had a boarding out rate (stock figure) which has been higher than most, if not all, other social services departments. That Warwickshire should have a foster placement flow rate as high as 84 per cent leads us to ask how this compares with that of other authorities. Official statements to date provide only partial information, but we can draw on the results of the large-scale study of placements in six representative authorities which was undertaken by Jane Rowe and her colleagues (1989). This important study collected details on 5000 different placements for over 2000 children. The six authorities included two London boroughs, one large city, one small metropolitan district and two counties.

Figure 4.1 gives details of the static stock figures and foster placement flow rates, over time, for each of Rowe's six authorities alongside the same figures for Warwickshire.

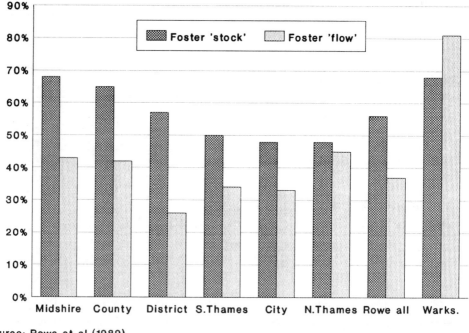

Source: Rowe et al (1989)

Figure 4.1 Warwickshire and comparisons: Foster placement stock and flow rates

Interestingly, unlike Warwickshire, the foster placement flow for each of Rowe's six authorities was lower than the foster placement stock (and in one case it was less than half the stock figure). Indeed, when we focus on flow rates, as shown in the second column for each authority, the differences between Warwickshire and these other typical authorities in the types of placements made for children in care are much greater than might have been anticipated. In

Warwickshire as many as 17 out of 20 placements experienced by our cohort were foster placements; in Rowe's authorities a maximum of nine out of 20 and a minimum of five out of 20 were foster placements.

We must be cautious about being too precise in our comparisons because, in Rowe's study, children of all ages were included whereas our study includes only children aged five and over. However, if we had included the under fives, then if anything the effect would have been to *increase* the foster placement rate, since residential care and residential school placements are a negligible resource for placements for under fives in the County.

In summary this analysis reveals, first, that Warwickshire is successful in its aim of making foster care its main resource for children in care. Second, the County makes significantly greater use of foster care than other local authorities, especially if we measure placement rates rather than take a more static view. And, finally, it would appear that in particular, the use of *short-term* foster care is especially prevalent. We shall consider some of the explanations for this later.

Let us now move on to consider what determined the type of placement children in our cohort experienced.

Factors associated with the placements made

Changes of placement

One factor which was strongly associated with the type of placements which were made for children in the County was the number of placement changes a child experienced. Table 4.2 shows the types of placement made for children at admission to care, in their second placement, and in their third and subsequent placements.

Table 4.2 Placement types and placement changes

	Admission placements (No.=72) (%)	Second placement (No.=43) (%)	Third or subsequent placement (No.=52) (%)
Foster care	94	91	60
Home on trial	0	7	10
Residential care	0	0	8
Residential school	0	0	4
Other	6	2	19
Total	100	100	100

What appears to happen at the first change of placement is that some children remain in care but return to their parents from foster placements or from other placements (home on trial). At the second and later placement changes, the proportion of children in foster care falls steadily, slightly more children return home on trial, and residential and other placements become increasingly used. How should we interpret these changes and how do these results compare with what happens in other authorities?

The types of placement made for children on admission to care in Warwickshire clearly distinguish the County from other authorities. As Table 4.2 shows, for our cohort, residential care placements and residential schools were only used when children and young people had experienced at least two other types of placement (usually foster care). Berridge (1985) identified children's homes as having a significant role in providing placements for children at the time they were received into care. In addition, Millham and his colleagues (1986) found that over half of the admission placements for children in their study were in residential facilities. In Warwickshire, in marked contrast, all but a handful of admission placements were in foster homes.

In Warwickshire, the procedures for securing approval for residential placements mean that, although in theory a residential placement would be available for a child on admission to care, in practice such placements are very seldom, if ever, made. The working assumption of social workers and their managers, which was confirmed in many interviews, is that approval for a residential placement would not be given unless alternative types of placement (usually foster care) had been tried first.

For those children who remain in care for more than a short time the picture becomes more complicated. Some children remain in their initial placements while others experience many moves. There is an increasing use of residential care but still at a low rate.

The age of the child

The other key factor affecting the type of placement made for children in care is age. Berridge (1985) in his detailed study of 20 children's homes found that almost three in every four of the residents of the homes were aged 12 or over. The Department of Health's most recent figures (at the time of writing) for placements according to age are shown in Table 4.3.

Table 4.3 Age-structure of childcare placements, England

	5–9	10–15	16+	Total%
Home on trial	15	13	20	16
Foster placement	74	50	30	49
Residential placement	8	30	28	25
Other	3	7	22	11
All	100	100	100	100

Source: DHSS, 1988, *Children in the Care of Local Authorities, England, 31 March 1986.*

Berridge's findings are supported by these figures. Residential care is predominantly used for the over-tens group. It is also interesting to note the rapid decline in the proportion of children in foster care among the older groups and also the high use of other types of placement for the 16+ group. We will return to these results later on.

Moving on from this static view of the stock of placements, placement flow rates *over time* show a different picture. Table 4.4 presents figures from Rowe's 1988 study and the Warwickshire study.

Table 4.4 Placement flow rates by age group

	5–10 (%)		11 + (%)		All ages 5+ (%)	
	Rowe	*War.*	*Rowe*	*War.*	*Rowe*	*War.*
Home on trial	7	6	11	4	10	4
Fostering	65	94	15	81	25	84
Residential	25	0	52	4	47	3
Other	3	0	22	12	18	10
All	100	100	100	100	100	100

Rowe's figures as well as those of the DHSS and Berridge confirm that the main role for residential care is with older children. Warwickshire's placement pattern reflected this but the scale of the placements was of a startlingly different order and to this extent childcare in Warwickshire clearly is exceptional. Only 11 of the placements (No.=256) in the Warwickshire cohort were residential (including residential schools) and these were all for children aged over ten. Over 81 per cent of the placements for this age group were foster placements, which is more than five times greater than the equivalent figure for Rowe's cohort (which was only 15 per cent).

The use of other types of placement

In Chapter 3 we saw that suggestions that the closure of children's homes by Warwickshire had led to increases in placements of children home on trial and in other types of placement were in fact unjustified. However, if we look at the types of placements which made up this umbrella category of placement, some important details emerge. Figure 4.2 provides a breakdown of these 'other' placements for the period 1979 to 1989.

Figure 4.2 shows that between the early and the late 1980s, that is the periods before and after the closure of the Children's Centres, the number of children in care in Warwickshire and accommodated in residential special schools rose. This issue will be examined in detail in Chapter 12. Furthermore, Figure 4.2 also reveals that throughout this period, Warwickshire, encouragingly, had relatively few children in care who were placed in penal establishments. From a

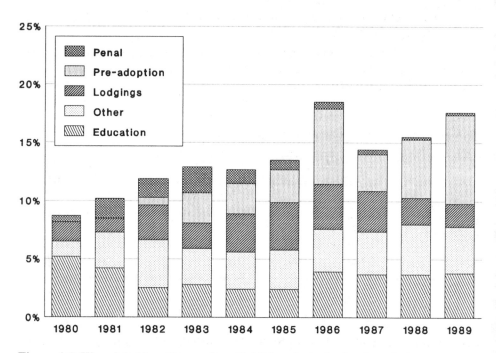

Figure 4.2 Warwickshire: Proportion of children in 'other' types of placement

peak of around two per cent in 1983 the numbers steadily declined until in 1989 they were less than half a per cent. In Jane Rowe's (1989) study the average of placements in penal establishments for all six of her authorities was four per cent. Warwickshire's success in reducing these already low figures is the result of their alternative to custody policy, as described in Chapter 3, and this is to be applauded.

Although we have rejected Parker's suspicion about a shift of children from residential care to home on trial placements, his concern does, however, lead on to a second and possibly more important question for this research. To what extent is foster care within the County able to offer satisfactory experiences to children and young people from a broad range of circumstances? As we have already seen, many of these children would have been deemed candidates for residential placement if they had lived elsewhere. We will return to this question in Chapter 6.

Priorities in the identification of placements

Case workers completing our questionnaires were asked to identify the priority they had given to a series of issues at the time they were making each new placement for our study cohort. Eight separate factors were described and the worker was asked to classify each as high, medium or low priority, or not applicable. These factors, detailed in Table 4.5, cover three main areas:

• whether siblings could be placed together;

- the skills and experience of the carers; and
- the location of the placement and the effect this had on the child's contact with parents, others and on schooling.

In the recent literature on childcare there has been considerable agreement on the importance, for children in care, of maintaining regular contact with their parents and other family members. As a consequence, this was enshrined in the Children Act 1989. Berridge and Cleaver (1987) demonstrated that foster placements are less likely to disrupt if they are 'inclusive' rather than 'exclusive'; that is, if they are able to involve the natural parents rather than keep them away. Millham and others (1986) identified the importance of maintaining links between children in care and their families and one reason they gave was the correlation found between the likelihood of a child remaining in care for a long period and a lack of parental contact. They also identified families as an important source of continuity for children in care; the care experience itself often being discontinuous and turbulent.

However, while arguing for greater social work commitment to maintaining links between parents and children in care, the Dartington Social Research Unit also recognised that the issue of links is not separable from many other aspects of social work policy and practice.

The ways that links are maintained, lost or regenerated are dependent on many other issues and different processes, each with different outcomes... Many barriers to contact are implicit on decisions made on placements, distance or a child's special needs ... [and on] changes in the child's natural family while he or she is away in care. (Millham and others, 1986)

For one group of children in care the benefits of parental and family contact has been the subject of some debate. Goldstein, Freud and Solnit (1973) and others in Adcock (1980) have argued that for some children in long-term substitute care placements – particularly younger children – terminating parental contact can improve the chances of success of the placement. Others have disagreed with this analysis even for children in long-term care (for example, Holman, 1975; Thorpe, 1980; Fanshel, 1978). Rowe and others (1984), in their study of long-term foster care, came down somewhere in the middle of this debate. Fewer than half of the children in their study had any contact with their natural families. For some of those who did have contact there were benefits; but overall, the best adjusted group of children were those who were at least five-years-old when they lost touch with their parents but who were no longer being visited. It should be remembered that the group of children in Rowe's study had been placed with foster families for at least three years. For children who have been in care for a relatively short period, however, there is little disagreement that for the majority family contact is beneficial and should be encouraged.

To a large extent the issue of maintaining parental contact is about ensuring continuity for a child admitted to care. Three of the other factors which we asked social workers to prioritise in terms of their bearing on seeking placements also concerned aspects of continuity through the admission process and care experience. For example, the desirability of keeping sibling groups together once admitted to care is identified as desirable by several of the authors cited above and, once again, is also an issue taken up by the Children Act 1989.

Furthermore, we asked social workers about the priority they gave to continuity of more general community links, such as contacts with friends, and to continuity of education. A number of studies (Millham and others 1980, Essen and others 1976, Jackson 1987) have clearly identified that children who have experienced care have lower educational achievements than children who have not been in care. However, more up-to-date work by Aldgate has shown that children in foster care did not perform worse educationally than a matched group of children not in care.

A variety of explanations have been identified for this poor educational achievement. In one study, social workers were shown to give little regard to the child's education when making decisions about placements (Melotte, 1979). Low educational attainment has also been linked with a lack of continuity experienced by children in care, both in the personnel involved in caring for them and also in the educational experience itself. There is also, of course, the fact that children entering care have often experienced multiple deprivations and many come from sections of the population that in any case are quite likely to underachieve.

The importance to children in care of a good education was recognised by the House of Commons Social Services Committee in their report on children in care (1984).

We consider that a child in care has a right to at least as good an education as any other child. In view of the disadvantage which being in care all too often represents, that may sometimes mean making a particular effort to ensure the quality of education given to children in care. (House of Commons, 1984)

Two of the other factors we asked social workers to prioritise, in terms of their influence on seeking placements for the Warwickshire cohort, concerned the ability of the placement or the care providers to address the child's specific problems – such as the ability to provide a framework in which a child's behaviour could be managed. And the final factor asked whether it was felt desirable to place the child at a distance from his or her family or community.

Table 4.5 summarises the responses to these questions. It details the number of placements where each of the factors was considered and identifies the proportion of placements where each factor was rated high priority. One of the key issues affecting the decision about priority of different factors in making placements was the reason for admission to care, or for continuing to be in care, and these differences are also shown in the table (*High priority by type of case*). The table also organises these factors into three larger groups, which are, those concerning placement with siblings; the location of the placement and issues of continuity; and the skills and abilities of the care providers. Let us consider each of these issues in turn.

Table 4.5 The priority of different factors when identifying placements

	No. of cases where considered or applicable	Cases where factor a high priority (%)	High Priority by type of case		
			Neglect/ abuse (%)	Poor care (%)	Child's behaviour (%)
Siblings					
To place with siblings	76	74	85	70	29 (N=7)
Continuity					
To be close enough for good access between child and parents/other relatives	217	54	55	61	48
To enable child to maintain other community links	215	42	33	51	40
To enable child to remain in same school	184	74	60	78	84
To provide physical distance from parents	143	27	20	29	26
The skills of carers					
To provide control over child's behaviour	216	54	45	47	84
To meet child's particular special needs	192	53	56	56	63
Placement where carers had skills or experience to address child's problems	233	71	80	65	82

Placing with siblings

In just over one third of all the placements the factor of placing a child with his or her brothers or sisters was an issue. Nearly all of the children in care with siblings were there for reasons of poor care or neglect/abuse; very few were in care for behavioural reasons. This finding is reflected in other studies (Millham and others 1986, Berridge 1985). Given that research has identified the desirability of keeping sibling groups together in care, except in very limited circumstances, it was noteworthy and encouraging that for our cohort no other issue received more high priority ratings from the social workers. The factor was rated as high priority much more for children under 11 (90 per cent) compared with older children (56 per cent). It was also the only factor which was associated with a preference by the social worker for a placement with relatives.

The continuity of the care experience and the location of placements

The second group of factors which emerged prominently in influencing social workers' choice of placements for the cohort concerned the continuity of experience for children in care. To some extent this overlaps with the location of the placement. Contact with parents, friends and continuity of education crucially depend, of course, on where the placement is in relation to home and school. Again the research findings and legislation are unanimous that continuity and location are crucial issues in making an appropriate placement for a particular child. Chapter 6 will examine in detail how the placements made for children in the cohort met these criteria but our concern is the placing social workers' attitudes.

In nearly two-thirds of placements the social worker thought that it was necessary to consider providing at least some distance between the child's parents and his or her placement, although for only a quarter of these placements was this issue rated highly. It was surprising that the issue of continuity of schooling rather than contact with parents was identified as a higher priority for placements – particularly in view of the research we reported earlier which suggested that, hitherto, educational considerations have played little part in care placement decisions. What was not so surprising was that the highest priority to education was given to those cases where the main concern was identified as the child's behaviour.

Providing a placement which enabled a child to see his or her parents regularly was identified as having a high priority for 54 per cent of placements and as being a low priority issue in only 11 per cent of placements. If we look at the age of the children in the placements, we discover significant differences between those aged under 16 and those who were older. For the under 16 age group contact with parents was rated as high priority for 63 per cent of placements. For those aged 16 or more, the figure was about half this. For these young people social workers were either identifying contact with parents as less important, or possibly they were assuming that travelling longer distances was not such a problem, as it could be undertaken by the young person or the parents.

The maintenance of links with friends was identified as of less importance, but was only seen as being a low priority for just over a quarter of placements.

The skills of carers

Three questions addressed the issue of the priority given to the skills which substitute carers in different types of placements could provide and these questions produced very interesting results. First, in very few cases was this issue not seen as relevant. Second, the skills and experience of carers were seen as much more significant for children aged over ten. Did social workers believe that the needs of the younger children could be met in less specialised placements or by less skilled carers? This might be true for children with behavioural problems but would it also be true for children with emotional problems, such as children who have been abused or neglected? The third finding was that providing a placement with skilled carers was most important where behavioural problems were the main issue or where the child had been admitted because of neglect or abuse. It was the group admitted for reasons of poor care (for example, illness or death of a parent) for whom placing with especially skilled carers was seen as less important.

Finally, there were strong associations between the placements where social workers identified the need for skilled carers and the type of placement identified as most appropriate for the child. The two types of placement identified as those most likely to fulfil the requirements for skilled carers were contract foster placements and, interestingly, given their unpopularity in the County, residential placements. Independent living, lodgings and home on trial were seen as the least likely, with ordinary foster homes coming somewhere in the middle.

In Chapter 6, where we begin to look at how successful the placements were, we will examine the extent to which these priorities were achieved.

Placement aims

The questionnaires which were used to examine each of the placements made for children in care included reference to placement aims. The responses to these questions are revealing, especially in the way they changed as children moved from one placement to another (see Table 4.6). Overall, more than two-fifths of all placements had the main aim of either providing a short-term placement during a family difficulty or providing a child with a roof over his or her head for a short period. Just over one in ten of placements was made while an assessment of the child's or family's situation was being carried out, and about the same proportion were made with carers who would be responsible for the longer term upbringing of the child.

Table 4.6 Placement aims by age group (No. = 189)

	5–10 years (%)	11–13 years (%)	14–15 years (%)	16+ (%)	Total (%)
Preparation for long-term family placement	12	2	7	0	4
Care and upbringing	25	21	11	1	12
Short-term care during family difficulty	34	30	39	12	26 ·
Assessment of child's or family's needs	15	14	11	13	13 ·
'Treatment' of child/family problems	0	12	9	3 ⁻	6
Emergency care, e.g. 'roof over head'	9	12	15	21	15 ·
Bridge to independence	0	0	2	22	8 ˛
Remand placement	0	0	4	21	8 ·
Other	3	9	2	7	6
Total	100	100	100	100	100

Age was clearly an important factor associated with placement aims. The average (mean) age of the young people in the bridge to independence and remand placements was nearly $16^1/_2$. The average age of children in placements where the aims were preparation for long-term placements, care and upbringing, short-term care or assessment, was under $12^1/_2$ years.

The sex of the child was associated with placement aims in two ways only. The first was the finding that for all 16 placements which resulted from a remand by a court, all the placements involved boys. (These 16 placements were for a total of six cases.) The second was that there were more than twice as many placements for girls where the aim was care and upbringing.

For all children in the cohort who were in care, we asked the case worker to identify 'the most appropriate placement' for the child at the time each placement was being sought. The workers were told to assume that all types of placement were available. This question was intended to get to the heart of the issues in Warwickshire. Table 4.7 presents the responses to this question with the types of placement organised into broad categories: therefore, foster placement with relatives, contract foster placements and ordinary foster placements are all subsumed under the broad heading of foster placements.

Table 4.7 Social workers' 'ideal' placements

	Ideal (No. = 193) *(%)*
Home on trial	9
Fostering	62
Residential care	6
Residential school	0
Other	23
All	100

The reader will be aware from the results presented in Table 4.1 that the figures presented here are very different from the actual pattern of placements which were made for our cohort and we will examine these differences in detail. However, before doing that, let us look at these figures as they stand.

Three things in particular stand out. First, in line with County policy, very few social workers identified a residential placement of any kind as their first choice. (This no doubt provides some assurance to senior management!) Second, social workers' first choice of placement in six out on ten cases was with foster carers. We will have already seen, in fact, that this figure is very much less than the figure for actual placements made. But perhaps the most perplexing result is the one which shows that in nearly a quarter of cases social workers' ideal placements were neither in foster nor residential care. This 'other' category includes:

- placements with relatives (but not fostering arrangements);
- in supportive lodgings;
- in ordinary lodgings;
- with friends; and
- in independent accommodation.

We will see later that, in particular, social workers were largely unsuccessful in being able to make placements with relatives and in supportive lodgings.

The determinants of social workers' preferred placements

What were the main factors associated with the types of placement social workers preferred? One was *age*. If we look at the three largest groups of placement types – that is with parents, foster placements (of all types) and residential placements (of all types) – we find that the average (mean) age for the first two groups was very close, but for foster placements and residential placements there was a statistically significant difference. The foster placement group was significantly younger (just over 13 years) compared with the residential placement group (nearly 16 years).

A second factor which related to the preferred type of placement was *the aim of the placement* when it was set up.

- Placements with parents were seen as appropriately used in a larger proportion of cases when the aims were care and upbringing, short-term care, preparation for a long-term placement or providing a bridge to independence; and a smaller proportion of cases when the aims were to provide emergency placements or remand placements.
- Foster placements were associated with the aims of 'treatment', assessment, preparation for long-term placement or emergency care; and were less often associated with providing a bridge to independence.
- Residential placements were seen as much more appropriately used for remand placements, emergency care and 'treatment'; least appropriately used for care and upbringing, preparation for long-term family placements, assessment and short-term care during family difficulty.

Age and placement aims were by far the most significant factors affecting social workers' assessments of the type of placements which would be best for children. The sex of the child did play a limited part, mainly in relation to residential placements with social workers identifying these as best for ten per cent of boys and only one per cent of girls.

There were also differences between the types of placement identified as most appropriate at admission and the type identified when placements changed. When a move was required for a child who was in care and who had one or more previous placements, social workers' preferences increased for home on trial, residential placements and contract foster placements. They were relatively less likely to identify placements with relatives or in ordinary foster homes than they were at the time of admission.

Matching preferred placements and actual placements

We now move on to consider how successful Warwickshire was in enabling social workers to place children in the type of placement they had identified as best for the child. Table 4.8 compares the social workers' preferred placements with the placements which they were actually able to make. Later on we will look at the results for different 'types' of placement by breaking down these broad categories.

Table 4.8 Ideal placements and actual placements compared

	Ideal (No. = 193) (%)	Actual (%)
Home on trial	9	4
Fostering	62	84
Residential care	6	2
Residential school	0	1
Other	23	9
All	100	100

The differences between ideal placements and actual placements are, in some categories, quite considerable.

- Nearly a quarter of the preferred placements fell into the 'other' category, but placements of this type were made in less than half this number of cases.
- The actual number of home on trial placements made was half the preferred number.
- Even though residential placements were preferred in a very few cases, the actual number of residential placements made was even smaller.
- In six out of ten cases, the placement of choice was fostering. However, foster care accounted for well over eight out of ten of the placements which were actually made.

Overall, foster placements were the only category where the figure for actual placements exceeded the figure for preferred placements. As we will see, the availability of placements was crucial for understanding these differences, but there were also other factors involved.

Table 4.8 and the analysis of it compared the accumulated results from questions which asked about ideal and actual placements, but we can carry out a more sophisticated analysis which compares the responses on a case by case basis. That is, each time a placement was being made, we can compare whether, on that occasion, the placement which the social worker wanted for the child was the same as the placement which was actually made. If we do this, we find that social workers were able to make a placement in the broad category of placement they preferred in seven out of ten cases.

Significantly, where a foster placement was preferred, the success rate in making a placement was near to perfect at 96 per cent. For all other categories of placement, however, social workers were successful in less than a *third* of cases. Statistically, this is a highly significant result.

This result would support our speculation that the *supply* of placements was a crucial factor. For all categories of placement other than foster care, there appeared to be a much more restricted set of options. However, as we shall see below, the supply of placements is only in part within the control of the local authority; placements with relatives obviously cannot be created if the relatives do not exist. Despite this reservation, however, the policies and practices of the authority remain as important factors in determining the availability of different types of placements.

In a quarter of the cases where a foster placement was the actual placement made, social workers judged that something different would have been more appropriate. Indeed, overall, the main types of placements which social workers would have liked to have made for the children and young people in our cohort but which they were unable to make were:

- Placements with relatives (fostered or not fostered)   91 per cent (No.=22) not made
- Residential placements in-county   100 per cent (No.=10) not made
- Contract foster placements   53 per cent (No.=32) not made
- Supportive lodgings   69 per cent (No.=13) not made

To what extent can we identify policy factors or practice issues which account for these large differences between ideal and actual placements? Let us examine the four types of placements separately.

The first of these four types of placement, that is placement with relatives, is one where policy changes would probably not have a profound effect on availability. (The exception to this is perhaps in the area of financial payments to relatives looking after children in care.) However, relatives cannot be recruited as carers if they do not exist – assuming of course that social workers routinely explore this option. We should, however, point out that the willingness of relatives to exercise caring responsibilities may be in some ways related to previous social work activities and attitudes.

However, different policies could provide more placements with contract foster carers, in supportive lodgings and in residential care. In-County residential placements could not be made because the Department no longer have any such facilities. However, the demand for such provisions, based on the figure of ten preferred placements for our cohort, would be low. Contract foster placements, as we will see with our case study of Chris Taylor in Chapter 5, are a restricted resource. We saw that the likelihood of having to wait for a contract foster placement is quite high, especially if a placement is required at short notice. There are only a limited number of contract foster placements in the County and, at any one time, most of them are occupied. However, it is important to point out that during the course of the research, the number of approved contract foster placements about doubled. In the light of our findings it is understood that further expansion is envisaged.

In relation to the supply of supportive lodgings, one Children's Services Team manager described the difficulties his team had in recruiting and retaining people willing to offer such facilities. Such landlords and landladies are required to go through a part of the foster carer approval process. In addition, there is only limited financial incentive for people to commit themselves to providing such a placement. An empty bed can usually be filled with an ordinary rent-paying tenant rather than keeping it free for social services' use. The problem of finding appropriate placements for older children and young people is one which we have identified before. Supportive lodgings were one of the main types of placement which social workers preferred for older children, but it was a type of placement which they were least successful in making. The issue of placements for older age groups has proved to be a particular problem for Warwickshire and is one to which we will return.

Making placements and placement aims

We began to look earlier at the aims which social workers had for placements at the time they were made. We identified there that particular aims were closely associated with particular types of placement. Given that social workers had less success in making some types of placements compared with others, what effect did this have on particular aims?

It was when the aims were treatment or care and upbringing that the preferred placements were most likely to be found. For both aims, over nine in every ten preferred placements were made. Least success was for placement intended to provide a bridge to independence (less than a third of preferred placements made), followed by preparation for long-term family placement and remands (both, four out of ten preferred placements made).

The options for residential placements and other placements were most restricted and these were seen by social workers as preferable to foster placements for some purposes. Indeed, if we look at the actual placements we can identify associations with particular placement aims. As we might expect, home on trial placements were strongly associated with the aim of care and upbringing; foster placements with treatment, assessment, preparation for long-term placements, and emergency care. Foster placements were much less frequently used where the aim was to provide a bridge to independence. Residential placements were particularly closely linked with remand placements and the aims of providing emergency care or treatment.

Rather disconcertingly, there were just about as many placements where the aim was to provide emergency care *after* admission as at the time of admission. This was also one of Rowe's (1989) findings and as she commented, 'This has to be seen as a salutary reminder of the instability of the care experience'. We will examine how and why placements ended in more detail in Chapter 8.

Placements for children from minority ethnic groups

For practical reasons, this research project was only able to examine a relatively small number of cases where the child was from a minority ethnic group or of mixed parentage. The reason for this was that relatively few Black children come into contact with Warwickshire Social Services Department. Jane Rowe's recent large scale placement study included a significant number of Black children, nearly 600, and their placements which numbered nearly 1500. Her main findings were:

- Overall, Black children were over-represented in admissions to care.
- Asian children were under-represented in admissions, African and Afro-Caribbean children over-represented, and mixed parentage children were the most likely to be admitted to care.
- African and Afro-Caribbean children tended to have shorter care episodes but more of these Black adolescents were still in care at the end of the project compared with White children.
- There were few differences in placement patterns or outcomes for Black children compared with White.

The cohort in our Warwickshire study included 13 Black children: one of African or Afro-Caribbean origin, two of Asian and ten of mixed parentage.

In 1989 Warwickshire began to monitor systematically the ethnic background of children in care. Excluding the cases in Warwickshire's childcare figures where the information was not available, Table 4.9 compares the data for all children in care in Warwickshire in March 1989 with our cohort of children admitted to care.

Table 4.9 Ethnic background of children in care

	Warwickshire March 1989 (No.=511) (%)	Study cohort (No.=141) (%)
White	94	91
African/Afro-Caribbean	1	1
Asian	1	1
Mixed parentage	3	7
Other	1	0
All	100	100

Given the small numbers of Black children in this study, it is unsurprising that there are some differences between our figures and those for all children in care in the County. However, both sets of figures in Table 4.9 suggest that Rowe's findings for her six authorities – that children of mixed parentage are the single largest minority group in care – also appear to be true for Warwickshire.

What can these figures tell us about the representation of Black children in care in the County? The best estimates of the Black population in Warwickshire were produced in a 1988 working party report. These figures suggest that overall, the Black population accounts for about three per cent of the total population, but this figure will include only a proportion of those in the County with mixed parentage. This overall figure also hides some marked differences between Social Services' divisions and even greater differences between electoral wards. The Black population in the divisions ranges from fewer than one per cent of the total population to almost six per cent. At ward level, the Black population in some areas rises to as high as 28 per cent. However, as we do not have reliable information on the ethnic background of *children* in the County, it would be unwise to attempt to assess whether or not Black children in care in Warwickshire are over-represented.

Given the small number of Black children in our cohort, few firm conclusions can be drawn about their care experience. However, what we were able to do was to monitor the race of foster carers as well as children to see how these compared. Such monitoring is not routinely carried out in Warwickshire and neither was this an issue which Rowe (1989) was able to address.

Though Tizard and Phoenix (1989) have recently provided some pertinent observations, the balance of evidence from research strongly suggests that, other things being equal, Black children in foster care are best placed in foster families where at least one parent is of the same ethnic origin – indeed, Department of Health guidance supports this line. This principle also applies to children of mixed parentage.

Table 4.10 shows the extent to which children in the cohort were placed in same-race foster placements. The details about foster carers' ethnic origins were taken from Warwickshire Social Services Department's records. Foster carers were asked to identify their ethnicity during the recruitment and approval process.

Table 4.10 Ethnic background of children and foster carers

Child	Foster carers			
	Both White	*One White one Afro-Caribbean*	*Both Asian*	*Both Afro-Caribbean*
White	189	1	0	0
African/Afro-Caribbean	2	0	0	0
Asian	0	0	3	0
Mixed parentage	14	1	0	2
All placements	205	2	3	2

The only instances where same-race placements were achieved in all or most cases were those for White children (189 places) and Asian children (three places). The one Afro-Caribbean child in the study had two placements with White foster carers but the children of mixed parentage fared worst. For these ten children, 14 out of 17 placements were in foster homes where both carers were White; in the other three there was at least one Black foster carer.

Warwickshire has a policy committing it to making same-race placements for children in care where possible (Warwickshire Director of Social Services, 1987). However, in this policy paper problems in making same-race placements are identified. These included problems in recruiting Black foster carers and problems in ensuring that Black foster carers are available for Black children when they need a placement, given the relative infrequency with which placements will be required because of the small numbers of Black children in care. Clearly, appropriate strategies are needed to break into this cycle.

Figures relating to the ethnicity of foster carers are not routinely collected in the County but from the information gathered about those with whom children in this study were placed, the following results emerged.

- In 95 of the foster families both parents were White.
- In two, one parent was White and one was Afro-Caribbean.
- In one, both parents were Afro-Caribbean.
- In one, both parents were Asian.
- No foster carers of mixed parentage were identified.

As the policy paper mentioned above recognised, same-race placements will only be possible in Warwickshire if more Black foster carers can be recruited and arrangements made to support them while they are not being used. This is an issue that needs to be confronted in many other English local authorities and requires a major reorientation of services. Given the fact that residential resources were not available as an alternative to an 'other-race' foster placement, this evaluation of Warwickshire's innovative approach must conclude that, at present, it is not meeting satisfactorily the needs of children and families from minority ethnic groups. This is an important conclusion from our research.

Planned or emergency placements

We looked earlier at the new admissions to care in our cohort and discussed the question of whether the admissions were planned or made in an emergency. We saw that recent research, in particular Packman (1986) and Millham and others (1986), was critical of the operation of a care system used as a last resort because this was identified as leading to too many unplanned and distressing admissions to care.

Whether a move, at admission or from one care placement to another, is planned or made in an emergency will affect the likely success of that placement. First, because unplanned moves more often lead to an inappropri-ate placement being made, that is a different type of placement from that preferred by the social worker. Second, because planning in childcare is rightly seen as the cornerstone of good practice: to have a clear idea of the purpose of an admission placement or a new placement makes 'drift' less likely. Having a clear plan also enables the social worker to prepare the child, parents and carers for what will happen in the placement. Moreover, having a plan also enables introductions to be carefully managed. Given this, the issue of whether placement changes were planned is an important one.

It is equally important that changes of placement once in care as well as on admission to care, should be planned as far as possible, rather than happen in an unforeseen and haphazard way. The consequences of not planning moves may include:

- disruption and upset for the child, the existing and new care providers and the social worker;
- unnecessary demands on fostering services; and
- probably less appropriate placements.

Overall, a half of placements were described by social workers as 'planned', the other half were made in an 'emergency'. Previous research would lead us to expect that the proportion of emergency placements would differ between placements on admission and changes of placement while in care. Millham and others (1986) identified 35 per cent of admissions, 'Where there was little interval between notification of the problem and actual reception'. The Dartington study excluded remands from its figures but in Packman's study (1986) remands accounted for just over one in ten of all admissions and, overall, she identified about 38 per cent of admissions as emergency admissions.

The best comparison with our study is Rowe's 1989 placement study and we used a similarly-phrased question to her's to enable valid comparisons. She found that no fewer than three-quarters of admissions placements were made in an emergency. This was made up of 16 per cent of new cases and 58 per cent of cases where the child or family was known, and Rowe described it as, 'rather depressing ... that only one child in four experienced a planned, unrushed admission'. In Warwickshire the picture was almost as bleak. Nearly seven out of ten admissions were made in an emergency; 16 per cent new cases but 53 per cent where the Department had previous involvement with the family.

If we look at placements made in the period after admission we find, not unexpectedly, that more of these placements were planned: overall 65 per cent planned and 35 per cent emergency placements. Unfortunately we have no directly comparable figures for all types of placement as Rowe (1989) presented figures for the category of foster placements only. Table 4.11 provides the details.

Table 4.11 Proportion of post-admission placements made in an emergency (foster placements only)

	Emergency (%)	Planned (%)
Warwickshire (No. = 160)	52	48
Rowe (1989 Study)	35	65

Why the proportion of emergency placements in Warwickshire should be so much higher than for the six authorities in Rowe's study is not clear. Two reasons could account for the difference. First, an overall higher rate of emergency placements for all types of placement; second, differences in the use of foster placements in Warwickshire. We will have more to say about the first possibility in Chapter 8 when we discuss placement endings and breakdown rates, but on the second point clear differences emerged from our data to identify some types of placement as being particularly associated with emergency placements.

- National Children's Home retained places (75 per cent, No. = 4 made in an emergency)
- Ordinary foster placements (53 per cent, No. = 135 made in an emergency)
- Contract foster placements (46 per cent, No. = 24 made in an emergency)

These results are interesting for several reasons. First, though dealing with very small numbers, three of the four residential NCH placements were of an emergency nature. Previous research on residential care (Berridge, 1985; Millham and others, 1986; Parker, 1988) has shown that one of the main functions of residential care has been the provision of placements in emergencies, which arise either because of an unanticipated admission to care or because of the breakdown of a previous placement. Warwickshire, even with its very limited use of residential care, still fits this pattern, but its access to residential facilities to use in emergencies is very limited.

The second point is that ordinary foster placements (that is foster placements other than those with relatives or contract foster carers) provided a disproportionately high percentage of emergency placements. Perhaps this should be expected in Warwickshire, but the consequences of this will be examined in Chapter 6. And finally, contract foster placements provided fewer emergency placements than ordinary foster placements. This is not a surprising result. We have already noted the inability of social workers to make contract foster placements in a large proportion of cases where they were the preferred option. However, given that one of the intentions is that contract foster placements should work at the sharp end of placement provision, this may be seen as surprising.

Though we are again only dealing with relatively small numbers, the types of placement most associated with *planned* placement were:

- home on trial (89 per cent, No. = 9 were planned)
- residential school (100 per cent, No. = 2 were planned)
- independent living (75 per cent, No. = 4 were planned)
- supportive lodgings (57 per cent, No. = 7 were planned).

Earlier in this chapter we noted the concern expressed by Parker (1988) that the movement towards closure of residential establishments might lead to increasing numbers of placements home on trial. That trend was not apparent in Warwickshire and we now see that home on trial placements for our cohort were the most planned of placements (although given the small numbers it is not possible to draw any firm conclusions). Similarly, no trend has been noted for greater than average use of supportive lodgings or independent living placements and, again, both these types of placement were planned to a greater extent than most placements overall.

The factor most strongly associated with placement planning was whether the placement resulted from a new admission to care or was a placement change while in care. When looking for other significant factors, we found that the sex of the child made no difference but that age was statistically significant. Older children experienced more emergency placements, as Table 4.12 shows.

Table 4.12 Proportion of planned placements by age group (No. = 193)

	5–10	11–13	14–15	16+	Total
Planned	64	64	35	47	51
Emergency	36	36	65	53	49

Nearly two-thirds of placements for children aged up to 13 were planned, compared with just over four in ten of placements for those over 13.

We also asked social workers how much time was available to find and make placements if they were planned. In a third of placements less than 48 hours was available; for almost half, up to two weeks; and for the rest more than two weeks. It is arguable that the 11 per cent of cases where the placement had to be made with less than 24 hours' notice might be termed emergencies. If this is the case, then over 60 per cent of the placements experienced by our cohort were made on an emergency basis. Less than a day, or even 48 hours, is very little time in which to identify possible placements, to consult the carers, to choose between the available placements, to prepare the child, and to arrange the move to the placement.

We do not envy social workers who so frequently have to tackle the unanticipated crises thrust upon them. Nonetheless, other research has criticised the lack of contingency planning that too frequently characterises childcare work. And the fact that such a large proportion of our cohort start their placements in such inauspicious circumstances does not, as we shall see, augur well for the success of their placements or their future.

Choice of placement

In the process of attempting to find an appropriate care placement for a child, a crucial factor is choice. We have already examined the extent to which social workers were able to make placements of the type they thought best, but to what extent did social workers have any *choice* between placements?

The answer to the question of choice, however, is not a simple one of either having no choice or of having a choice between, say, two or three different placements. The complications arise because of the overlapping roles and responsibilities of community team case workers and Children's Services

Teams. As the case studies show (*see* Chapter 5), the process of finding a placement varies between divisions and, even within divisions, different social workers in the Community Teams and the CST will adopt different practices.

One factor affecting the process is the time available. When a placement change is planned or a planned admission considered, then there will usually be a Community Based Assessment (CBA) meeting at which the type of placement a child requires, the preferred location and other factors will be discussed. This discussion will then be used as the basis for the CST Resources Team's search for suitable placements. If a placement is required in an emergency, this process will be foreshortened. The case worker will contact the CST Resource Team duty officer, provide details of the case and the child's needs, and will then await the response.

It is at the point at which possible placements have been identified by the CST that practice seemed to vary most. At one extreme, the CST staff, on the basis of the information they have available from the CBA or verbally from the case worker, will use their judgement to identify what they think is the best placement. This will then be offered to the case worker. At the other extreme, the CST will identify *all* available placements which, very broadly, meet the known requirements and then these placements, with details about each, will be offered to the case worker. He or she will then be expected to make the final choice.

Most day to day practice appeared to fall somewhere between these two extremes. Often there appears to have been little or no choice to make because of a shortage of placements. In other cases more of a dialogue occurred between the CST and the case worker, in which the respective merits of available placements and the needs of the child were discussed until a shared decision was reached. In the cases of planned placements, as the case studies show, considerations might include visits to various placements by the case workers, introductory meetings between child and potential carers, and discussions between potential carers and CST staff.

The questions we asked about the making of each placement covered both the issues of choice and process. These issues were also addressed by Rowe in her 1989 placements study and so we have some comparative data. We excluded cases where the child was placed home-on-trial when there could be no choice (or if there was any choice, it would be very circumscribed (Farmer and Parker, 1991)). Table 4.13 identifies the extent to which there was a choice between placements for each new placement episode.

We can draw a number of conclusions from these figures.

- In nearly two out of every five placements the choice was made by the CST. We do not know whether there were alternative placements which were also suitable.

Table 4.13 The availability of choices between placements

	Number	(%)
Yes – CST offered alternatives	6	(4)
Yes – but choices limited	12	(7)
No – but placement seemed suitable	40	(24)
No – only placement available	45	(27)
No – choice made by CST	63	(38)
All	166	(100)

- In only 11 per cent of cases did the case worker feel that he or she had any choice. This figure compares unfavourably with responses to the same question in Rowe's study (1989). In her six authorities at least a third of social workers, and as many as a half, felt that they had a choice about their placements. These results did not seem to depend on the size of specialist fostering services in the authorities, nor in the way these services were organised.
- An important finding for Warwickshire was that in as many as a *half* of the cases there was no alternative to the placement made – it was the only one available. This is one of the most important conclusions from our study.

These findings, especially the last, tally with the comments of social work staff in Community Teams and in CSTs, including those who were interviewed for the case studies. Other evidence from within the Department also supports these findings. In some divisions cross-divisional placements, made out of necessity rather than choice, have reached as high as 20 per cent; in most divisions foster carer vacancies are in single figures.

We anticipated that choice would be most limited for older age groups. However, this expectation was in fact not realised and shortages were more widespread. There were some other interesting results:

- Not surprisingly, where there was a lack of choice between placements, fewer were identified by the case worker as their preferred placement.
- Perhaps unexpectedly, there were approximately equal proportions of planned and emergency placements where there was some choice between placements, but there were three times as many planned placements where the response was 'no choice but placement suitable' compared with emergency placements.

Having little or no choice in the placements made for children in care can only have negative effects on the likely success of placements in meeting children's needs. In the longer term, the resulting intensive use of fostering and other resources would also be expected to have damaging effects on the foster carers, and others who provide substitute care. The pressure on resources means that carers are often given little chance to recuperate between placements, which some of the foster carers we interviewed were at pains to point out.

Summary

This chapter contains some of the key findings of our research. It examined: the pattern of placements made for children in care in Warwickshire; social workers' priorities in making placements for children in care in Warwickshire; and, more importantly, the extent to which it was possible, after the County closed its children's homes, for social workers to provide children with the type of placement which would best meet their needs. The main findings are summarised below.

- Warwickshire succeeded in making foster care the main placement for children in care. Over 80 per cent of the County's placements were foster placements compared with an average of just 37 per cent for six other typical authorities.
- Foster care was used for all but a few admissions to care, including emergency admissions. For the children and young people in our study, residential placements (of all types) were only used after they had previously lived in two or more foster placements.
- Closing the children's homes did not lead to increases in home on trial or 'other' types of placement.
- Social workers' priorities in making placements were: to keep sibling groups together; to maintain community links; and to ensure continuity of education for children in care.
- Older children and those admitted to care for behavioural reasons or because of neglect or abuse were seen to need placements with more skilled and experienced carers. Contract foster placements and residential placements were seen as most likely to provide such skills and experience.
- Social workers' preferred placements for children were 60 per cent for foster care, and just six per cent for residential care. In seven out of ten occasions, social workers were able to make their preferred placements. When the preferred placement was home on trial, residential or 'other', only one in three could be made.
- Warwickshire failed to make same-race placements for the large majority of Black children. The County clearly has too few Black carers.
- Warwickshire has a high proportion of new placements made in emergency circumstances but the figure is no higher than those for comparable authorities. However, the County does have a higher than average number of foster placements made in an unplanned way when children change placements – clearly a problem for a County so dependent on foster care.
- Placement matching was often not possible in Warwickshire. In half the cases where a placement was made, that placement was the only one available. This finding compares unfavourably with authorities examined by other researchers.

5. Three case studies

In Chapter 2 we explained that the large scale survey approach would be complemented by a more intensive study of the issues – in the form of a series of case studies. The benefits of case studies are many. They can provide a voice for those involved: the children, parents and foster carers as well as the social workers. Case studies undertaken once the results of the survey work are becoming clear can focus on what are emerging as the key issues. For instance, our study examined the effects of placement changes on all those involved, not least the children and young people themselves, and case studies enabled issues which arose out of the general study to be pursued in depth. Of course, case studies cannot claim to be statistically representative in the way that large scale surveys may, but carefully selected case studies can shed a different kind of light and that is their justification. Our complementary approach, using both the survey method and the case studies, was intended to benefit from the advantages of each.

This chapter, therefore, introduces our case studies – Angela Collins, Becky Johnson and Chris Taylor. In particular, we look in detail at some of the issues highlighted in Chapter 4 concerning the selection and making of placements.

Case study selection was approached as follows. We decided to undertake *three* case studies; if there had been greater opportunity, more would have been included. However, we decided to pursue three in depth rather than a larger number more superficially. In each case it was our intention to interview:

- the child or young person (having established with his or her social worker that it would be appropriate to do so);
- the child's parents (again having checked this with the social worker);
- the child's case worker;
- as many as possible of the foster carers or other substitute carers;
- the social workers providing link work support to the foster carers; and
- social workers in the Children's Services Team Direct Work Teams who had undertaken work with the child.

Social workers were positive about us undertaking interviews with the young person concerned in each of the cases which were selected but in one case, despite considerable efforts to establish contact, the young person was not interviewed. At this time this young man was very close to leaving care and was not responding to requests for meetings from his social worker. Parents' perspectives are, however, less well represented in our intensive work. We were not particularly encouraged by social workers to make contact with the parents of any of the people in the study: relations between Social Services and the parents had frequently reached a sensitive stage and it was feared that involvement by a third party might damage the relationship. Therefore, we were unfortunately restricted in the amount of information we were able to gather, and therefore present, from parents.

Nevertheless, a substantial number of interviews was undertaken for each of the case studies. All interviews were undertaken by the researcher, in confidence, with no third parties involved. Each of the interviews lasted for at least an hour and many lasted two hours or more. Foster carers in particular had a lot they wanted to say about the young person who was or had been in their care, about their role more generally and their relationship with the Social Services Department. Interviews were undertaken using a semi-structured schedule. Information from case files and from the survey results were also used to identify issues of particular interest.

Below we outline the way in which we identified the cases for the study. This is followed by introductions to each of the cases which describe the current circumstances of each of the three young people and give details of their family background and the reasons why they came to be in care. We also look at the process of selecting placements. Chapters 7 and 8, examining placements' progress and their endings, return to the three case studies after the broad analysis of Chapter 6.

Identifying the case studies

The three case studies were selected from the cases in the cohort. There were advantages in choosing the subjects for the case studies in this way. The intensive study followed on immediately after the completion of the extensive work which meant that the body of data relating to each of the 215 children and young people in the longitudinal study was available to be used as a basis for selection.

A number of criteria were developed for the selection process. Only children who had been admitted to care were considered. We also restricted the categories from which the case studies were selected to the 'new admissions to care' group, plus those children in the 'not admitted' group who came into care during the course of the follow-up period. The 'long term in care' group was excluded because, for many children, it would have been difficult to have effectively examined some key issues because of the passage of time.

The next criteria which were used to identify possible individual cases for more detailed examination were of a different type. The policy changes in the County had a greater impact on some groups of children than others. In particular, the closure of the children's centres and the much more restricted use of residential care was more significant for adolescents in care than it was for younger children. Residential care had been used to only a very limited extent for younger age groups for several years before the closure of the children's centres. Almost exclusively in their last years, the centres were used for older children, and a large proportion of these were reported to have had emotional or behavioural problems. Some had also previously been in substitute family placements, which had ended either in a planned way or as a result of a placement breakdown. Given the significance of these features (adolescence, emotional and behavioural problems and multiple placements) in the context of the County's new childcare policies, it was decided that these features should be well represented in the selection of the case studies. Indeed, it can be argued that these types of cases provide the major challenge to the effectiveness of Warwickshire's innovative policies.

A further criterion concerned the type of placements made for the children. The cases selected broadly reflect the use of placements identified in the longitudinal study, that is the majority are foster placements. However, it was also an aim in the selection process to highlight cases which, if possible, would also allow some exploration of other types of placement such as contract foster placements; residential care (provided under the retained places arrangement with a voluntary agency); home on trial; and finally, those often erroneously seen as something of a residual category, living in supportive or ordinary lodgings, or trying to cope independently.

These criteria were applied to the cases in the longitudinal study and this resulted in a shortlist of about 30 cases. The eventual three were chosen:

- by ensuring that the features identified above were reasonably represented taking the case studies as a whole;
- by selecting cases from the different divisions of the Social Services Department;
- by trying to check that the key people involved in the cases (in particular the child and the case social worker) were likely to be available; and
- by checking that, in the social worker's view, interviews with the child, his or her current carers and others could be carried out without any adverse effects on the child or the case.

When reading these case studies, it is important that the above considerations be borne in mind. In particular, the criteria ensured that the cases selected were among the more difficult that any social services department is likely to face and even more so for a department with a policy of making extremely limited use of residential care. That said, however, and accepting that every child's situation is essentially unique, we will see that many of the themes and issues identified in the extensive study are reflected in these cases.

In the remainder of this chapter, we will briefly outline the background of the three young people who are the subjects of the case studies, together with the reasons why they came into care. We will then look at the process of finding placements for them. Throughout this report, all names have been changed, together with sufficient other details to ensure the anonymity of the young people and others involved in the cases.

Angela Collins

When first encountered, Angela Collins was nearly 16-years-old and had been living with her third set of foster carers – Mrs and Mrs Clowes – for 14 months.

We talked about what had happened to her since she had come into care nearly two years earlier. Angela was naturally suspicious of this stranger who was asking her questions, however, she soon relaxed and began to talk easily and frankly about her experiences. She discussed her school and the courses she was studying on day release at the local further education college (the rather imaginative combination of domestic science and welding). She was very fond of her foster carers and although she called them 'Mum' and 'Dad', she also saw her own mother every weekend. 'It is brilliant here ... they love me and include me in the family ... I hope I will stay here until I am 18.' Angela, therefore, seemed rather more comfortable about relating to two families than some childcare observers may sometimes assume.

Angela's hope that she would be able to stay with the Clowes until she left care at 18 was certainly in line with the current social work plan. It was not envisaged that Angela would return to live with her mother but, because of Angela's age and because contact with her mother was regular and seen as important by all parties, neither were there any plans for the Clowes to become Angela's adoptive parents. However, while social work staff shared Angela's hope that the current placement would last, there was some doubt about that because of the fact that her previous two placements had ended mainly because of the demands which Angela placed on those caring for her. We will hear about these demands as they were experienced by the Clowes (and in later chapters about the earlier foster placements) but first let us examine the circumstances which led to Angela being admitted to care in the first place.

Before she came into care Angela had lived all her life with her mother in a modernised council house on a small estate in a medium-sized town. Mrs Collins was 17 when Angela was born. Angela was Mrs Collins' only child but there was a large extended family of grandmother and aunts and uncles living in town, and many on the estate. The Social Services Department had been involved with the wider Collins family on and off for many years. There had been considerable involvement with Mrs Collins at the time of Angela's birth and while she was a baby and the Department had helped Mrs Collins secure her current tenancy.

Other agencies were involved as well, in particular, in relation to Angela, the Education Department. Angela had been assessed at the age of ten as being in need of special educational provision for her learning difficulties. As a result of this assessment she was attending a day special school, which was just a few miles away from her home, and she had been there since soon after the educational assessment. This school was to become an important source of continuity for Angela from the time she was admitted to care; with the staff of the school providing more than educational support for Angela. Importantly, the later searches for foster placements for her took this into account.

Particular concern about Angela was initially raised with the Warwickshire Social Services Department by her mother. She made contact with the Department because she was worried about Angela's behaviour and also about the difficulties she had imposing limits which Angela would accept. Mrs Collins told the social worker that Angela was socialising with boys from the town who were considerably older than herself. She was also sometimes felt to be behaving in a sexually provocative way at home towards male members of the family. At this time Angela was a physically mature 12-year-old.

The social worker met Angela and spoke to her, both in the presence of her mother and on her own. It was felt that the case needed pursuing. After consultation with her team manager the social worker planned to continue monitoring the situation by remaining in contact with Angela and her mother, and with the school. A decision was also made to refer Angela to the Division's Children's Services Team for help in making an assessment of her situation and in planning future social work involvement. The CST was able to respond quickly to this referral and within two weeks Angela was attending a Girls' Group. The purpose of this group was to come to an assessment of Angela's needs as they were revealed in this setting of a peer group of the same sex.

This CST involvement will be described in more detail later, but for now let us move forward a few months to the next significant turning point in the case. This happened when Angela and Mrs Collins turned up at the Social Services office. Mrs Collins complained that Angela was verbally abusive and defiant towards her. Angela, barely 13, had spoken about having sexual relationships with young men and boys on the estate and, indeed, the police were investigating these relationships.

A decision about what action to take was required and a Community Based Assessment Meeting was chaired by the Manager of the Children's Services Team. This was attended by Angela and her mother as well as staff from the Social Services and Education Departments and Health Service. The breakdown of the relationship between Angela and her mother, her mother's loss of control and the perceived risk to Angela if she remained living on the estate resulted in the decision to seek a Place of Safety Order. Angela was to be placed with foster carers while a further and more detailed assessment could be made and a longer term plan drawn up. Angela's social worker described the initial foster carers, Mr and Mrs Abbott, in the following way, 'They have an enormous degree of tolerance, patience and understanding ... I have tremendous respect for the Abbotts'.

Once in care, the behaviour which Mrs Collins found difficult to accept and control continued, and possibly became worse. Promiscuous sexual behaviour and inappropriate sexual attention towards men was the everyday experience of those who knew Angela. By this time it had also been reported by Angela that she had been sexually abused by members of her own family, possibly over a period of years. By the time she came to live with the Clowes there were some members of her extended family with whom contact was not allowed. By this time Angela was also subject to a full care order (Children and Young Persons Act, 1969, 'moral danger'). The plan was that she would remain in care until 18, hopefully living with the Clowes, and that she should receive support in preparing herself for living more independently.

The Clowes were prepared by Angela's social worker for the difficulties they might face but they were still willing to provide a home for her on a long-term basis. Angela, the Clowes and their 18-year-old daughter got on well, and this helped them in their decision to offer a placement for Angela. Let Mrs Clowes describe in her own words how the placement went initially:

We were naive about what Sheila (Angela's social worker) told us; we thought she could not have done all these things ... We had six months of heaven compared to what it is now and then Angela accused John (Mr Clowes) of sexually abusing her.

Angela had made this accusation at school and although, when she was questioned about it she volunteered that she had made it up, there was still a thorough investigation of the accusation which involved the Police among others.

The outcome of the investigation was that Angela stayed with the Clowes and had to try to face up to the distress she had caused to her foster carers. From that point on Mr and Mrs Clowes were, on their own assessment, more realistic about the problems Angela presented: 'Without Angela knowing it, we are careful that John is not on his own with her', said Mrs Clowes. But there was at least one other occasion when Mr Clowes found himself in a vulnerable situation. He and Angela were, unusually, alone in the house when Angela appeared in a flimsy nightdress and asked him to give her a kiss and a cuddle: 'He blew his top and sent her up to her room and then he telephoned our daughter who lives just down the street and she came round.'

The Clowes' youngest daughter, who had moved out temporarily, moved back home, at least in part to provide her parents with some support by ensuring that there was a second female in the house in addition to Mrs Clowes. Angela disliked this move. Consistently, she had been jealous of the Clowes' attention:

They asked me how I would feel if they had another foster child. I said, 'No', because I did not want to share them ... I think it is hard if there is another child or foster child in the house.

Apart from issues surrounding her sexuality, it was Angela's demand for constant attention that Mrs Clowes found most wearing:

She will talk at you for hours ... and then when you think you have sorted things out she will start again on the same thing ... We have no privacy at all ... we have had to make our bedroom out of bounds.

The Clowes' link worker summed up her feelings about the way they had cared for Angela:

They had not fostered teenagers with Angela's difficulties before and initially they were playing down her problems ... But I think they have been excellent with Angela.

And what of the future? We have seen that Angela wanted to remain with the Clowes until she is 18 and this was also the social work plan. But what of the Clowes? As Mrs Clowes said, 'I would like to think we would keep her until she is 18 but that depends on Angela, doesn't it?'

We have now seen how Angela came into care, and discovered something of her background and the problems she can present to foster carers, of whom the Clowes were her third set. Let us now examine in some detail the circumstances surrounding the identification of all three placements and how each of these placements benefited Angela. (*See* Table 5.1 which schematically sets out Angela's movements while she was in care.)

Very little time was available to make a placement for Angela after she and her mother turned up at the Social Services office and the resultant decision was made to seek a Place of Safety Order. (As she did not appear to be in imminent danger, it is unclear why this rather drastic step was taken.) While a Community Based Assessment (CBA) Meeting was quickly convened and then a magistrate contacted to request the POSO, the Division's Children's Services Team (CST) began the search for a suitable placement on the assumption that an order would be granted. But there were only a few hours available from the time the CST was notified to the time when Angela must be found a bed for the night.

The CBA decided that a short-term placement was required for Angela while a full assessment was carried out. It was not clear at this stage whether the POSO would be followed by an application for a Care Order or, if such an application was made, whether it would be successful.

What type of placement was Angela's social worker, Sheila, asking for at this time? A foster placement was the first choice with foster carers who could provide some control over Angela's behaviour and who could ensure a period of some stability while the assessment was undertaken. Limiting the disruption to other areas of Angela's life was also a central part of Sheila's plan. The placement should be close enough to enable Angela, her mother and other members of her family to maintain regular contact but a placement at least a short distance away from Angela's estate was felt to be desirable, to get her away from the boys and men with whom she was said to have been sexually involved. School was Angela's social worker's other main priority. As we have seen her school provided Angela with stability and support, and it was important for that to continue.

Table 5.1 Angela Collins – movements in care

Timing	Plans and placements	Legal status
October	Angela aged 13 years and 10 months. Emergency 'admission to care'. Short-term placement with the Abbotts (foster carers).	Place of Safety Order
		Interim Care Orders
February following year	Planned move to long-term placement with the Browns (foster carers).	Full Care Order
June	Placement with the Browns had become problematic ... planned move to other long-term placement with the Clowes (foster carers).	"
September following year	Placement with the Clowes continuing.	

So what was the CST able to offer as a placement for Angela with so little notice? After a few hours the CST had been able to identify just one placement which was available and which fitted at least some of the criteria. The Abbotts were foster carers who had been fostering for six years and had previous experience of providing care for adolescents. They lived in the same division as Angela and her family and at a distance which certainly removed Angela from daily contact with her previous sexual contacts. However, there was no direct public transport between the Abbott's village and Mrs Collins' home and travelling to the placement by public transport took Mrs Collins about two hours each way, although the social worker did have some success in arranging volunteer drivers to take Mrs Collins there. There was also a problem with travel to and from school and the Department had to hire taxis for these trips.

For other reasons Angela, in retrospect, stated that she did not enjoy this temporary placement or particularly like this foster family but events were moving quickly and we will look at these issues in more detail later. Meanwhile, as the case plan developed it became necessary to look for a more permanent placement for Angela.

One week after a magistrate granted the Place of Safety Order, the Department went to Court with a successful application for an Interim Care Order. It was agreed that Angela's interests would best be served by her remaining in care and it was not anticipated that the court would disagree when an application for a Full Care Order was presented. So within a week of her arriving at the Abbott's, the CST was asked to find a long-term placement for Angela and they had a few weeks to do so. The search was for foster carers who were geographically better placed to enable Angela's mother to make visits more easily and to enable Angela to attend school without the need to use a taxi; but it was still thought important that Angela was not too close to the estate where her mother lived. Equally important, given that this was intended as a long-term placement, was the foster family's ability to cope with the kinds of behaviour Angela was presenting. They would also hopefully be able to begin to work with her, in cooperation with social work staff and others, to develop greater self-control.

This time there was some limited choice of foster placements but one stood out as particularly appropriate. The Browns had been fostering for 14 years and had provided a home for over 30 children of all ages, some short- and others long-term. They had one other foster child, a boy aged 14, living with them on a long-term basis at this time but they were approved to provide two foster places. The Browns actually lived in a different division but, geographically, their home was quite close both to Angela's school and to her mother.

Angela's change of placement was carefully discussed and planned. Sheila, the social worker, met the Browns to give them some background details, although the latter said they preferred to know as little as seemed necessary so as not to pre-judge the child. Angela made two visits to the Brown's home before the final move and these went well. The actual move to the Browns was also carefully set up as a two-week trial but after one week the move was confirmed and Angela was there, 'Settling in quite well but very quiet', according to Mrs

Brown. The prospects looked good. However, within a few weeks problems developed and considerable social work support was required to maintain the placement for as long as it lasted; which was about four months in the end.

Three weeks from what turned out to be the end of this placement, Angela went to stay with the Clowes while the Browns went on holiday. On their return the Browns found Angela increasingly difficult to cope with; she had enjoyed her two weeks stay with the Clowes and was pushing for a permanent move there.

Was any other alternative considered once it was clear that the placement with the Browns would not be permanent? The social worker did explore the few other options which were available but none of these seemed particularly suitable, whereas the Clowes met most of the requirements outlined before:

- proximity to mother and extended family and school;
- foster carers who possibly had the skills to assist Angela and to provide some control; and
- a household where Angela could have her own bedroom and where there was only one other child living – meaning that it would be possible for the foster carer to provide Angela with more of the time and attention which she demanded.

Angela's social worker gave Mr and Mrs Clowes more details than they had needed for the holiday placement and, after some thought, they agreed to take her on a long-term basis. They had been fostering for four years and had provided a home for six children previously, although none of these prepared them for the difficulties Angela presented.

Just over three weeks after she had stayed with them while the Browns were on holiday, Angela moved back to the Clowes and she was still there 15 months later.

Becky Johnson

Our second case study subject, Becky Johnson, had been living with her foster carers, Mr and Mrs Gardner, for just over three months when first visited. She was fashionably dressed in clothes which looked new and not inexpensive. She obviously took considerable pride in her appearance and was an attractive 13-year-old who looked more like 15. Although Becky's father was Afro-Caribbean, it was usually assumed that she was White. Indeed, she had grown up in a White family and community with no contact with her Black father. Placing Becky with foster carers who were Black had not been a priority.

The conversation with Becky was quite difficult to get going. Having been reassured of her anonymity, Becky demanded the opposite and almost threatened to withdraw unless her real name figured prominently! Having broken the ice somewhat by this brief skirmish over research ethics, Becky began to talk about her life and the various foster carers she had lived with. The Gardners were the *fifth* foster family she had lived with since first coming into care four years ago when she was just nine-years-old. Becky saw this as a temporary placement while the Social Services Department found her a long-term one. She was clear that, as far ahead as it was possible for her to see, she would be in care and would not be returning home to live with her mother. The Gardners also saw Becky's stay with them as temporary although when she might move on was unclear – the Department had not set a date for a move.

The reason why a date had not been set was because the Department was having considerable difficulty in finding a long-term placement for Becky. As one member of staff at the Children's Services Team said,

Placements for adolescents are what we are shortest of ... if a child has got behaviour problems and you're looking for a long-term placement then that makes it even more difficult.

In relation to Becky, a recognition of these problems had led to a decision, which needed senior management approval, to advertise in the local press for foster carers specifically for her. Details of Becky's needs were included in an advertisement (using a fictional name) which was inserted in a number of local papers. The response to those advertisements was nil – not even one telephone or written enquiry. For Becky's social worker, John, and for the staff of the Children's Services Team who were involved in trying to recruit long-term foster carers for Becky, the failure of the advertisements came as a considerable setback. Much time, effort and hope had been put into this strategy. In our interview Becky was not asked how the failure of the advertisements had affected her, as it was thought the question might be too sensitive to ask. The rejection could hardly have boosted her self-confidence.

For social work staff in the Community Team and the CST some rethinking of plans was taking place. It might be possible to find Becky a long-term foster placement from among the families currently going through the approval process but that was not an option for the near future because of the length of time taken to make final approvals. Alternatively, an existing foster placement might become available but that was very unpredictable. Even then Becky, with an existing placement, might be in competition with a child with no placement at all. The option of considering a long-term placement outside the Division or even outside the County was not seriously considered by Becky's social worker. There were strong arguments for keeping Becky in the area, not least the need for at least some contact with her mother, but also for reasons of educational continuity. Becky was about to be offered a place in a small special educational needs unit on the site of a local secondary school, and this seemed like the most promising way of reintroducing her to mainstream education and was too important a consideration to ignore.

A further option, which was being considered at the time of interview, was the possibility of the placement with the Gardners becoming longer term but neither the Gardners nor Becky had yet been presented with this possibility.

What were the reasons which had led to Becky's three periods in care and to her living with five different sets of foster carers over a period of slightly more than two years? The first social work record in Becky's file was dated early 1977 when she was about one and a half years-old. At this time, Becky's name was added to the Non-Accidental Injury Register and Becky went to live, temporarily, with her grandmother. Becky's mother, Tracey, was then herself only 19-years-old. Becky's father was no longer present and the concern about Becky centred on the man who was currently living with Tracey in her council flat.

John had been Becky's social worker for over a year when we met; he had taken over the case when he arrived in the team as a newly qualified social worker. The previous social worker was still in the Team and from her and the case records, and from the other people involved in the case, John had been able to build up a picture of the circumstances which had led to Becky's first admission to care.

Tracey was a young single mother with poor parenting skills. Becky's dad was off the scene and Tracey has had a number of other more or less unstable relationships ... Generally, the care Becky got was poor and she was left [to her own devices] from an early age ... [When she got older] Becky just used to wander the streets. Tracey lost control. There was conflict between them and Becky was involved in stealing.

The Department had been involved on and off with the family since Becky was born, but during the year or so before Becky's first admission to care most of the Department's involvement was from the Direct Work Team of the CST. This involvement was at times quite intensive and focused on preventing a family breakdown. From this time, and to date, one member of staff at the CST was involved with Becky.

Despite the CST involvement, things came to a head between Tracey and Becky; Tracey told the Community Team social worker that she couldn't control Becky and that she wanted her to be received temporarily into care. The social work assessment was that this would be the best option; it would provide Tracey with some time during which she might be able to sort out some of her other problems. The break would also allow some work to go on with Becky, to help her reflect on her behaviour and possibly to modify it.

Becky was placed with foster carers on the other side of the County. At the time a placement was needed, this was the only one available and at all suitable. The intention was that this placement should be short-term and that Tracey and Becky should be reunited quite quickly. In the event, Becky remained in this placement for nearly nine months. She started at a new school and appeared to settle in well there, she got on with her foster carers (both in the judgement of social workers and Becky herself) and her behaviour improved.

By the time Becky returned home, all appeared promising as Tracey's life was somewhat more stable and both Tracey and Becky wanted to be reunited. However, the return home lasted for less than four months. On Becky's return, there was a short-lived period of calm but then Becky reverted to her previous behaviour – refusing attempts by her mother to set limits on her behaviour, staying out late and possibly getting involved again in shoplifting. Tracey's limit was reached one night when Becky didn't return home at all. Tracey reported her missing to the Department's emergency duty officer (coincidentally the CST social worker who knew her well), who responded to Tracey's refusal to have Becky home by agreeing to a second voluntary admission to care. An emergency placement was arranged with an experienced foster family by the name of Donnelly, but this placement was again out of the Division at the other end of the County, not out of choice but because it was all that was available. This location meant that, for the social worker, nearly two hours travelling time was involved in every visit to the placement. For Mrs Johnson regular contact with Becky was difficult and for all those involved in the case planning, an additional dilemma was introduced – was it best to attempt Becky's rehabilitation from this distant placement or should a closer placement and an additional move to another set of foster carers be pursued? At the time of her move to the Donnelly's, Becky was nearly 12. It was the end of August and in September she was supposed to be starting at a new secondary school near her home.

We will look in more detail at this placement and at Becky's subsequent placements later but for now let us return to the present and the placement with Mr and Mrs Gardner.

As we saw earlier, Becky's placement was seen as short-term and a written agreement, drawn up between the Gardners, the CST link worker and the Community Team social worker, stated that it would last for between three and six months – which was as long as it was estimated that it would take to find Becky a permanent placement. Before the placement was confirmed, John brought Becky to visit the Gardners and to see their home. The visit lasted for about one and a half hours, and both Becky and the Gardners expressed their willingness to go ahead on the understanding that the placement was short-term. According to the Gardners, Becky settled-in very well and quickly. They described her as, 'Really chatty and friendly' and Becky described them (a couple in their late twenties) as, 'A good laugh'.

How had the placement gone? The Gardners described three phases to the placement. From May when she arrived until the beginning of the school holidays, Becky was attending the CST every weekday. She had been excluded from school in February; part of the day was taken up with work with her home tutor and, some of the time, with other activities mainly involving a sessional worker recruited by the CST. Next came the Summer which seemed to be full of activities – a holiday with the Gardners, another with a group of young people involved with the CST and other CST-organised day activities. The period since the end of the summer holidays had proved more difficult. Becky was no longer being provided with any home tutor hours because the Education Department was considering providing a placement in a special unit on the site of a secondary school. This placement was awaiting the decision of an Education Department Panel which would meet early in the Autumn term. This gap was leaving Becky with a lot of time to fill and the Gardners commented, 'Becky finds things to do ... but we're worried about her getting into trouble [with the Police]'. At this time, however, Becky was seeing more of her mother and the Gardners thought that they, she and Becky, were getting on much better.

The Gardners summed up their relationship with Becky in these words.

We get on well most of the time, we've had no big rows ... What's annoying about Becky are not things like staying out late, it's little things; she's very untidy and she won't take responsibility for her actions.

This quite possibly underestimates the difficulties Becky presents. John, the social worker, said that foster carers couldn't know what they were taking on. The words he used to describe the worst behaviour which could be expected were, 'insecure, aggressive, criminal and lying'. Becky had once attempted suicide and had been excluded from school for, 'truanting, being disruptive in class, disobeying and being abusive towards staff'. The difficulty which Becky was expected to present to foster carers was reflected in the allocation of a banding level of six; only a small proportion of the children in foster placements were on Band Six – the highest banding on a scale of one to six. However, John went on to say that in previous placements Becky's behaviour had deteriorated as time went on but with the Gardners this had not happened ... yet.

The future of Becky's placement with the Gardners was, as we saw earlier, in some doubt after the failure of the advertising campaign to recruit any long-term foster carers for her. The Gardners had been concerned and were also unsure what it meant for them. At the time of writing Becky was still there but the plan continued to be that she should move on. The possibility of her staying had not been raised either with the Gardners or with Becky.

Having now provided a general introduction to Becky and her circumstances, let us now look in closer detail at how each of her care placements was selected. A summary of Becky's experiences since she was received into care is presented in Table 5.2. We will not consider the placement with the Hastings, which was made on Becky's first admission to care. That placement began before the data collection for the survey was under way and, in addition, personnel changes meant that detailed information would be difficult to obtain.

Becky returned home from the Hastings to her mother but her return only lasted for four months, after which Becky was re-admitted to voluntary care by an Emergency Duty Officer (EDO). Whether Becky would have been received into care at all by her own social worker or, if admitted, whether that would have been on a voluntary basis was not clear. But the EDO who admitted Becky also organised the placement with the Donnellys. If this had been a planned placement, Becky's social worker said that its purpose would have been as a short-term intervention while difficulties between Becky and her mother were resolved. Ideally, the carers would have been skilled and experienced enough to cope with Becky's problems including her behaviour and, furthermore, be able to begin to address these problems directly. The placement would also have been close to Becky's own community so that contact with her mother, other family and friends could easily have been maintained and so that Becky's education (her secondary school career was about to start) would not be disrupted.

The Emergency Duty Officer knew the circumstances of this case well but, having to find a placement out-of-hours, there was nothing available in the Division and the only suitable placement which could be found was with foster carers some distance across the County who were willing to offer a short-term placement. These were the Donnellys, foster carers who already had one older female foster child placed with them, but who had, in the words of the link worker, 'Had more difficult placements before and coped with them'.

Table 5.2 Becky Johnson – movements in care

Date	Plans and placements	Legal status
July	Becky aged 9 years and 2 months. Becky beyond mother's control. Planned short-term reception to care – placed with Hastings (foster carers).	Voluntary care
April following year	Planned return home to mother.	Not in care
June	Becky absconded. Emergency reception. Short-term placement with Donnellys (foster carers).	Voluntary care
August	Placement broke down. Move to other short-term placement with Edwards. Case plan still to return home.	"
January following year	New placement needed. Return home attempted. Living with mother.	Not in care
February	Return home unsuccessful. Search for long-term placement. Placed with Contract Foster Parents, the Floods.	Place of Safety Order
		Interim Care Orders
May	Time limited Contract Foster Placement ended. Move to short-term placement with Gardners (foster carers) while long-term placement sought.	Full Care Order
October	Placement with Gardners continuing.	"

The main problem with this placement was its location. 'The Donnellys felt very sorry for Becky, she didn't know anyone in the area', said the link worker. Mrs Johnson could not easily visit and when the placement was going badly it was very difficult for John, the social worker, to be supportive. In addition, in order to ensure that Becky was able to attend her new school, the Department was having to provide a taxi twice a day.

We will consider in more detail later how this placement worked out and why it ended, but, for the reasons identified above, when it was clear that Becky couldn't return home, a placement nearer to home was required. The requirements remained the same as when the placement at the Donnellys was made and the CST was asked to see what it could find. The CST worker who oversaw this search described it in the following way.

The aim was still to attempt rehabilitation of Becky with her mother so we were looking for a short-term placement ... but as I remember it we had little or no choice. The Edwards had some previous experience [of teenagers] but they were approved for one settled teenager who was still with them ... with Becky there was a rapid reapproval [so that they could take two foster children].

The Edwards lived only a mile or so from Becky's mother and the journey to school was not difficult, so on geographical grounds the placement was very suitable. Their link worker made the initial contact and this was followed up by two meetings with her social worker. He gave the Edwards detailed information about the reasons why Becky was in care and about the problems they might face. When interviewed, several months after Becky had moved on and after they had been through a very difficult time, they nevertheless stated that they thought they had been well prepared for Becky's placement with them.

The question mark was perhaps over the Edwards' experience. They had been fostering for two years before Becky arrived and six children in all had been placed with them temporarily, one of whom had stayed on as a more permanent placement. In the event, as seen in Chapter 7, the Edwards made up in commitment what they may have lacked in experience.

The Edwards lived in quite a large house with their own two children (one older and one younger than Becky) and one long-term foster child, who was also older than Becky. The process of moving Becky from the Donnelly's to the Edwards' happened quickly once the decision was made since there was agreement on everyone's part that Becky needed to leave the Donnelly's as soon as possible. Becky was collected with her possessions and taken to the Edwards by the CST Direct Work Team social worker, whom she knew well. She had only known John, in the Community Team, for the short time since he had taken over the case.

No-one involved in this case was confident, even in retrospect, that the placement with the Edwards would succeed or that the plan of rehabilitating Becky and Tracey would work. In the end, the placement lasted for five months (but was not without difficulties as we shall see) and Becky left the Edwards to return home to her mother.

It was possible for Becky to return home because there had been some improvement in Becky's behaviour while she was with the Edwards and Tracey's attitude had changed again so that she was willing to have Becky back home. However, there was doubt on the part of social work staff about whether this reunion would succeed and, with a degree of foresight, contingency plans were made in case it did not. It was decided that there would be little point in receiving Becky into care for a third time on a voluntary basis; such an arrangement meant that it was difficult for Becky's social worker to make plans for her other than in the short-term. Because of this the CST was unwilling to commit any of its scarce long-term resources to meet Becky's needs. The social work plan decided upon was that, if Becky's return to her mother was unsuccessful, then Becky would be re-admitted to care on a Care Order. This would enable the Department to find a longer term foster placement for Becky, while building in regular contact with her mother.

After just a couple of weeks at home, relations between Becky and Tracey had deteriorated and reverted to their previous style. It was clear that the situation would not last much longer and preparations were made to implement the contingency plan described above. The CST were notified that Becky would require a placement with a foster family, that the placement should be local and that the foster carers should be able to cope with Becky's behaviour. However, although the social work plan was for a long-term, 'inclusive' foster placement for Becky, this depended on success in convincing the courts to grant a Care Order. Therefore, at this stage what was required was a short-term placement – but one sufficiently open-ended to cover the period of the court proceedings and the time involved in finding Becky a long-term alternative.

In the event, Becky's return home lasted only three weeks despite considerable social work input. After Tracey refused to have her home again, a magistrate granted a Place of Safety Order, which was followed by a number of Interim Care Orders and then by a full Care Order about two months later. In a report to the court during this period, Becky's social worker wrote,

It became apparent that the home situation was not good ... Becky's behaviour had regressed. She was argumentative, out for considerable periods of time ignoring Mrs Johnson's attempts to control her and continuing to truant ... Mrs Johnson was insistent that Becky should be received into care ... She also saw little hope of pursuing rehabilitation in the future.

So what placements were the CST able to find for Becky, at relatively short notice and with the overriding need for the placement to be local?

John, Becky's social worker, remembers being, 'Offered a choice of two placements ... But one was completely inappropriate'. The CST worker involved remembered the events as follows,

There was a sudden request for a placement but there was nothing appropriate available ... We looked at placements out of the Division but (John) wanted a local placement ... We made the placement with the Floods out of desperation.

The Floods were one of two families in the division who were approved as contract foster parents. They certainly had experience of working with difficult adolescents so why was this placement made 'out of desperation'?

The first reason was that it was seen as an inappropriate use of the limited contract fostering resources in the Division. 'There was no need for the assessment of [Becky's] needs or for the development of plans; the plan was clear.' More importantly, however, was the fact that contract foster placements are used as a strictly time-limited resource with a maximum stay of three months, and it was clear that court proceedings to secure a care order and then the identification of a long-term placement for Becky would not be achieved inside this deadline. The consequence for Becky would, therefore, be an additional change of placement. The placement with the Floods was a compromise, caused by the lack of foster placements from which to choose.

The Floods themselves were initially confused as to why Becky was being placed with them and were also critical of the lack of preparation for the placement and the way in which introductions were managed. Mrs Flood said:

We didn't really know what was going on. We knew very little about Becky ... There was one short phone call before she arrived ... She was brought over by [the social worker] ... He only stopped a short time ... We found a very frightened 13-year-old girl.

In the end, Becky stayed with the Floods for four days more than the three month maximum stay. This placement was followed by the planned move to the

Gardners, details of which we considered earlier.

Before we move on to our third case study, let us consider the answers given by those involved in the case when asked whether a residential placement would at any stage have been of benefit to Becky. In the series of questionnaires used to monitor this and other cases, the following question was asked on the occasion of the making of each of Becky's four placements:

If the Department had retained four children's centres, would you have considered placing this child in one at the time you were seeking this placement?

On each occasion, Becky's Community Team social worker, John (or at the time of Becky's first placement, his predecessor) answered, 'Yes, definitely'. John's predecessor expanded on her answer:

Becky has been in care previously with foster carers. She found it difficult to handle the divided loyalties to her foster carers and her mother. Her mother tuned in to this and exacerbated the situation to the detriment of Becky. A 'neutral' residential placement might have avoided this.

Becky's current social worker expressed arguments in favour of and against using residential placements.

Becky needed a positive experience of a family environment. Residential care out of the County would have meant Becky being swept under the carpet [but] intensive work in a small group home in the Division at the time of Becky's second reception could have prevented a lot of her later problems.

Neither of these two social workers had been employed in Warwickshire when children's homes were still open but the CST social worker who best knew Becky had for a time worked in one of the homes and he added a warning.

I'm not sure Becky will ever make a full commitment to any foster placement because of her commitment to her mum ... Residential would have been better in some ways for Becky but not in others. I'm certain she would have got involved in more offending because of the peer group pressure [in the homes].

Chris Taylor

This case study differs from the previous two in several respects. First, Chris Taylor was no longer in care when we were completing the study. Second, we failed to meet Chris despite making several attempts to contact him both directly and via his social worker. This case study therefore, unlike the previous two, is unable to present the events as they were experienced by the person at the centre of it all. Nonetheless, we decided to include it as it highlights a number of very pertinent issues. It is also interesting to note that this case study involved a residential placement, one of only two cases in the whole of our cohort which did so. Indeed, Chris was selected, in part, precisely because his case provided an opportunity to consider in great depth the experiences of the relatively small number of children and young people for whom residential care is chosen by Warwickshire Social Services Department.

At the time of our scrutiny, Chris had been out of care for about four months and he was 17-years-old. His social worker – Liz – had not seen him for some weeks and the most recent address she had for him was a small bed and breakfast lodging house in the centre of town. Liz had been intensively involved with Chris for nearly two years. How did she see him and his prospects now?

Chris is a survivor ... He sees himself as streetwise. Over the Summer he got himself into arrears with his rent but he seems to have sorted that out. He's learning to be independent but the risk is the possibility of putting him in the position of being at risk of offending.... Since he was discharged [from care] he has been cautioned. Prior to that there was no involvement in offending ... Now he is planning to start on a pre-vocational FE [further education] course.

But Liz was not confident that he would stick with this course. He had a history of starting courses, training schemes and jobs and persevering with them for only a few days. Liz's possibly optimistic hope – it seems also rather a curious rationalisation – was that being out of care and not being able to rely on parental support Chris would begin to settle down and commit himself to something. As she said,

One of the reasons Chris was discharged was because he had been through all we had to offer without any appreciation of the situation he was in. It was not until he was discharged from care that Chris actually did do something for himself.

The first contact between Chris' family and Warwickshire Social Services Department was when Chris was 15½-years-old. His mother and stepfather entered the Area Office and spoke to the duty social worker (who happened to be Liz, the social worker to whom the case was allocated and who has held it ever since).

Chris' family had only moved into Warwickshire a year or so previously, when his mother had remarried. Prior to that she and her two children (Chris and a younger sister) had lived a few miles away in a neighbouring county. Mr and Mrs Taylor had separated when Chris was five; Chris' father had remarried and had other children; and Chris and his sister saw him infrequently.

The reason Chris' mother and her new husband arrived at the Social Services Office was because their relationship with Chris had deteriorated since Mrs Taylor had remarried. Mrs Taylor described Chris as unmanageable: he stayed out late, would not do anything asked of him and picked arguments constantly. The couple had visited the Social Services office that particular day because a fierce argument that morning had ended with Chris' stepfather hitting him, although Chris had then gone off to school. Later that day the school telephoned the department to report that Chris had turned up with obvious bruising, the cause of which he had explained. In their meeting with the social worker Chris' mother and her husband said that they had reached the end of their patience with him and did not feel they could have him back home. They were asking for him to be received into care.

Problems with Chris were not new. Investigations revealed that the family had been involved, on and off, with the social services department in the neighbouring authority over a period of years, dating from the time of Chris' parents' separation. However, the family had had a more substantial involvement with the education department of that authority. At the age of six Chris had been identified by education psychologists as having both educational and behavioural problems. The educational psychologist had become involved after a referral from Chris' school within his first year of attendance. At the age of eight Chris was transferred to a special educational day unit where more individual attention was available. At 12 he was reassessed under the 1981 Education Act, which led to a statement identifying Chris' special educational needs as primarily 'emotional and behavioural difficulties'. As a result of this assessment, Chris was educated at a residential special school not far from his home. From the age of 13 Chris continued to attend this school but as a day pupil and it was this school which he was still attending after the family's move to Warwickshire; the school was not too far away, just across the County border.

What action did Liz, the social worker, take after her meeting with Chris' mother and stepfather? She set up, for later that day, a Community Based Assessment meeting which was chaired by the CST manager. She also notified the CST that an emergency placement would probably be needed for that night. And she informed the NSPCC Child Protection Team of the circumstances of the case because of the report of physical abuse. The NSPCC team had (at least at the time of our enquiry) an agency agreement with Warwickshire Social Services Department to manage the Child Protection Register for the whole County on their behalf. The result of this referral was that several days later a Child Protection Case Conference, which involved NSPCC and Social Services personnel, postponed a final decision about whether Chris' name should be placed on the Register. At the second Child Protection Case Conference, held after the Department had assessed Chris' situation, it was decided that his name should be placed on the Register.

The plan decided upon at the earlier Community Based Assessment meeting was that Chris should be received into voluntary care on a short-term basis. This time would be used to make a thorough investigation of the circumstances surrounding the referral in order to decide whether any work with Chris or his family should be undertaken and, if so, what work.

In a period of less than 18 months following this decision Chris went from never having been in care to having short, turbulent placements with three different sets of foster carers and then to being one of the few young people placed in residential care by Warwickshire. While in this National Children's Home resource the Department made attempts to identify a longer term, 52-week, therapeutic residential placement for Chris but their attempts failed. From the NCH establishment Chris returned to lodgings in his home town and, three months later, he was discharged from care.

Let us now look more closely at the series of placements which Chris experienced while he was in care; Table 5.3 provides an overview of Chris' moves.

We have seen how Chris and his family suddenly came to the notice of Warwickshire Social Services Department. At a Community Based Assessment meeting called on the day of the referral, it was decided that Chris should be received into care as a short-term measure while an assessment of the family's situation was made and a plan of action drawn up. At such short notice, what type of placement was found for Chris and what type would have been best?

Table 5.3 Chris Taylor – movements in care

Timing	Plans and placements	Legal status
October	Chris aged 15 years and 3 months. Emergency reception into care after problems in family. Short-term placement with Imlotts (foster carers) while assessment undertaken.	Voluntary care
October	Returned to mother after two weeks in care	Not in care
December	Family relationships broke down. Emergency reception. Placed with Jones family (foster carers) on short-term basis while awaiting Contract Foster Placement.	Voluntary care
February following year	Planned move to Contract Foster Placement with Kennedys. Plan to work with Chris and parents to secure return home.	"
March	Placement with Kennedys broke down. Move to residential placement with National Children's Home while looking for long-term residential placement.	"
October	Plan changed from seeking long-term residential to finding independent accommodation in home town.	"
January following year	Return to home town to self-contained bedsit.	"
January	After one week Chris asked to leave. Move to bed and breakfast hostel found by local voluntary agency.	"
February	Move to other lodgings found by Chris himself.	"
March	Move to live with 'friends' (the Jones family who had been foster carers to Chris).	"
April	Chris left care aged nearly 17.	Not in care

Given that a short period in care was anticipated while an assessment was undertaken, the most appropriate type of placement, according to the case worker, Liz, would have been with contract foster parents. As we have seen, contract foster parents only deal with placements of brief duration and are more actively involved in the social work process than other foster carers; their involvement in assessments is, therefore, seen as particularly valuable. Since the plan was that Chris would return home quickly, it was also important that a placement should be reasonably close to his mother's home so that contact could easily be maintained. The third key factor was Chris' schooling; he needed to be living where getting to and from school was not difficult.

So, where was Chris placed? There were no placements with contract foster parents available. The Division had two sets of contract foster parents, both of whom were heavily used. The chance of either of these families having a vacancy at short notice was slight and on this occasion neither was free. Chris was placed with an ordinary foster family, the Imlotts, who lived where visits from Chris' mother and the journey to school were quite easy. The Imlotts were a couple who were approved for fostering teenagers and who had considerable experience of providing a home for difficult adolescents. The Imlotts had another foster child living with them as a long term-placement. He was an 18-year-old boy with severe learning difficulties. Chris' social worker said that, at the time, the presence of this other foster child made the placement a less than ideal choice but that there was no other placement available.

After the Imlotts were identified as a possible placement initial contact with them was made by a member of the CST staff. Given their willingness to consider the placement, Liz, the case worker, then spoke to them at length on the telephone and gave them what details she knew. The Imlotts' link worker later said that they felt adequately prepared by the social worker for Chris' placement with them. Liz collected Chris from his school, having already collected some of his clothes and personal possessions from his mother's house. She explained what had happened during the day, although Chris already knew some of it from staff at the school. She explained to Chris that his mother had agreed that he should be received into voluntary care for a short period while the Social Services Department assessed the case and that then he would return home, possibly with some input from the Department to help sort out relationships between the family members. Liz then drove Chris to the Imlotts and, after making sure he was settled in, left him there.

We will see in the Chapter 7 how this placement went and how it ended after two weeks when Chris left the Imlotts and returned home. During these two weeks Chris' name had been put on the Child Protection Register and a package of work with the family had been planned. Despite the input from the Department, after Chris returned home relationships between Chris and his mother and stepfather did not improve. The Community Team Social Worker was involved in trying to resolve a number of crises and it became apparent that Chris would probably have to return to care at some point. The plan agreed in discussions between the case worker and the CST was for a planned reception into care with a placement in a contract foster home. Once in such a placement it was planned that more intensive work would be undertaken, both with Chris and his family, with the aim of effecting a more sustainable rehabilitation.

However, this plan required that Chris' home situation was maintained until a contract placement became available and, to this end, additional direct work input from the CST was planned. This would involve individual work with Chris in the evenings and at weekends, with the aim of providing some respite for Chris and his family from the intense situation at home.

The other part of the plan to readmit Chris involved a decision that, if care again became necessary, then it should be on the basis of a second voluntary reception. Arguments against a second voluntary reception were that it could lead to Chris returning home or moving elsewhere without the Department having any control, or to other decisions affecting Chris being taken by his parents, possibly against social work advice. The argument in favour of voluntary reception was precisely that it would maintain a greater degree of parental responsibility and, therefore, hopefully involvement in planning for Chris' future. A return home, at some point, would therefore be more likely.

The planned reception into care never happened. Another crisis led to Chris' mother and stepfather formally asking for Chris to be admitted to care. A CBA meeting was called which agreed to the request on the basis planned – voluntary reception. The Department asked and was given an agreement by Chris' parents that they would not interfere with plans drawn up for Chris once he was in care.

By the time this CBA meeting was held it is worth noting that Chris' social worker was beginning to question the appropriateness of placing Chris in a foster family, even a contract foster family.

I do not think it is always appropriate to place children into family circumstances ... especially when there is enough information about the background to decide that the child was not ready for a family ... I said at the CBA that serious consideration should be given to a residential placement.

However, those at the CBA meeting, including Liz, decided that the previously formulated plan should be put into effect and so, for a second time, Chris was received into care in an emergency.

Again the need was for a short-term placement, in the right location, with foster carers who could cope with the demands which experience had shown Chris would impose. A placement was found with the Jones family. They lived in a village several miles away from Chris' home town. This was not a problem for visits for Chris' mother, who had a car, but did make the journey to school more difficult; a taxi had to be hired for the trips in both directions.

Mr and Mrs Jones were among the Division's most experienced foster carers. They had been fostering for 11 years and had mainly cared for teenagers on short-term placements. However, they were approved for two placements and they currently had another boy, aged 11, living with them. It was intended that this boy would stay with them on a permanent basis.

Mrs Jones was contacted by telephone and she spoke to both CST staff and Chris' social worker before agreeing to the placement. In recognition of the expected difficulties which Chris would present, it was decided that the Jones would be given payment on Band Six (the top rate of the foster payment scheme). This level of payment is the same as is made to contract foster parents.

Chris was collected from his parents' home by one of the CST Direct Work Team Social Workers whom he had got to know (the case worker was ill) and he was taken, with his personal possessions, to the Jones' house. Chris, of course, had not met the Jones family before. There had been no time for planned introductions and, according to Mrs Jones, he did not settle in very well or very quickly. She described a 15¹/₂-year-old boy who did not seem to appreciate the difficult position he was in; he expected, quite unrealistically, that he would be returning home to his mother after only a short stay with the Jones. He did not seem to be aware of the seriousness of his situation, that the social work plan for rehabilitation was not seen as involving just a few days in care and that, in fact, he would be moving to stay with contract foster parents when a placement became available.

The contract foster placement, which the plans had been built around, took a further seven weeks to materialise. It had not been anticipated that it would take this long; the delays were caused by court proceedings involving the child currently placed with the family (the Kennedys). The Kennedys were described by a CST worker as:

Very experienced and well trained ... They have an excellent record of achievement with many children.

The move to the Kennedys meant a move back into town for Chris. This was an improvement in terms of both contact with the few friends he had and it made the journey to school simpler. The Kennedys also lived within easy travelling distance for Chris' mother. The primary aim of this contract placement was to provide a period of stability while longer term plans for Chris were worked out. The plan of a few months before, that is short-term involvement leading to Chris' rehabilitation home, had not worked out. The state of relationships between Chris and his family, which had declined, and the experiences with Chris over this period, needed to be taken into account while a reassessment of the case was undertaken.

The main requirement was for a placement where the care providers could at least cope with the kinds of behaviour which Chris was presenting. Additionally it was hoped that they might also be able to work with the Department to begin to address some of the family problems. However, at this stage serious consideration was being given to the possibility of identifying a long-term residential placement for Chris. The main idea at this stage was to find a residential school for Chris to begin in the Autumn to allow a natural move from his current school. This was the plan even though, it is important to point out, Chris' problems were *not* primarily school-based. It was now February. This plan would involve maintaining Chris in other placements until the Autumn but the search for a possible placement was begun by the CST.

Because the move to the Kennedys was planned, it was possible for the case worker and the CST link worker to meet them to fill in the background and outline expectations. It was possible for Chris to meet the Kennedys before his final move and the transfer was in fact undertaken by the Jones who took Chris over to his new placement. However, the hopes for this placement did not materialise and, within six weeks, it broke down. Liz, the Community Team Social Worker observed:

We were looking for a placement where we could do an assessment ... but events took over. Whatever plans you tried to make, Chris was always going off in his own direction ... When the placement with the Kennedys broke down there was a decision that a residential placement was the most appropriate and so he was placed at the NCH while we were looking for a long-term residential placement.

Chris, therefore, was moved to one of the four places reserved for Warwickshire children under the terms of the agreement between the County and the National Children's Home (NCH).

Why, by this stage, was a residential placement seen as most appropriate? The first set of reasons revolved around the expectation that the staff in a residential setting would be better able to meet Chris' needs:

- because of their experience and training;
- because of staffing levels; and
- because of the different, that is, non-family and more structured environment.

The most pressing of Chris' needs was the control and management of his behaviour, as a prerequisite to undertaking any other work with him.

There was a second reason which was more pragmatic. Placing Chris in three different family settings had not succeeded for Chris and neither had it worked out for the three families concerned. In fact, their experiences had been very difficult and possibly damaging. There was, therefore, a reluctance on the part of social work staff to put further foster families through a similar experience when there was, to say the least, no guarantee of success.

Having seen how the decision to place Chris in a residential setting came to be taken, why was he placed at the NCH establishment and did this meet his needs as his social worker assessed them? The placement with NCH was made because no alternative longer term residential placement had been identified; the search had begun but had been overtaken by events. Residential placements, other than placements with NCH, require the approval of the Director of Social Services (or his nominee) on the basis of a detailed written submission. Placement with the NCH can, if necessary, be used in an emergency with the verbal approval of the Director (or, again, his nominee). In this case the CST Manager made contact with the Director by telephone and his approval was given after a brief summary of the circumstances of the case.

The main problem with this placement, according to Chris' social worker, was its location. The NCH establishment was on the opposite side of the County from Chris' home town, not a difficult journey by car but a tedious one by public transport. Being placed there meant that Chris' links with the town were disrupted, as was his education. The social worker was a part of the group which made the decision to place Chris in a residential setting but her ideal option would have been a local, in-County residential placement, 'providing an appropriate structure and a therapeutic environment'. She was *not* saying, however, that she would have placed Chris out of choice in one of the County's Children's Centres. By implication she was saying that the Children's Centres as they were in the period before the closures would not have provided the environment she identified as necessary.

The job NCH saw itself doing was providing a short-term, holding placement while a long-term residential placement was found for a boy of nearly 16 who had been in several foster home placements which had broken down. What happened while Chris was at the NCH facility will be described in Chapter 7 but for reasons which will be explained, the intended short-term placement lasted considerably longer than had been planned (for nearly 10 months in fact). The plan to place Chris in another longer term residential placement was dropped, and he was brought back to his home town to a placement in semi-independent accommodation. Liz explained how the change of plan had come about.

We had to reassess what was happening with Chris. He wanted to come back to the town and live independently ... We agreed to look at that as a possibility and Chris agreed that he needed some sort of independence training ... We advertised twice for self-contained accommodation in somebody's property but we got no suitable responses... The decision to return Chris to the town was because NCH was not offering him anything further and he was not spending any time there. Then some supportive lodgings became available and we brought him back and placed him there.

The idea of trying to find self-contained accommodation in someone's house was so that Chris could be independent, would impinge to only a limited extent on the owners, but there would be people around to keep an eye on him. In the supportive lodgings Chris had a room of his own but shared other facilities with the owners. At the CST they felt certain that there was, 'No possibility that it would last'– and it didn't. Within a week Chris was asked to leave because of his unacceptable behaviour. This was the last placement that was found for Chris by the Social Services Department. He went from these supportive lodgings to a bed and breakfast hostel (found for him by a local voluntary project which worked with homeless and rootless people). He stayed there for a few weeks and then found himself another bed and breakfast room which lasted for a few more weeks. His last move while in care was back to the Jones', but this was not a foster placement arranged by the Department but a private arrangement set up by Chris himself. Mrs Jones described what happened:

It was Easter and we took Chris in because he said he had nowhere to go ... It was only later that his social worker told me she had set up lodgings for him.

Chris stayed with the Jones family for a week or so and then moved on, but by then the Department had made the decision to discharge him from care. He was discharged from care not because he was returning to his mother but because he was determined to be independent and to live in the town. He did not want to be in a residential home miles away and he had avoided that option by refusing it in a very determined way. The Social Services Department had tried all it had to offer and Chris had only accepted the options which suited him. There was little else the Department felt it *could* offer and, they argued, no rationale for continuing the pretence that Chris was in their care.

When Chris left care he was three months short of his seventeenth birthday and, as we have seen, six months later Chris appeared to be surviving without the help of the Social Services Department.

Let us now leave the case studies and return to the survey data, this time looking at what actually happened during the course of placements.

6. Meeting the needs of children in their placements

In Chapter 4 we focused on the process of finding placements for our cohort of 215 Warwickshire children when they were admitted to care or when, for whatever reason, they needed to move from one care placement to another. We have also just looked in greater detail at how this process affected three case studies. Having found somewhere for a child in care to live the social work task shifts; it focuses on the reasons why the child is in care, but views these in the context of the overall plan for the child. In the majority of cases the long-term plan will be to reunite child and family. In a much smaller number of cases the aim will be to provide the child with a long-term alternative home, or for some young people the focus will be on enabling them to move towards more independent adulthood.

The skills and the expertise as well as the decisions made by social workers are key factors in determining the extent to which these aims are achieved. But the practice of individual social workers is not our focus here. Equally important for the outcome of each case will be the effects of the placements which are made for the child. A placement in the right location, with experienced and sensitive carers will minimise the disruption experienced by the child, and will ensure the best possible chance that the social worker will be able to achieve his or her aims for the case. A placement of the wrong type, in the wrong place and with less than sensitive carers will make the social work task that much more difficult; not least because social work effort will go into simply maintaining a placement rather than being able to use the placement as a means to an end – for example, as a secure but temporary base for a child who will return home to his or her parents. It is these placement factors on which this chapter will concentrate.

There are a variety of ways in which the effects of particular placements on individual children might be assessed. One method is to use social and psychological adjustment scales. These are applied to children at the beginning and end of (and sometimes during) placements, and attempts are then made to quantify the effects of the placement on an individual child over time.

An alternative approach is more quantitative. It involves identifying a series of criteria which are commonly held to be indicative of good practice, and which are supported by research findings, and then applying these criteria to a range of cases. We can consider the extent to which these criteria are met and then try to identify factors which affect the degree of success. For example, in relation to making placements for children in care, other than in exceptional circumstances, siblings should wherever possible be placed together. The Children Act 1989 emphasises this point. In Warwickshire, this leads us to examine how the more limited range of available placements affects the ability of social workers to make placements for groups of siblings, rather than to separate them.

In our study, we predominantly adopted the second of these two methods, for two reasons. First, on the grounds of pragmatism, the quantitative method is more appropriate to a large-scale study because it is easier to apply and less time-consuming than adjustment scales would be. Such scales need to be applied periodically and are usually completed through observation or interview. This project did not have the necessary resources or time available to use such an approach in relation to well over 200 placements.

The second reason why the quantitative method was more appropriate for our study was that so many of the placements with which we were concerned were of very short duration. This would make adjustment scales, which essentially measure changes *over time*, difficult to apply. It would also be complex to distinguish placement-related factors (which is what we are most interested in) from other factors, such as for instance the effects of the separation from parents, especially for children newly admitted to care. In dealing with our survey data in this chapter, the issues we focus on are:

- The numbers of changes of placement which the children and young people experienced.
- The extent to which placement aims were achieved.
- The effects of placements on children's links with parents, siblings and other community contacts.
- The consequences of placements for children's education.
- The extent to which, in the view of social workers, the carers had the skills and experience necessary in the particular case.
- The extent to which children were settled and comfortable in their placements.
- And finally, we look particularly at the experiences of children from minority ethnic groups in Warwickshire.

Throughout, we examine the results in the light of what we know about good practice but, where possible, we also compare the results for our cohort against what we know of experience in other authorities.

Placement stability

Placement changes while in care can occur for a variety of reasons: in line with a social work plan, because a placement broke down or because of other factors. However, it is possible to say that, in general, frequent placement changes are undesirable. Individual moves from one placement to another may or may not be to the benefit of a child in care but it is difficult to envisage circumstances in which a large number of moves in a relatively short space of time will be in a child's best interests.

The House of Commons Social Services Committee in 1984 (The 'Short' Committee) was so convinced on this point that one of its recommendations was that:

Priority in policies for children in care be given to reducing the number of changes of placement which children in care presently undergo. (House of Commons, 1984)

The possible effects of placement changes were shown in our case studies. In the period immediately before he left care at the age of 17, Chris Taylor lived in a number of placements including supportive lodgings, bed and breakfast hostels and with friends. He would no doubt have been better off if a single placement could have been arranged where he lived independently or with a minimum of supervision, although it was not Chris' social worker's assessment that these moves were particularly damaging for Chris.

If, however, we look at Becky Johnson, it was the unanimous view of those who knew her that each of her moves from foster placement to home to foster placement and then to another foster placement had been damaging. When we left Becky, the Community Team and Children's Services Team social workers were attempting to identify a long-term foster placement which would work for Becky and, meanwhile, were putting in considerable effort to maintain her existing placement.

Wedge and Phelan (1988), in their study of children in care in Essex, discovered that half of the children, admitted to care during their four-year monitoring period, experienced three or more placements. They argued that it is desirable to reduce not only the numbers of unplanned movements but also the total number of movements between care placements.

Measures which reduce the demands made on individual foster carers and members of staff or which reduce the degree of turbulence must be good for children. Steps which reduce the amount of work involved in the transfer of children between placements should benefit not only children but staff too. (Wedge and Phelan, 1988)

Research from the Dartington Social Research Unit supports this general point but also makes specific comments about the effect on the parents of children in care.

Social workers, mindful of the unsuitability of many of the actual placements in which children end up ... protect themselves from inevitable parental reproaches by vagueness of plan and misplaced optimism. Hence, frequent movements of children between placements come to be viewed by parents as a demonstration of their child's difficulty rather than as a reflection of the inadequacy of the care offered. (Millham and others, 1986)

The base for our analysis in this chapter was the 72 children in the new admissions to care group. Children in the long-term in care group – that is the 56 children and young people already in care for at least one year when their cases were selected for this study – accounted for just six changes of placement and are not included. The 14 children from the not admitted group, who were admitted to care during the course of the follow-up and who accounted for 14 placement changes, are also excluded since some of them were admitted to care very late on in our monitoring period.

For the 'new admissions' group, a home on trial placement was counted as a move. If, however, a child left care temporarily to return home, the period at home was not counted as a placement; but the placement made on re-admission was counted. Our definitions of a placement and a placement move are, therefore, deliberately the same as those used in Rowe's 1989 study. The main difference between our study and her's was the length of the follow-up period; 12 to 23 months for Rowe and 12 to 18 months for us. We would, therefore, anticipate that the results for Warwickshire would show fewer placement changes because of the shorter monitoring period.

Figure 6.1 summarises the number of placement changes experienced by Rowe's cohort (aged five years or over only) and the Warwickshire cohort, which covers the same age range. Despite the shorter monitoring period and our consequent expectations outlined above, it is noticeable that the children in Warwickshire experienced considerably more moves to new placements while in care. Whereas just 40 per cent of the Warwickshire children experienced no placement changes, in Rowe's study the figure was 57 per cent. A third of the Warwickshire children had two or more placements compared with only one in five; and the number of children who had five or more placements was *twice* as high in Warwickshire compared with Rowe's six authorities. (On this measure, these six authorities showed little difference one from another.)

Surprisingly, in Warwickshire age did not appear to be a statistically significant factor in differentiating between children who moved frequently and

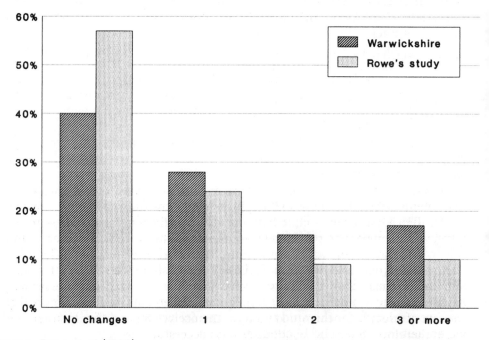

Source: Rowe et al (1989)

Figure 6.1 Warwickshire and Rowe compared: Number of placement changes

those who did not. The reasons why the children came into care were also not particularly strongly associated with the numbers of moves.

In the introduction to this section, we outlined the reasons why large numbers of placement changes were undesirable. These results, therefore, which are among the most important for this study as a whole, give strong cause for concern about childcare in Warwickshire. We expected fewer placement changes in the County compared with Rowe's study because of the shorter monitoring period, but we found considerably *more* changes of placement. And the higher rate of placement changes appeared to apply to *all* age groups. The reason for this large number of moves is an issue which we will examine further.

Placement aims and the achievement of those aims

Apart from having an overall aim for each child in care for whom they are responsible, social workers should also have more specific expectations for each placement. What we will examine here is the extent to which social workers judged these placement aims to have been successfully achieved and we will try to identify the factors which are associated with success.

For reasons discussed earlier, the descriptions of placement aims we used resembled those of Rowe's placement study (1989). The first significant finding is that the frequency with which particular aims were identified for our cohort in Warwickshire was very close to that in Rowe's study of 9335 placements in six authorities.

We asked social workers to assess the extent to which the placement aims had been achieved by the time the placement had finished, or while the placement was continuing for those which had not ended when we ceased monitoring. The question was phrased to give the social workers a range of responses from 'aims fully met' to 'not met at all'. Although this kind of question is a matter of some subjective judgement, there were sufficient consistencies in the responses (for instance more or less success with particular aims or with particular age groups) and responses broadly tallying with Rowe's study, for us to feel that the results were valid and important.

Overall, it was encouraging that seven out of ten of the Warwickshire placements were felt to have met the placement aims fully or in most respects. Fewer than a tenth were said to have not achieved the aims at all. These results were, within one or two percentage points, similar to Rowe's. However, within this overall pattern of success and failure we found some marked differences.

To some extent, the results in Table 6.1 obviously reflect the fact that some aims are, in themselves, more easily achievable: for instance where the primary aim was simply to provide a short-term home. Placements made with more than the aim of providing accommodation set themselves more difficult targets and were, therefore, likely to be judged as less successful.

If we combine the 'fully achieved' and 'achieved in most respects' responses, we find that the aims assessed to have been best met were: emergency care (87 per cent); care and upbringing (81 per cent); and short-term care (66 per cent).

Table 6.1: Success in achieving placement aims

Aim	Fully achieved (%)	Achieved in most respects (%)	Partially achieved (%)	Not achieved at all (%)
Short-term care (No. = 50)	46	20	22	12
Emergency care (No. = 30)	50	37	10	3
Treatment (No. = 12)	8	50	25	17
Assessment (No. = 28)	18	43	29	11
Bridge to independence (No. = 17)	6	30	41	23
Care and upbringing (No. = 54)	44	37	17	2
Remand (No. = 15)	40	13	47	0
All (No. = 206)	36	32	23	8

Least success was with placements where the aims were: bridge to independence (36 per cent); remand (53 per cent); treatment (58 per cent); and assessment (61 per cent).

Did other factors, apart from the nature of the task itself, affect the extent to which aims were achieved? In particular, from the point of view of our research, we want to know whether the availability or use of particular types of placement meant that aims were achieved to a greater or lesser extent. These are complicated questions to answer because there are several dimensions to them. First, we need to know whether different aims were associated with different types of placement or whether, for example, we were as likely to find a foster placement made with the aim of care and upbringing as we were to find a residential placement with the same aim. The results show that particular types of placement were indeed associated with particular aims.

- Residential placements were particularly associated with 'treatment', emergency care, assessment and remand.
- Foster placements were linked with short-term care, care and upbringing and assessment.
- And 'other' types of placement (which were predominantly in lodgings and independent living) were associated with aims of providing an emergency placement or a bridge to independence.

These associations were also true of Rowe's much larger number of placements although, of course, considerably more were residential placements.

We can compare the extent to which placement aims were achieved for our cohort in Warwickshire and in Rowe's study but only for foster placements where we have sufficient cases to make the comparison valid. Table 6.2 gives details of the placements where aims were achieved in most respects.

Table 6.2 Foster placements: aims fully achieved or achieved in most respects (aged five or over only)

Aim	Warwickshire (No.=160) (%)	Rowe (No.=1722) (%)
Short-term care	65	88
Emergency care	87	83
Treatment	55	46
Assessment	58	57
Bridge to independence	37	53
Care and upbringing	82	66
All	70	69

How are we to interpret these results? First, we can see that the task-centred aims met with less success in both studies and that the 'success rates' in both studies were, for most aims, broadly similar. The relatively few cases in the bridge to independence group means that we cannot draw too many inferences from differences which appear there. The relatively more straightforward aims, that is short-term and emergency care, and possibly also care and upbringing, were achieved to a much greater extent. Warwickshire appears, from these figures, to have been noticeably more successful with foster placements where the aim was care and upbringing but less successful where it was short-term care. We will see if we can identify any factors which might explain these, and the other, differences.

Having isolated the foster placements, should we expect aims to be achieved to a greater extent in Warwickshire than in other authorities? The County does put considerably more resources into supporting foster placements, via Children's Services Teams link work and direct work inputs. Should this be seen to have an effect on outcomes? On the other hand, as we have seen, Warwickshire does use fostering to a much greater extent than other authorities and places a great number of 'difficult' children in foster care.

Children's adaptation to placements

Social workers were also asked to identify how well adapted and integrated each child was to each of his or her placements. They were asked to code their responses on a five point scale ranging from 'fully integrated' to 'not integrated at all'. The question was asked about all placements which had ended and, also, about placements which were continuing at the point at which we ceased to monitor the cohort. The base for our analysis here is all the placements made for all the children in the cohort who spent time in care.

Like other issues in childcare, integration into placements is not straightforward to analyse. We cannot simply measure the degree of integration without considering the context of the placement and, in particular, the aims and purpose of the placement. We would obviously not expect, for example, a young man in a remand placement to be integrated to the extent to which we would hope a child would be integrated where the aim of the placement was care and upbringing

Overall, in more than four in ten placements, children were identified as being in the two highest of the five categories of integration. In placements with different aims, however, the figures varied – from remands (fewer than one in ten), emergency care and short-term care (two in ten) – to placements where the aim was adoption or custodianship (nearly 70 per cent) and care and upbringing (nearly 90 per cent). In Warwickshire, the type of placement where children were best integrated was, perhaps not surprisingly, home on trial: in only one placement out of 16 was the level of integration assessed outside the top two categories. Significantly, all other types of placements were rated on a similar level with about 40 per cent of foster placements, residential care and 'other' placements placed in the top two categories.

It is important to point out that this result for foster placement compares very unfavourably with the results from another study where direct comparisons are possible. Research carried out by the Dartington Social Research Unit (Millham and others, 1986, p.160) examined the degree to which children in foster placements were felt to be integrated compared with children in residential placements. Their research was carried out in five authorities, all of which had a more traditional balance of residential and foster provision. In residential placements they found that fewer than 40 per cent of children were reasonably well integrated, compared with over 80 per cent of children in foster placements. However, more of the residential placements were 'holding' or temporary placements where less integration would be expected. A larger proportion of the foster placements had longer-term aims.

Comparing the two studies, we have a figure of *39 per cent* of children in Warwickshire who were at least reasonably well integrated in their foster placements, in contrast with over *80 per cent* overall for the five authorities in the Dartington study. However, we must be careful how we interpret this finding. We know that the degree to which children are integrated in their placement is, to a large extent, dependent on the aims and purpose of the placement. It is, therefore, reasonable to conclude that the much reduced level of integration of children in foster placements in Warwickshire is, at least in part, a consequence of the much greater use of foster placements for difficult to achieve and task-centred aims. This can be compared with other authorities where the residential sector provides a greater proportion of placements which have such aims.

However, if we compare the results for *all* types of placement for our Warwickshire cohort, we find a figure of fewer than 40 per cent for children who were reasonably well integrated in their placements compared with a figure of 54 per cent in the Dartington study. The conclusion we must draw from this is that the results in Warwickshire cannot be completely accounted for by the greater use of foster care in the County, and that this pattern of placement has other, unintended consequences for children's integration in placements. These results are disquieting.

In Warwickshire, other factors did appear to be associated with the degree to which children were integrated in their placements. The reason *why* children were admitted to care or remained in care was strongly associated with the level of integration of children. Between three and four times as many of children in care for reasons of neglect or abuse, or poor care were well integrated compared with the group where the main concern was the child's behaviour. This last group tended to be older.

Another significant finding was that integration was less successfully achieved as children experienced *changes* of placement. In nearly half of initial placements children were what we have termed well integrated, but when we look at third and later placements, the figure was only just over a third. In Chapter 4, we also identified a comparatively high proportion of emergency placements in Warwickshire compared with the results of research in other authorities. It is, therefore, of concern that many fewer children were identified as successfully integrated when placements were made in an emergency (18 per cent) compared with planned placements (45 per cent).

We can now venture an explanation for the lower levels of integration in placements which we found in Warwickshire. The explanation must remain hypothetical because, given the size of our data set, we cannot apply the more sophisticated statistical analyses which would make it possible to identify more rigorously the relationships between the different factors. However, given that reservation, we found that lower levels of integration were associated with changes of placement and with unplanned moves to placements. In the earlier part of this report we identified that our cohort experienced both more moves and more unplanned changes than children in other authorities. Our speculation, therefore, is that there is a connection between these two factors and the low levels of integration we found.

The continuity of the care experience

In Chapter 4, we examined a number of issues of good practice in childcare. We looked at the extent to which social workers had a choice about the placement they made for children; we considered the extent to which it was possible to plan admissions to care or changes of placements; and we looked at the importance which social workers attached to a range of issues when they were making placements. These issues were: keeping sibling groups together; the skills and experience of the care providers; and the continuity of the child's experiences through the process of being admitted to care and moving from one care placement to another. We shall now examine these issues in greater detail in relation to our Warwickshire sample.

Many studies have described the disruption to children's lives which is the result of even the best planned admission to care. The Department of Health summary of research into childcare (DHSS, 1985) referred to, 'the deep, emotional problems generated by the care experience'. The least disruptive admission to care might be one in which a child is placed for a few days with foster carers while her (for example) mother is in hospital. The event may be anticipated and the child well prepared for the separation in the knowledge that she will be back with her mother within a very short time. She and her mother may previously have visited the foster carers so that the child was not going to strange people or into an unfamiliar home. Her mother might have taken her to the foster home, ensuring that she had her own clothes, favourite toys and photographs. All of this might have happened and it will have reduced the level of anxiety felt by the child. But she will nonetheless still have felt shocked by the separation and will have harboured real doubts about whether she would return home, until she actually did.

Imagine a different case. And this time one of our case studies, Becky, is appropriate to consider. After worsening relationships with her mother, Becky at the age of nearly 12 was admitted to care for the second time. The admission was made very quickly; there was no time to match Becky's needs with available placements because only one placement was available. No introductions were possible and Becky, with very few possessions, was taken to the placement by the emergency duty social worker, who knew Becky but had never met the foster carers. She was in a new house with strange people and she didn't know how long she would be there or whether she would ever return home.

To help reduce the anxiety for the child, one aim of social work practice should be to focus on the maintenance of continuity in the child's life in as many areas as possible. In Chapter 4, we summarised the responses of social workers to a series of questions which asked them to prioritise factors relating to issues of continuity. In this section, we will examine how well continuity was maintained in placements made for the children and young people in the cohort. The three factors we will concentrate on are: placement with siblings (where applicable); contact between parents and children; and the maintenance of other community links, such as those with friends. Continuity of education is an additional related factor which will be examined in the next section.

Siblings

Our results disclosed earlier revealed, encouragingly, that where a child was admitted to care with brothers or sisters, or had siblings in care and was moving to a new placement, then social workers considered that no other issue was more important than finding a placement in which they could be united.

The group who were in care with siblings was different in many ways from other children. The sibling placements involved much younger children (69 per cent were aged 13 or under compared with just a third of those where there were no siblings to consider); eight out of ten were placements where the reason for care was neglect/abuse or poor care while these reasons accounted for just six out of ten of the non-sibling placements; and 61 per cent of the sibling placements had the aim of short-term care or care and upbringing, compared with less than 40 per cent of the placements which did not involve siblings. We also found that in the cases where placement with siblings was a consideration, the children had considerably fewer placement moves (partly because, on average, they spent less time in care). Of the children in care with siblings only two per cent experienced three or more placement changes, compared with more than five times this number of the children in care without siblings.

All these factors as they applied to the sibling placement group (age, reasons for care, placement aims and numbers) are ones which, in the last chapter, we discovered were associated with success as measured in terms of being able to make the preferred type of placement and having a choice between placements. Did the fact that placements were being sought for sibling groups mean that these advantages were lost?

In over 80 per cent (No.=65) of placements, the social worker was fully satisfied that the aim of placing siblings together was achieved. In the other cases, pairs of siblings were separated or larger groups split up.

The types of placements made for children with siblings are compared, in Table 6.3, with placements for single children.

Table 6.3 Placements for children with and without siblings

Placement type	Children with siblings (No.=65) (%)	Children without siblings (No.=162) (%)
Foster care	82	79
Home-on-trial	12	6
Residential	0	7
'Other'	6	9
All	100	100

Residential care was not used for sibling groups in Warwickshire unlike in other authorities, as shown in research such as that by Berridge (1985) and Millham and others (1986). In Warwickshire siblings were more often placed with foster carers and home-on-trial. Significantly, placements for two-thirds of the sibling groups were more often the social workers' placements of choice (67 per cent of placements) compared with just a half of the placements for children without siblings in care.

Siblings were also better integrated in their placements, with 55 per cent being rated in the top two of the five point scale of integration compared with 39 per cent of the placements for children without siblings. Furthermore, if we look at social workers' assessments of whether placement aims were achieved in the placements for siblings, 83 per cent were identified as achieving the aims fully or in most respects. For the other children's placements the equivalent figure was just 68 per cent.

We have no information about the size of the sibling groups in our cohort but clearly, for larger groups of siblings (say three or more), Warwickshire's dependence on foster home placements might result in sibling groups being separated. Berridge identified the facility for keeping large groups of brothers and sisters together as one of the roles which children's homes could fulfil (Berridge, 1985). However, given this reservation, in summary, we can say two things about children in the cohort with siblings who were admitted to care or who moved to a new care placement. First, a large majority of these children were successfully placed with their brothers or sisters, which would be the desired outcome in all but exceptional circumstances. And second, on most measures of assessing the success of placements, the sibling groups did better than those children without siblings in care. On this dimension, therefore, Warwickshire's policies seem to have a positive effect on the quality of care provided for sibling groups.

Links with parents

As discussed in Chapter 4, there is general agreement in the childcare literature that, with few exceptions, children in care should be encouraged and enabled to maintain regular contact with their parents and other significant relatives (including grandparents and siblings). The Children Act 1989 endorses this view. Contact includes visits, telephone calls and letters. The exceptional cases would include some where children, especially very young children, are placed for adoption and some, but by no means all, where children are in care because of physical or sexual abuse in which either or both parents were involved.

The evidence and arguments identifying the importance of maintaining links come from the fields of developmental psychology and social work research. In 1986 the Dartington Social Research Unit carefully examined the problems which exist in maintaining links between children in care and their absent parents, and they summarised the body of writing on these issues which has appeared in the post-war period. They concluded:

The maintenance of links between separated child, parents and wider family is important: (a) because research evidence suggests that the absent child is happier and functions better when parents remain in contact; (b) because frequent contact with home is the clearest indicator that the child will leave care quickly; (c) the majority of very young children who enter care do not stay long, thus long-term substitute parenting is not a dominating issue; (d) stable, alternative care placements for children are very difficult to ensure, thus parents and family ... may prove to be the only enduring relationships the child has; (e) increasingly, older children and adolescents tend to enter and stay in care, and they have well-forged family and friendship links which they wish to maintain. (Millham and others, 1986)

More recent research has also shown that limited contact between children in care and their family is associated with the breakdown of foster placements (Berridge and Cleaver, 1987). Encouragingly, we saw earlier that most Warwickshire social workers rated the maintenance of contact with parents as a high priority when making placements and that exceptions mostly concerned young people aged 16 or over.

Here we will report not only the level of satisfaction among social workers with the frequency of contact between children and parents, but we will also report 'harder' data on the frequency of contact by identifying both the distance of the placements from the child's home and the time it took parents to travel to the placement.

The authors of Lost in Care (Millham and others, 1986) usefully distinguished between 'specific restrictions' on contact between children in care and their parents and 'non-specific restrictions'. By specific restrictions they referred to conscious and deliberate decisions by social workers to deny access by the child to particular people. In their study they found that over one third of children were subject to specific restrictions on contact with one or more people (usually parents). In our new admissions group, only one child out of 86 was allowed no visits at all by parents, but we do not have information about how many more were subject to more limited restrictions on access. A more useful comparison comes from Packman's study (1986). She found that overall, nine per cent of the children admitted to care had a ban on contact with one or more members of their family, but this overall figure disguised the fact that children admitted compulsorily were twice as likely to be subject to such restrictions compared with children in care on a voluntary basis.

Overall, excluding the home-on-trial placements, in only four per cent (No. = 204) of Warwickshire placements was contact between the child and his or her parents not permitted. Table 6.4 details the frequency of visiting between parents and children.

Table 6.4 Frequency of visits

Frequency	(No. = 204) (%)
More than once a week	23
Once a week to once a month	44
Once a month to once every three months	10
Less than once every three months	6
No visits occurred	13
No visits permitted	4
All	100

These results cannot be interpreted in a completely straightforward way, not least because of the fact that a substantial proportion of the children spent a very short period in care and, for them, the question of organising regular visits would not have arisen. However, we can find comparisons with these results in other research studies. Overall, for example, if we consider visits taking place at least once a month, then the figure of nearly 70 per cent for our study is broadly similar to the Dartington Research Unit's study (Millham and others, 1986) and to Rowe's placement study (1989).

Nevertheless, it is important to try to see the issue of the frequency of visits through the eyes of those most affected – that is the parents and, even more so, the children. For a child who has spent all, or most, of her (say) life in daily contact with her parents, to be in a situation where she is only seeing them once a month, quite likely seeing them in strange and not necessarily comforting surroundings, and is seeing them without familiar routines to support the contact, the experience will inevitably be difficult if not distressing. The child, her parents and the carers will all have different problems to face in managing such monthly visits. Problems would be less likely if visits were more regular and routine but in our study, in fewer than a quarter of placements were parents and child seeing each other weekly or more frequently.

Social workers certainly thought that there was a difference between weekly visits and monthly or less frequent visits. In nearly one in five placements where the frequency of visits was between less than once a week and up to once a month, social workers said that more frequent visits would be better. Where the visiting was even less frequent, social workers commented that more visits would be better in a third of placements.

Is this figure showing only a quarter of children having weekly visits low? Compared with Rowe's findings (1989) the answer is in the affirmative. In nearly twice as many of the placements in her study, children and parents were seeing each other at least weekly. Why the level of contact should be so low in Warwickshire we will explore later, but first it will be important to identify the particular circumstances which were associated with greater or lesser contact between parents and children.

Time in care and the frequency of parental visiting

The length of time children and young people had spent in care was strongly associated with the frequency with which they saw their parents. Two different groups can be identified.

The first group was those children who spent only a short period in care and who were also more likely to be separated from home because of their parents' inability to care for them, perhaps because of illness. These children accounted for most of the two in every ten first placements where there were no visits at all. In only one in ten of third or later placements was there no visiting. It was this poor care group whom social workers thought would benefit from more regular contact. Interestingly, it was the group of children admitted for reasons of behaviour who had the most regular contact with their families.

Children who had been in care for more than six months, and even more so children in care for over a year, had considerably fewer visits from parents than children who had been in care for shorter periods. The authors of *Lost in Care*, which we have frequently referred to because of its importance, made a similar point in their study and they went on to express considerable concern that, after six or 12 months, the level of social work activity in most childcare cases declined considerably. This included work put into rehabilitation. The status quo appeared to become increasingly accepted by all parties, even where long-term care was not the plan. Our study would support this assessment: for those children who had been in care for longer periods, even though the level of visiting was much reduced, social workers were not expressing the opinion that increased parental contact would be desirable.

The location of placements and parental visiting

Where children were placed was the second major factor which affected the frequency with which they saw their parents. For example, children in residential care had very limited contact with their families. Table 6.5 compares the frequency of visiting for children living in different settings.

Table 6.5 Family contact with children in different types of placement

	Frequency of visits			
	At least weekly (%)	*At least monthly* (%)	*Less often* (%)	*No visits* (%)
Foster care (No.=167)	25	71	15	14
Residential placements (No.=11)	0	36	55	9
'Other' (No.=15)	27	73	13	13
All (No.=193)	24	69	17	13

(Results from the first column are subsumed into the second.)

Even though only small numbers of children were in placements other than foster care, the lack of contact between children in residential placements and their families compared with children in other types of placement is obvious. None of the children in residential settings saw their families weekly or more often, compared with over a quarter of children in other types of placements. Only a third of the children in residential settings saw their families even once a month. Twice as many children in 'other' settings saw their parents this often. These differences between the frequency of contacts between children in different types of placement were statistically significant.

Why did children in residential placements see their families so infrequently? The distance of the residential placements from the children's homes seems to have been the primary factor. In social workers' judgements, in half of the cases where children were in residential placements, 'A placement which was closer to the natural family home would have been better'. For children in foster placements the figure was fewer than one in five, and for children in 'other' placements only seven per cent.

Social workers were also asked how easy it was for parents to travel to their child's placement. Some parents would have had transport of their own which would have made visiting much easier, especially in a county authority like Warwickshire with large rural areas and comparatively poor public transport services. However, even taking this into account, for only 22 per cent of residential placements did social workers describe the journey for parents to visit their child as 'easy'. They described over half of the trips to foster placements and three-quarters of trips to children in 'other' placements as 'easy'.

We have seen that Warwickshire's most commonly used residential care facility was that run by National Children's Home in Sutton Coldfield – a location not easily accessible from any part of the County. Other residential facilities which were used were even less easy to reach. The County's Education Department has only a limited number of places in residential schools for children with special educational needs but, as we will see in Chapter 12, most children in care and placed in residential schools are located out of the County, which inevitably means that visiting is difficult.

It is interesting that Rowe found very little difference between the frequency with which parents visited children in foster homes and children in residential placements (Rowe, 1989). There were two main differences between Rowe's six authorities and Warwickshire. The first was that four out of the six were urban areas, where travelling to and from placements would presumably be much easier than in County areas because of the shorter distances involved. The second difference was that each of these authorities retained considerable residential childcare facilities (residential placement rates ranging from 28 per cent to 52 per cent of all placements). With a range of residential facilities within the authority, local residential placements which do not make visiting difficult for parents, are much more likely to be made.

This finding was reflected in Packman's research (1986), which identified a possible link between the proximity of residential units and the frequency of visits to children in these units by their parents. However, the Dartington study (Millham and others, 1986) came up with a somewhat contradictory finding; social workers viewed foster care more positively than residential care in relation to maintaining links between children and parents, mainly because foster care could be more local. However, they go on to say, 'There are considerable barriers to contact in foster homes as well as in residential care, but these impediments are different.' We will look at some of these other issues shortly.

If we return to look at *all* types of placements made for the children in the study, we find a strong and statistically highly significant relationship between those placements where social workers felt that a different placement, closer to the child's home, would have been better, and those placements which were the most difficult for parents to travel to. The implication of this result is that, as far as social workers were concerned, the locality of placements is a key issue. We also found that placements made in an emergency rather than planned were also associated with more difficult travelling for parents and with less regular visiting by parents.

The effects of the type of placement on parental visiting

Childcare research into contacts between parents and children in care has examined a second major theme in addition to the one of distance between home and placement. We have seen in our case studies that for parents, some substitute carers make visiting their child a comparatively comfortable and acceptable event, whereas visits to other placements can make parents feel unwelcome, inadequate and guilty. The most substantial study of the links between children in care and their parents goes so far as to say that, when comparing barriers to contact:

The attitudes of foster carers and residential staff to family contact were far more significant than problems of distance and transport. (Millham and others, 1986)

What is it about particular placements that can make visits to children more or less difficult? One aspect is the style of the placement. Staff in better organised residential homes will have routines and structures which are flexible enough to make visitors welcome and also give them a role. On the other hand, however, in more institutional establishments the routines and structures can act as barriers to contact rather than enable it.

These comments also apply to foster placements. Good foster carers will be welcoming towards the child's parents and will make every effort not to appear judgmental. They will make sure that the child and his or her parents can be alone together and, if possible, will ensure that the parents have some role relating to the care of their child. However, foster carers will not always act in ways which encourage visits either because they are relatively inexperienced, because they are unclear about their role or even, perhaps, because they are hostile. Children in one study described foster carers who wouldn't leave them alone when they had visitors. The foster carers did not want the child to have any secrets (Kahan, 1979).

Other studies have described particular problems in foster placements for children under ten, with the foster carers seeing themselves as taking over the role of natural parents and thus making it very difficult for the parents to visit (Millham and others, 1986). Residential settings, with their greater territorial neutrality, may have certain advantages in this area (Berridge, 1985). Children under ten are also more likely to be visibly upset as a consequence of parental visits: a natural reaction but one to which foster carers (and social workers) can sometimes respond inappropriately by restricting access, either by formal or informal means.

The role and attitude of social workers must also be taken into account when we are examining visiting patterns and restrictions on visiting. In their study, Berridge and Cleaver (1987), described cases where social workers imposed restrictions on visiting in response to what they saw as foster carers' difficulties with visits:

However, when foster couples were then interviewed, we seldom perceived there to be this degree of antipathy [to visits]. Instead, the absence of parental contact was explained as the social worker's preference.

In the research studies we have mentioned so far and in others (for example Colton, 1988) there was broad agreement about the relationship between the type of placement and the extent to which parental contact was encouraged or discouraged. All of this research has shown that there were both foster placements and residential homes where visits were encouraged and made as easy as possible, but there were others where styles and attitudes were very discouraging. However, while accepting that individual placements varied, the general conclusion was that residential establishments, overall, encouraged contact between parents and children to a greater extent than foster homes.

This is one of Colton's conclusions in his comparative study of children in residential homes with those in specialised foster care, but he goes on to ask a series of questions about whether the role and function of foster care can change to take over some of the roles currently seen as more effectively carried out by residential homes. In particular, while conceding the fact that residential care rather than foster care is more conducive to maintaining family contact, he asks whether this needs to be the case. Some of his findings would suggest otherwise (Colton, 1988).

This is the key question for Warwickshire. Having closed their Children's Centres and only having access to residential establishments to which visiting is difficult because of the travelling distances, are the main substitute care resource in the County – foster homes – any more encouraging to parental visiting than research suggests is true of other authorities? We asked social workers to rate each placement in terms of how encouraging it was to the maintenance of parent-child contacts, ignoring the issue of distance between the child's home and where she or he was placed. There are naturally problems in relying solely on the judgements of social workers but we do also have the evidence from our case studies which we return to in Chapter 7.

Excluding the home-on-trial placements, placements with relatives and the few other placements where, for example, there were no parental visits because parents were ill, Table 6.6 gives the overall results to the question which asked how encouraging the placements were to visiting.

Table 6.6 Placements and the maintenance of contacts between parents and children

	Proportion of placements (No.=164) (%)
Very encouraging to good and regular links	34
Quite encouraging	36
Both encouraging and discouraging	23
Quite discouraging	5
Very discouraging	2
All	100

Overall, in seven out of ten of the cases, the placement was said to be encouraging to the maintenance of links and in very few cases was the placement described as discouraging. In relation to the effects of the type of placement on the responses, we cannot come to firm conclusions because of the small numbers of placements in residential settings (No.=8) and 'other' settings (No.=9), where the question was applicable. Given this reservation, we can only make the following points tentatively.

- All of the 'other' placements were identified as 'encouraging' to contact. This result is perhaps not surprising; the 'other' category consists mainly of children living in lodgings or in independent accommodation. We would expect that the kinds of barriers to contact we have been describing would be less likely to be present in such placements.

- There was little difference between the proportion of foster placements and the proportion of residential placements where the setting was described as 'encouraging' to contact.
- Only nine placements were described as 'discouraging' to contact, but all of these were foster placements.
- We expected, from previous research results, to find that there would be particular problems relating to younger children, that is those aged ten or under, placed in foster care, especially given that Warwickshire places more children of all ages in foster placements. The responses to our question did not confirm this expectation and age was not a significant factor.

Overall then, it would seem that the lower levels of visiting of children in care in Warwickshire, compared to research results from other authorities, are less attributable to the style of placements and the attitudes of carers. Instead, the distance children are placed from home seems to be a major factor, with the consequence of complicated and time-consuming journeys parents would have to make. This applies particularly to the, albeit small, number of children placed residentially.

The continuity of other community links

As we have seen, high priority was given by social workers to ensuring that children and young people in care could maintain regular contact with their brothers and sisters, their parents and other family members, although with adults in particular this proved difficult to deliver. But the lives of children and young people do not simply revolve around home, family and school. There are a range of other links with their communities which are important. Primarily these are their friendships with individuals and their involvement in peer groups and organised leisure activities – contacts which are probably more important for older children.

Potentially, these contacts are the ones which are likely to suffer more if a child in care is placed at a distance from home. Parents and siblings will be expected to maintain contact and may be helped with transport by social workers. Over a quarter of the placements, as we will see, involved more difficult journeys to school. A few children were taken from their care placement by taxi at the Department's expense. But friends will generally not be expected to visit children in care and will seldom be helped to do so. On top of all the other disruptions, which being admitted to care or moving to a new placement often entails, the loss of one's friends can only lead to more distress for the child. Furthermore, being denied access to pets, though it may seem trivial to some, can be very hurtful for children who have been unable to find love and solace in other people. Children in care when interviewed frequently refer to this point, although we have yet to see it mentioned in any other research study.

This general point about broader contacts was recognised by social workers. As we saw in Chapter 4, there were very few cases where they identified the maintenance of community links as of low priority in their practice, although contacts with siblings and parents and continuity of education were all rated as more important. It transpired that in nearly three in ten placements, children were able to maintain their community contacts 'very well'; in over half the cases the response was 'very well' or 'quite well'. Nonetheless, this leaves a large number whose broader social contacts were restricted.

The key factor which decided whether these contacts could be maintained was, as we anticipated, the distance of the placement from the child's home. When the travelling time from the child's home to the placement was less than half an hour, half the children were able to keep in touch with friends 'very well'. When it was more than half an hour only six per cent were able to maintain contact 'very well'. An equally significant result was obtained by comparing those placements which social workers felt were close enough to home and those where they thought that one nearer would be better. For the former placements, children were able to maintain community contacts 'very well'. For the other placements there were no children whom social workers said were able to maintain those contacts 'very well'. In half the cases the placements meant that children were able to maintain these contacts 'badly'.

As we have come to expect by now, where children were placed affected the extent to which they experienced some degree of continuity when they were admitted to care or when they moved to a new placement. Table 6.7 clearly shows the effects of the type of placements on children's ability to stay in touch with their communities.

Table 6.7 The type of placement and the effect on general community links

Maintained links:	Foster care (No. = 150) (%)	Type of placement Residential (No. = 9) (%)	Other (No. = 18) (%)
Very well/quite well	51	11	78
Not particularly well/badly	49	89	22
All	100	100	100

Disconcertingly, nearly half the children in foster placements had difficulty in keeping in touch with their friends. For young people in lodgings or their own flat the figure was only two in ten; reflecting, in part, the fact that those living in such placements were an older group and could travel to see their friends more easily. However, these 'other' placements did on the whole seem to be much closer to the young people's communities. In only one in ten of these cases did social workers say that a placement closer to the parental home would be better and this was the lowest result for any type of placement. When we look at residential placements, we have to be careful about what we can claim because of the small number of children involved. But the results above suggest that it is precisely these placements which make it most difficult for children to keep in touch with broader social contacts. This parallels the earlier finding about the problems of maintaining links between parents and children in residential care.

In summary, we can say that social workers recognised that maintaining links with friends is an important issue for children in care but that the unavailability of placements meant it was impossible to facilitate this. The distance of placements from the original neighbourhood was what made these links most difficult to maintain and the problem was most acute for those young people who were placed in residential care establishments or in residential schools.

Continuity of education

In Chapter 4 we saw that, over a period of years, researchers and official bodies had expressed concern about two aspects of the education of children in care. There was concern first that in the process of admitting children to care and finding placements for them, too little consideration was given to the effects of decisions on the child's education. The second aspect concerned findings that the education of children did not seem to be particularly enhanced if they came into care, but for reasons which were not always straightforward to understand.

We also reported in the same chapter our finding that the social workers who were responsible for the children in our study gave a high priority to maintaining continuity of education for the children and, especially, those who were in care for reasons which were mainly to do with behaviour.

There are of course a whole series of other considerations around the issue of education for children in care. For instance, it has been well established that children's educational success is closely tied to their parents' attitudes, expectations and support but what happens to children in care who are not living with their parents? In our case study of Becky Johnson, one of her foster carers (Mrs Edwards) had taken an active role, had discussed Becky's problem with the school and had almost certainly delayed the decision to exclude her. However, in our discussions, Mrs Edwards also said that she was not at all sure if this level of involvement in Becky's education was what was expected of her as a foster carer.

In her summary of the available evidence from Britain and the USA, Jackson (1987) concluded that, with very few exceptions, the routines in foster homes and in all types of residential children's homes, and the attitudes and expectations of the carers in these places often ensured that children in care achieved poorly in educational terms. Berridge (1985), in his study of 20 children's homes, found limited educational achievements among the children. The explanations he put forward were educational disadvantage associated with their home backgrounds; a climate and attitudes within the homes which were not conducive to educational progress; and changes of school which followed on from changes in placements while in care. More recent work by Aldgate (1990) has shown that although entry to care may not in itself necessarily lead to a deterioration in educational performance, neither does it bring about the significant improvements that one might expect.

In our study we were obviously not able to examine all of these issues. What we focused on was the location of placements and the extent to which it was possible to find placements for children in care which led to as little disruption to their education as possible. Berridge and Cleaver (1987), in their study of foster placements breakdowns, found that children in long-term foster placements whose education was disrupted by an otherwise unnecessary change of school also experienced twice the rate of placement breakdown compared with children who had been able to remain in the same school.

Table 6.8 shows the effects which the location of the placements had on the schooling of the children and young people in our cohort.

Table 6.8 Effects of placements on schooling

	(No. = 184) (%)
Child remained at same school, easy journey	34
Same school, more difficult journey	26
Same school, very difficult journey	3
Change of school necessary	16
Not previously attending, still not attending	7
Not previously attending, has started at new school	14
All responses	100

In a small number of placements the move to a new placement was associated with positive educational developments. Some children (14 per cent) who had not previously been going to school, started to attend. In four out of ten cases the placement change had a neutral effect on the child's education, either because she or he continued not to attend school or because the journey to school was an easy one. But in the remaining 45 per cent of placements the effect on the child's education was negative, in that the journey to school became more difficult or because the child had to change school.

When we talk about a more difficult journey we should remember that, as with two of our case studies, this can involve long journeys by taxi – sometimes from one side of the County to the other. The consequences, for the child, include making it difficult to become involved in out-of-hours activities. It could also be very tiring for the carers, and such an arrangement makes it even more difficult for them to take an active interest in the child's education. However, for short-term placements it is clearly more desirable to resist the temptation to change schools, even if the journey is difficult (and expensive).

The decision about whether to maintain the child in a school, even though the journey was difficult, or whether to change schools, was mainly based on the purpose of the placement. Placements where long-term care and upbringing was the aim accounted for only a quarter of all placements, but they accounted for over 60 per cent of the placements where the child had changed school. Most of the other placements had aims which were more or less short-term, but even so, in one in ten of these the child had been required to change school. Care and upbringing was, as we saw in an earlier chapter, an aim mainly applicable to younger children. It is, therefore, no surprise that those children who had had to change school were significantly younger than children with different educational experiences.

Social workers' assessments that placements were having a negative effect on children's schooling were strongly associated with their opinion that a placement nearer to the child's home would be better. Five times as many social workers expressed this opinion when the journey to school was described as difficult compared with when it was easy.

In conclusion, it must remain a concern in Warwickshire that, for approaching half of the children in care and of school age, their education is disrupted to some extent because of the location of the placements which are found for them. As Parker said in his report for the Wagner Inquiry into residential care:

Both educational progress and emotional security depend upon a reasonable degree of stability. Moving children from one placement to another and at the same time obliging them to change schools is a multiple burden on them. (Parker, 1988)

The skills and experience of carers

Earlier we saw that the attitudes and experience of those providing care for children away from their own families was an important factor in relation to parents' visits to their children. The carers needed to be sensitive to the difficult position which parents feel themselves to be in when visiting their own child in the place where someone else is looking after him or her. The carers also needed to have the experience to know how to handle these difficult circumstances.

It is also obviously important, for a whole range of other reasons, that those who are providing a home for children in care should be skilled and experienced. All children and young people in care carry their distress, anger and guilt with them, and these feelings need to be handled with sensitivity. Some children will arrive with more severe problems and then it is particularly important that those providing the care 24 hours a day can at least cope with these problems and, at best, can begin to work on them with the child. The amount of time which social work staff, either from the area teams or the specialist teams, spend with children in care is, in the vast majority of cases, very limited compared with the time the child and carers spend together.

In our case studies, with Angela for instance, foster carers were being asked to provide a home for a child who had been sexually abused and who could make life, for those she was close to, very uncomfortable or threatening. With Becky, carers were looking after a girl who had been admitted to care because she was beyond her mother's control, but her difficult behaviour continued while she was placed with different sets of foster carers.

In Chapter 4 we saw that the social workers responsible for the children in our cohort were very aware of the importance of placing all children with carers who were skilled and experienced. But in particular they identified two groups as needing the most experienced carers. The first was older children and the second was the group including children in care for behavioural reasons or those who had been neglected or abused – those who in other areas would comprise the bulk of the residential population.

Social workers were asked two questions in which they had to assess the skills of the carers in relation to each child's placement. The first asked how well the placement had met the child's needs in so far as the carers had the skills and experience to address the child's problems. The second question focused specifically on the issue of control and management of the child's behaviour (if it was a problem). Table 6.9 gives the responses to these two questions.

Table 6.9 The extent to which carers met children's needs

| | Met the child's needs: | | | |
| | Very well | Quite well | Not particularly well | Badly |
	(%)	(%)	(%)	(%)
Provided skilled and experienced carers (No.=205)	29	39	21	11
Provided control over child's behaviour (No.=199)	40	39	14	7

Overall, these results indicate quite high levels of satisfaction with the way in which carers were able to provide the skills which were required. In three or four out of ten cases social workers were saying that the child's needs were 'very well' met; in seven or eight out of ten cases, 'very well' or 'quite well' met. Three factors were associated with different levels of satisfaction with the way in which placements were able to meet children's needs in these two areas. The factors were age, the reason why the child was in care, and the type of placement.

Age

There was a clearly expressed view that placements met the needs of younger children well and older children less well. The average (mean) age of children whose needs were met 'very well' or 'quite well', in relation to the specific question of controlling behaviour, was about 13 years. The group whose needs were met 'not particularly well' or 'badly' were significantly older at 15 years. This same trend was also found in response to the other more general question about the skills and experience of the carers.

Reasons for being in care

We have already reported that social workers identified the need for carers who were particularly experienced when children were in care for behavioural reasons or because they had been abused or neglected. However, satisfactory placements for these children appeared difficult to find. In eight out of ten placements where the child was in care for reasons of poor care, the carers were said to have the skills to meet the child's needs well; but for children who had been neglected or abused the proportion was only just over six out of ten. Where behavioural problems were the issue, in only half of the cases were the needs well met.

The type of placement

We have already seen that in cases where social workers identified children as needing a placement with particularly skilled carers, their placement of choice was more often a residential setting or with specialist contract foster carers. To what extent did the workers assess carers in different placements as being more or less skilled? Table 6.10 identifies the differences between three different types of placement; ordinary foster homes; contract foster homes and residential settings.

Table 6.10 Placements and the extent to which children's needs were met

Placement	*Very well*	*Needs met:* *Quite well*	*Very well and quite well*
	(%)	*(%)*	*(%)*
Ordinary foster care (No.=150)	28	39	67
Contract foster care (No.=20)	30	50	80
Residential Care (No.=11)	45	40	85
All (No.=181)	29	40	69

As can be seen from figures in Table 6.10, in 45 per cent of the residential placements the carers' skills and experience were rated in the highest category compared with fewer than a third of the placements in ordinary or contract foster homes. Overall, both residential placements and contract foster homes were judged to have had carers with the skills the children required in over four out of five cases, compared with two-thirds of the ordinary foster carers. However, the trends identified above were not strong enough for the differences to be identified as statistically significant. That is, as far as the results from our cohort are concerned, and based upon social workers' judgements about how cases turned out, children were no more likely to be with carers who had the skills and experience to meet their needs in residential care or contract foster care compared with ordinary foster homes. Our results could have come about simply by chance.

Was it really true that the people in the specialist resources (contract foster care and residential care) were no more skilled than the people who provided the bulk of foster placements? This would be an unexpected finding which would go against both the expectations of the Department and against the experience of social workers. The explanation for this apparent anomaly may be found in the fact that the more difficult cases (for example children who had been neglected or abused or children with behavioural problems) were disproportionately placed in residential care and contract foster care. The assessment that carers in these facilities were no more successful than carers in ordinary foster homes must be seen in the context of the more difficult tasks being asked of them.

A surprising result was thrown up when we compared the priorities which social workers had expressed at the beginnings of placements with their assessments of how successfully the placements achieved these priorities. When, for example, we examined the placements where having skilled and experienced carers was identified as a high priority, we discovered that the placements which were made were no more successful in meeting these particular needs than placements where this factor was considered to be of less priority. This finding was also repeated when we examined priorities and outcome in relation to the issue of placing children and young people with carers who could provide some framework for managing their behaviour problems.

We were surprised by these results because our hypothesis had been, perhaps naively, that there would be at least some matching between the needs which social workers prioritised and the placements which were made; and that, therefore, there would be some measurable association between placements which were made with a particular priority and some success in meeting that priority. Since this was not the case, how are we to understand these results? The explanation probably lies in some of the findings reported already. Characteristically in Warwickshire, at the point at which a placement was being sought, there was either only one placement available or a limited choice between placements. Given this, the issue of matching needs or priorities with resources hardly arises.

A major conclusion of our evaluation in Warwickshire, therefore, is that placements are made essentially with whichever carers are available at the time. Whether or not they have the skills or experience necessary to meet the contingencies of a particular placement will, therefore, to a significant degree be a matter of chance. The consequence of this will be that the extent to which outcomes are successful or not will also be essentially a matter of chance. This was the result we found. Warwickshire is not alone in being in this situation (*see* Berridge and Cleaver, 1987). However, given the extent to which the County has deliberately chosen to be reliant on foster care, this does give grounds for concern.

It would be an improvement to move to a situation where there was more choice at the time placements were made and, therefore, more likelihood that needs and priorities could be matched with what particular placements have to offer. However, there are so many factors which have to be taken into account that 'perfect' matching in all cases is not a realistic target. Wedge and Phelan (1988, p.19) made this point in their study of children in care in Essex.

There are so many uncertainties and so many variables in the circumstances and predicaments of children coming into care that any system has to be flexible, and carers need a range of skills and supports to help them in their difficult task. However, there are possibilities for improvement.

We would certainly agree with this last point in so far as it implies that at least some choice and, therefore, some possibility of matching is vital. But the comment by Wedge and Phelan about the need for support for carers is also an important one. This is one of the roles which the Children's Services Teams take on. We will be examining this later.

Before leaving this issue it is worth seeing how it applied to our case studies. For most of the placements made for all three young people there was only a limited choice, if any at all, and so matching was only possible to a small extent. However, even when moves were planned and the young people's needs were matched with the skills and experience of the carers, the outcomes were not necessarily better than when placements were made with no choice and no matching. With Angela for instance, the move to the Browns was planned and all concerned felt they had the experience to successfully provide a long-term placement. But the placement did not work out. Her next placement was with the Clowes. They were less experienced than the Browns but, in the end, they coped much better with Angela and provided her with a home in which she was much happier – and which lasted.

Similar comparisons can be drawn from the other two cases, but the important point to note is that matching will, in theory, improve the chances that a placement will be a success. In practice, there are so many factors which cannot be predicted or accounted for, that success cannot be guaranteed.

The outcome of placements for Black children in care

In this chapter we have examined the experiences of all of the children in our research group. Were the experiences of Black children different? This is the important question we will try to answer here. Social work practice in the UK has not addressed adequately the needs of Black service users, nor has it confronted the racism which exists within its institutions (Hutchinson-Reis, 1989; Small, 1986; Ahmed and others, 1986; Coombe and Little, 1986; Frost and Stein, 1989; SSI, 1988). Research has been equally negligent, in avoiding these issues. Most of the major large-scale research projects which were funded and reported in the 1980s had little to say about services to Black people or about racism. Given that research should aim to be at the leading edge of practice and policy formation, it should perhaps bear particular responsibility for the fact that we still know remarkably little about what happens overall to Black children in care. We live in a diverse society and, therefore, should undertake research that reflects this. With the Children Act 1989, it is unacceptable to practice 'colour blind' social work – the same should apply to researchers.

Jane Rowe and her colleagues (1984) were among the first to examine in detail the experiences of Black children in care, in their study of the experiences of children who were in long-term foster care. In their book, the information was based on a relatively small sample and mainly came from interviews with children, foster carers, parents and social workers. At the end of the 1980s Jane Rowe and her colleagues (Rowe and others, 1989) took a different look at childcare in England, but this time their methodology allowed them to make statements about the experiences of Black children in care, which can reasonably be assumed to be representative of the experiences of Black children across the country. These results were discussed in Chapter 4, but to remind ourselves:

- Afro-Caribbean and, in particular, mixed parentage children were over-represented in admission to care.
- There was little difference between the different groups in terms of the frequency of contact between parents and children.
- The pattern of placement moves was complicated by differences in age and in placement aims between groups, but what differences could be identified were very limited.
- More Asian and mixed parentage children in care with siblings were placed together with their brothers and sisters compared to Afro-Caribbean and White children.

The small number of Black children identified for our cohort – which reflects the low numbers of children in care in Warwickshire who originate from minority ethnic groups – makes it difficult for us to come to firm conclusions, and the points we do make mostly apply to all Black children and do not distinguish between different ethnic origins. Nonetheless, the following are some of the main points:

- There were too few cases to identify whether there were different aims for the Black group compared with the White group, but there was no difference between the two groups in the extent to which the aims were achieved.
- In terms of distance and the time it took for parents to travel to placements, there appeared to be no difference between the Black and White children. Social workers were satisfied with the level of contact between children and parents for the same proportion of both groups. The same applied to the proportions of children's placements which they would have preferred to have been closer to home.
- In nearly three-quarters of the placements made for White children the carers were said to be encouraging visits from parents. Only half the placements for Black children were encouraging to links. With so few cases, however, this result is not statistically significant. We compared placements for Black children where there was at least one Black foster carer, with placements for Black children with White foster couples. We found no measurable difference in the extent to which carers in the two groups were said to encourage links between parents and children.

- Black children were generally identified as more successfully integrated in their placements than White children. Again, however, these differences did not achieve statistical significance. Three out of four of the Black children in same-race placements were identified as more or less well integrated compared with less than half of the Black children placed with White foster carers (No. = 15). A larger scale study would be required to identify whether this finding could be generalised.
- Overall there were no identifiable differences between the extent to which social workers identified carers as having the skills and experience required to perform the task in the placements for Black children and those for White. Nor could we identify any differences on this issue between those placements where Black children were placed with Black carers and those where they were placed with White carers.

Summary

This chapter has focussed on how well the needs of children in care in Warwickshire were met. A summary of the main findings follows.

- Children in care in Warwickshire were found to have significantly more moves while in care than children elsewhere. A third of our cohort had three or more placements in our 15-month monitoring period – this is approaching double what has been found in other studies.
- In about seven out of ten placements, social workers judged that placement aims had been met fully or in most respects. These results are comparable to findings elsewhere.
- However, children were found to be less well integrated in placements compared to results from other authorities. It would seem that there is a link between this finding and the level of discontinuity in care in Warwickshire, reported above.
- Warwickshire's policies do not seem to have an adverse affect on the care of sibling groups: social workers were able to place together four in every five siblings. This figure compares favourably with other research.
- Only a quarter of our Warwickshire children were seeing their parents weekly. This is about half the proportion of Rowe's (1989) nationally-representative study. Children who had been in care longest saw their parents least.
- A major problem for the County was the distance separating children's placements from their parents. This was a considerable impediment to contact and applied particularly to the small group of children in residential settings.
- A disconcerting finding was that for approaching half the school-age children in our study, journeys to school were made significantly more difficult by the location of their placements. For a similar proportion, there were also greater difficulties in maintaining links with friends, neighbourhood and wider social contacts.

- High levels of satisfaction were reported by social workers in the extent to which carers' skills enabled them to meet children's needs in placements.
- Owing to the relatively small number of children in care in Warwickshire from minority ethnic groups, specific results are inevitably inconclusive. Nonetheless, many findings appeared similar for both White and Black children. However, there were some indications that where Black children were not in same-race placements, they were less well integrated and carers were less welcoming to parental contact.
- A major conclusion from the research is that there is a serious shortage of foster carers in Warwickshire – as in many other local authorities. However, this is particularly serious for the County owing to its chosen policies. Children in Warwickshire were largely placed where there was a vacancy, which leaves too much to chance and accounts for many of the problems of distance between home and placements.

7. Progress in placements – Angela, Becky and Chris

Having looked at our survey data, let us now cover similar ground but in greater detail, and see how Angela, Becky and Chris fared in their placements.

Angela Collins

We saw in Chapter 5 how a Place of Safety Order was secured and Angela was placed on a short-term basis with the Abbotts. Within a week or so the Department had identified the need to provide care for Angela on a longer term basis and had begun to look for a long-term foster placement for her.

For the four months the placement with the Abbotts lasted, how well did it meet Angela's needs and how did it end? The Abbotts lived at a distance from Angela's school, which meant that a taxi was needed to get her there and back. There was no complaint about the financial cost of this on a short-term basis, but there was some concern (which never materialised into a problem) about Angela being unaccompanied on these trips with the taxi drivers who were usually male.

The location of the Abbott's home had the desired effect of distancing Angela from the sexual involvements which had developed near her home but, as we have seen, it made travel to the placement very difficult for Mrs Collins, who was dependent on public transport unless volunteer drivers could be found. Mrs Collins made regular visits, about every two weeks, to Angela while she was at the Abbotts despite the problems she had getting there. This regular contact was seen as important by Angela's social worker. However these visits were felt by all concerned to be unsatisfactory. These were Angela's memories:

Mrs Abbott did not like my mum. I did not like the way she treated me in front of my mum ... she cuddled me in front of her ... How do you think my mum felt when Mrs Abbott cuddled me?

Angela's impressions were also confirmed by her social worker who described the Abbotts as, 'Insensitive to Angela's needs ... critical of her natural family and too possessive'. Angela had never been away from home before; she was not at all clear why she had been removed, and she was trying to find some way of understanding these events and of coming to terms with them. Mrs Abbott's attitudes did not help in this.

The other feature of the placement which Angela disliked was the size of the Abbott's family: there were two sons and three daughters all living at home and

Angela had to share a bedroom with the three girls; they complained about Angela's standards of personal hygiene. The size of the household was also a problem in that it seems that the foster carers were unable give Angela sufficient attention. Symbolic of this was the sad fact that while she was there Mr and Mrs Abbott forgot Angela's birthday.

This placement came to an end when it had been possible to find and gradually introduce Angela to a placement which was intended to be long-term. But Angela remembers the reasons for the ending differently:

I asked to be moved and my foster mum asked for me to be moved and then I went to the Browns.

After the placement had finished a number of issues emerged, some of which were identified in the end of placement report to which the Abbotts, their link worker from the Children's Services Team and Angela's social worker contributed. It appeared that the Abbotts had been given different messages by the two social workers involved about how to respond to Angela and to her family.

After the placement had ended it also became clear that there were problems within the Abbott family, in particular in relations between two of the daughters and their parents. After Angela's placement with them the Abbotts decided to retire, temporarily, from fostering. Some months later they were formally reassessed as foster carers and reapproved, but only for young children. They had no other children placed with them and later they withdrew from fostering altogether.

Angela next moved to the Browns – very experienced foster carers who lived close to Angela's school and within easy travelling distance for Mrs Collins (*see* Chapter 5). This placement was made with the intention that it would be long-term; Angela was now in care and it was anticipated by her social worker that she would remain in care until she was 18-years-old. However, this placement lasted only four months. Why? Let us hear the various participants' reflections on the placement.

First, Angela herself. She said that the Browns were alright at first and that she had been glad to move there. She saw her mother and her grandmother most weeks. However, soon after the move, 'They [the Browns] kept pressurising me, told me I could not get on with their children.' The Brown's had two children – two daughters aged 13 and 15 and a son. 'I had to share a bedroom with the daughters ... I did not like that.' About the daughters, Angela also said, 'They used to leave me out of things ... I did not like that either'. The placement came to an end soon after Angela had spent two weeks with another set of foster carers – the Clowes – while the Browns were on holiday. As Angela said, 'They [the Clowes] treated me as one of their own ... I started behaving badly (with the Browns) so I would get moved.'

What about the Browns themselves, very experienced foster carers, how did they view the placement? After a quiet start Angela (now aged 14) began to be more demanding. 'She followed me about the house ... she could not get enough attention', said Mrs Brown. The Browns encouraged Angela to go out with their daughters and their friends but that did not last very long; neither the

Brown's children nor their friends liked Angela – they were embarrassed by her. 'She was just too sexually explicit ... her behaviour was totally inappropriate.' The fact that the Browns lived within walking distance of Angela's school also led to problems because she could see boys from the school very easily.

You could not relax with Angela if she was in or if she was out ... Every time she went out of the house she was having intercourse, we just could not control her ... By this time we did not know what we were supposed to do with her ... We could not provide the control she needed. We were saying [to the social worker] that Angela needs help and we need more support.

The feeling that they were not helping Angela and the effects that her presence was having on the family were the main problems as far as the Browns were concerned.

I was getting very edgy with Angela, I could not take her out in the car on my own ... I just realised how vulnerable I was and that was the crux of the matter.

The two boys also found the situation very uncomfortable. 'Angela would run around in front of them with no clothes on ... she just could not recognise that her behaviour was inappropriate.'

The issue of Angela's behaviour culminated when a 17-year-old boy, an ex-pupil of Angela's school, was questioned by the Police and admitted having sex with her. Under questioning Angela herself also provided a list of her other sexual partners all of whom were subsequently seen by the Police and cautioned. The Browns summed up Angela's placement with them this way:

We have had difficult children before and have been able to cope but Angela was beyond us ... We could not cater for Angela as a family.

What was Angela's social worker's view of the placement? Initially she was very hopeful – the placement was in the right location and the Browns were very experienced. Angela also seemed to settle down better at the Browns who were much more accepting of Angela's mother. She visited Angela regularly at the Browns and they took Angela to see her mother and grandmother most weekends. In the end Sheila said that her hope that the Browns would have the skills and experience to begin to meet Angela's needs was not borne out. She also thought that, because both the parents were working and because there were four other children in the house, Angela probably did not get the time and degree of attention she required.

The Brown's link worker's view was slightly different. He remembered the placement as going, 'exceptionally well early on ... but she just wore them down'. He thought that Angela had gained a lot from this placement. 'I think the females were a good example for Angela ... but she needed more attention than [the Browns] could provide ... in the end I am not sure the placement fully fulfilled her needs.'

Becky Johnson

We saw earlier that Becky had been received into care for a second time after the situation at home broke down again. She had been placed by the Emergency

Duty Social Worker with an experienced foster family who lived some distance away on the other side of the County. This location led to problems in terms of social work contact and necessitated the use of taxis to get Becky to and from school.

At least as importantly, Becky's mother was not able to visit her even once in her placement during the four weeks it lasted and, because of the transport arrangements for school, neither was Becky able to visit her mother. Given that the social work plan was then focusing solely on work with Becky and Tracey to bring about Becky's return home, this lack of contact was, presumably, highly detrimental. Using public transport, the journey from home to placements would take up to two hours each way. This provides a good illustration of the more general problem we highlighted in the last chapter.

Apart from the issue of distance, how satisfactory was the placement? The Donnelly's link worker made the following assessment.

The Donnellys already had an older child, another girl, placed with them and this led to problems for Becky. [The other child] egged Becky on and her behaviour problems increased ... She was very difficult to control and was absconding ... We had no choice about making a second placement [with the Donnellys] because there was a shortage of places ... We [the Children's Services Team and the foster carers] soon realised it was a mistake placing Becky with an older child. The problems weren't their [the Donnelly's] fault.

The comments made by the Community Team social worker reinforced this assessment but he made some additional points. First, he was not sure to what extent the deterioration in Becky's behaviour should be attributed to the influence of the other foster child. The effects of the isolation of Becky from her mother and the rest of her family and friends could not be ignored. In addition, there remained some doubts about the foster carers' abilities; certainly Becky never felt settled there. She described them as, 'Old people and they lived in a very small house'. In the end, this placement lasted for just four weeks, too long for Becky's best interests and generally unhelpful in her social worker's estimation.

The next placement found by the Children's Services Team was with the Edwards. This time the location was right but they were worried because the Edwards not only had two children of their own but also had a long-term foster child placed with them. In addition, the Edwards had limited experience and certainly had not had to cope with a child as difficult as Becky.

Becky was more positive about the Edwards than about any of her other placements.

It was a big family and they were used to kids like me ... I could talk to her [Mrs Edwards] and it was close to my mum's.

Looking towards a future long-term placement while she was living with the Gardners, Becky said, 'I'd like a foster placement like [Mrs Edwards] ... big, with lots of people and near home'.

How did the Edwards experience Becky's time with them? Mrs Edwards said that Becky had fitted in alright but was a little slow to settle down:

She needs a lot of attention and she can be very devious ... If she can't get her own way she's a spoiled brat.

Mrs Edwards described problems with school, mainly because of non-attendance. She had considerable contact with the school staff about Becky, in particular over a suspension which Mrs Edwards persuaded them to reverse.

Mrs Edwards was also concerned about Becky's out of school activities. She spent a lot of time with previous friends who lived near to her mother's home but most of these friends had been in trouble with the police. During this period, Becky herself was picked up by them.

She made no new friends round here ... she couldn't keep friends because of the way she treated them.

Mrs Edwards' main concern was about the effect that Becky's presence was having on her own eight-year-old son. She described how Becky teased and bullied him; he often became very upset. The Edwards' link worker spoke about his concern for the Edwards' family.

They were struggling to meet Becky's needs ... she wasn't going to school ... her behaviour, bullying, stealing, staying out. The main problem was with Becky bullying their son who was several years younger ... I was amazed they stuck it out ... the bullying overrode everything. I was all for pulling her out because I didn't want us to lose the Edwards.

The placement lasted in all for four months. Mrs Edwards said that they wanted to give Becky a home but they couldn't because of the effect on their son but, 'We agreed to hang on until somewhere else was found'.

As we have seen, however, no other placement materialised. Doubts had grown about the likelihood of any attempt at rehabilitation succeeding but long-term planning, it was felt, was being hampered by the voluntary status of Becky's care. In the end, the opportunity was taken for what was stated to be a last attempt at reuniting Becky and her mother.

In retrospect, Becky's social worker rated the care that the Edwards had provided very highly. Becky had been well integrated with the family and they had been very encouraging towards links between Becky and Tracey. On all counts, including managing (or at least coping with) Becky's behaviour and in meeting her needs with skill, this placement was rated as, 'Very helpful' to Becky's welfare. As with the Edwards' link worker, there was surprise that anyone could have coped so well.

Becky's return home lasted just three weeks and then she returned to care, initially on a Place of Safety Order, then on Interim Care Orders and finally a full Care Order. The placement found for her was with the Floods, who were contract foster parents. We have seen that this placement was made because it was the only one available and that there were doubts because it was a time-limited placement, but how suitable was it?

According to Mrs Flood, Becky didn't settle easily, she didn't seem comfortable with the foster carers. Her introduction was not helped by the fact that Becky arrived before the Flood's previous foster child had left and for one night she and Becky had to share a room. Mrs Flood felt that this was unfortunate and should have been avoided if at all possible. The Floods were unable properly to take leave of one child or to welcome the next. Becky's unhappiness with this placement was demonstrated by the fact that after only a few days she stayed away overnight without letting the Floods know where she was.

The Floods found some of Becky's behaviour very difficult to accept. Mrs Flood described truanting from school, stealing and causing problems with neighbours. She also made one of the Flood's children (both of whom were younger than Becky) very unhappy. 'She hated [their daughter] and had it in for her ... She tried to get her into trouble ... she's very clever.' Mrs Flood described her husband losing his temper with Becky on one occasion. 'He's never done that before [with a foster child].'

While she was in this placement, Becky was suspended and finally excluded from the secondary school she had begun to attend the previous autumn. It was now Spring. The Education Department provided a home tutor who worked with Becky at the Children's Services Team's premises. The CST also provided some daytime sessional input, among other work, for Becky.

Becky's placement with the Floods, therefore, ended when she moved to the Gardners at the end of the three months. Overall, Mrs Flood wasn't sure that they had been able to offer Becky very much; she agreed that what she needed was a long-term, well-supported placement, but that was not the basis on which Becky's next move took place. At least the Gardners had no children of an age close to Becky's: as had been seen in previous placements, relationships with children near to her own age had been problematic. Such problems, incidentally, have been consistently identified in research studies which have looked at factors associated with successful and unsuccessful placements (Trasler, 1960; Parker, 1966; George, 1970; Berridge, 1987).

Reviewing Becky's three periods in care, her social worker described the main problem as not being able to place Becky in a long-term placement because none was available. In the report for a review of the case he wrote:

When I picked Becky up [for the move to a new placement] her comment was, 'How many times is this?' ... The moves she has experienced have left her confused and unsettled. It's very important for the next few months that things are more settled.

These moves were mainly necessitated by the lack of availability of suitable placements. At the time the interviews for this case study were being completed, Becky was in her fifth short-term placement and the Department had failed to find a long-term placement even after advertising specifically for foster carers for Becky.

Chris Taylor

Chris' first placement with the Imlotts was made in an emergency and lasted just two weeks. It was not planned that the placement should be so short but Chris' behaviour meant that it had to end. Chris was described by the Imlotts as generally uncooperative, he was truanting from school and staying out late without letting the foster carers know. However, the behaviour which proved unacceptable was towards the Imlotts' own children and in particular towards the 19 year-old foster child who was also living with them. This boy had a mental handicap and Chris was said to have teased, threatened and bullied him. The Imlotts described Chris as, 'Attention seeking ... He tried to dominate the other children especially the other foster child'. While he was in this placement the Imlotts found no way at all of successfully managing Chris' behaviour, despite being experienced in working with adolescents. It is interesting to observe how conflicts with other children resident in foster homes has been a recurring theme of our case studies.

Chris' mother visited him once at the Imlotts but Chris also went to see her. Chris returned home from the Imlotts but, as we have seen, he was soon received into care for a second time. At little or no notice Chris was placed with the Jones family. This was intended to be short-term while waiting for a placement with contract foster parents to become vacant. This took seven weeks and Mrs Jones described their experience as follows:

He was impossible to live with ... he plays you off one against the other. He had a taxi to school but often he did not attend ... He spent his time in arcades, he is a real machine addict ... He was very naive at the time, I worried about him. He had spent all his money and we sometimes had to pick him up late at night.

The Jones' link worker commented that after visiting his mother Chris would be, 'really hyped up'. He sometimes visited her and spoke to her quite often on the telephone, but that only led to rows according to Mrs Jones. 'She and her husband visited us once ... They looked down on us.'

Mrs Jones was one of many who described the way in which Chris' life centred on the town:

He has always got a deal on the go ... everything revolves around the town ... He knows everybody but he has got no real friends, only acquaintances.

Like the children in the Imlott family, Mrs. Jones' children (aged eight and 18) found Chris very difficult to cope with and for them, as well as Mr and Mrs Jones, the seven weeks of the placement seemed a very long time. 'The family could not have coped any longer.' But the Jones' had a real concern for Chris' future:

He needs help, more than you can give him, but he was the most difficult, demanding placement we have ever had.

What did Chris get out of this placement? No one thought that he had settled in at the Jones' but the family's commitment seems to have impressed him.

We have heard that by the time Chris was placed with the Jones', questions were being raised about the appropriateness of foster placements for Chris and initial investigations into the availability of residential care were underway. However, the plan remained that Chris should move to stay with the Kennedys, the contract foster parents, when a place with them became available. When Chris went there how did it work out?

As Liz, the social worker, expected on the basis of the experience of the previous two placements, it did not work out well at all. The same behaviour patterns were repeated – truanting, staying out and so on – but this time there was even physical damage to the Kennedy's house. Chris' behaviour had become worse if anything and he did not integrate at all with the family. The Kennedy's own children, like the children in the previous placements, found Chris particularly difficult to cope with. Mrs. Kennedy said:

Chris avoided contact with the family ... He seemed bent on self-destruction ... We regret not being able to help him in any way.

That the placement was of no help to Chris was also his social worker's assessment but, she added, not because of lack of skill or experience on the part of the Kennedy's; it was because it was the wrong type of placement.

Chris' behaviour reached a point where the Kennedys found it unacceptable and a decision was taken to move him. The search for a long-term residential placement met with no success and so Chris was placed in the National Children's Home residential facility. On the NCH site there are two purpose-built units, each housing eight children in their own rooms and each independently equipped. Children placed by Warwickshire normally reside in one of the units.

If a marked difference in behaviour was anticipated or hoped for when Chris was placed with the NCH rather than with foster carers, it did not take long for these hopes to be dashed. In some respects Chris' behaviour continued along the same lines as previously, but in some ways it got worse. The overall assessment of the NCH placement by one of the CST staff was:

It held the situation but on Chris' terms. It did not do him any good ... it is an ordinary residential provision and it was not able to meet the needs of a lad like Chris ... it was basically a holding placement.

Staff at the NCH described the two sides of Chris' character:

He has a very engaging personality and at times he can be a charming character ... He is a highly articulate, intelligent youngster ... There was no violence or aggression from Chris.

But his relationships with the other young people in the home (as in previous placements) was a constant problem:

He has manipulative skills of a very high order ... He was constantly winding up younger more vulnerable people ... The cruellest things he did was to use young people who had far less ability than himself.

Another serious problem for the staff of the NCH establishment was that Chris was constantly absconding, once for two weeks, but more usually overnight or for a couple of days. He would telephone the NCH when he had had enough and ask them to collect him, or he would arrive at the Social Services Department and insist on his fare to get back to the NCH. Usually when he absconded it was to return to his home town. Mrs Jones had noted this habit, a trait also independently identified by Liz, his social worker.

Chris' contact with his family while he was placed at the NCH was infrequent, less than once a month in Liz's estimation, and those meetings took place when Chris returned to the town. However, Liz considered that this level of contact was about right. None of the issues which made the relationship between Chris and his family so difficult had been resolved. Travel to school also ceased to be a problem. Chris moved to the NCH at the end of March and his sixteenth birthday was in July. He had been attending school infrequently while in his foster placement and by the time of the move to the NCH, 'He had effectively left', according to his social worker.

We heard above that one member of the Social Services Department described the placement at the NCH as holding the situation but on Chris' terms. How did Chris' social worker assess the benefit of the placement for Chris?

Chris used the NCH as a base but he only stayed there when it fitted in with his plans. He only cooperated with the NCH staff when it suited him and limited pieces of work which they attempted to undertake with him failed because he simply wasn't interested.

As far as Liz was concerned, the NCH placement did not modify Chris' behaviour, although expectations had never been that it would. Also it did not involve any 'therapeutic' work with Chris, although again the placement was not set up to do that. It was planned as a short-term arrangement while a longer term plan was developed and implemented. Overall, Liz assessed the placement as having been unhelpful to Chris and certainly she thought that it had lasted much too long in terms of meeting Chris' best interests.

Chris went to the NCH while a long-term, therapeutic residential placement was found for him. This plan was given senior management approval, and Liz and Children's Services Team staff began to identify a number of possible placements. These were narrowed down to two or three options and visits were arranged. One residential school was visited by Liz, a CST worker and Chris. The visit was unsuccessful. Whether or not the school could have helped Chris, he made it obvious to the school staff that he was unwilling to move there. The school was a considerable distance from Chris' home town and that was one of the reasons for his objections; his life continued to revolve around the town, even after he was placed at the NCH. A visit to a second possible placement had very similar results.

After considerable time and effort had gone into trying to find a residential placement for Chris, the plan was not working and an alternative had to be found. What was needed was a plan which Social Services felt would benefit Chris and which would also be acceptable to him – he had demonstrated beyond doubt that nothing would be achieved unless *his support* was forthcoming. A new plan was, therefore, devised which aimed to introduce Chris gradually to independent living. Chris supported this plan, primarily because it would get him back to his home town, which was where he wanted to be. The plan had two parts, the first to find suitable accommodation for Chris and the second to develop a training package to prepare Chris for independence. We heard about the search for accommodation in Chapter 5.

Staff at the NCH, who were involved in the discussions which resulted in the changed plans, agreed to provide the training for Chris. How did it go? NCH staff said:

He started and stopped jobs and schemes one after the other. He just would not stick with them. It was the same with the independence programme.

Despite Chris' failure to take up the planned training he moved back to town but, as we have seen, to far from ideal accommodation and that placement lasted only a week. After that Chris lived at several different addresses before he was discharged from care. Most of these were bed and breakfast accommodation, which was arranged by Chris himself and which met his housing needs but nothing else.

We have now looked at how Angela, Becky and Chris coped in their placements, and we should remind ourselves that these three were deliberately selected as likely to be problematic and, if they had lived in other local authorities, probable candidates for residential care at some stage. Let us now return to our broader survey, and focus on the conclusion and termination of placements.

8. Placement endings – successes and failures

We began the analysis of our survey data by examining the process of finding and making placements. Then we moved on to assess the extent to which these placements were able to meet the needs of the children and young people in care. We now turn to look at how and why the placements ended and how satisfied social workers were, in retrospect, with each placement.

Why is it important to look at placement endings? It is important for a variety of reasons; because the manner of the ending is significant for the child or young person concerned; how and when the placement ended can help us to reach an assessment of the value to the child of that period in care; and, particularly important from our point of view, it provides us with more comparative data for our main aim of identifying the consequences for children in care of the pattern of placement provision which, in Warwickshire, is so different from other authorities.

We can see something of the effects of placement endings if we think of our case studies. Chris Taylor was found a placement in residential care but only after spending some time with three different foster families. Two of these three placements, including one with contract foster carers, did not last as long as had been planned, and the moves from each of these to the next placement were necessarily extremely hasty. This allowed little or no time for Chris to be introduced to the new carers; nor was there time for other preparations for the move. In retrospect, Chris' social worker wondered whether a residential placement should have been made sooner. It was certainly her opinion that these placements (which, together with a period with his mother, lasted in all for about five months) provided nothing positive for Chris. In addition, each of the three sets of foster carers had found the experience of trying to provide a temporary home for Chris difficult or even distressing. The circumstances of these three placement endings suggest that at least some of the decisions about where Chris should live might have been inappropriate.

Let us compare this with one of the other case studies – Angela Collins. Angela had lived with three sets of foster carers over a two-year period and she was still with the third set. The moves from the Abbotts to the Browns and then to the Clowes were both less abrupt, and therefore less unsettling for all concerned, than were Chris Taylors' transfers. Angela's first move was in line with the social work plan (from a short-term to a long-term placement) and it had been possible to arrange a gradual introduction to the Browns over a period of weeks. Her departure from the Browns to the Clowes was not in line with the original plan that Angela would be staying with the Browns on a long-term basis. However, it was still possible to manage the transfer to the Clowes gradually and smoothly once a move had been identified as necessary.

Unlike Chris Taylor's social worker, Angela's did not question the appropriateness of placing her with foster carers, nor did she see the manner of the placement endings as damaging for Angela. However, as in Chris' case, Angela's first two foster families had found Angela difficult to live with, and both families needed considerable support and counselling both during and after the placements.

These two cases provide us with a good idea of the kinds of questions we should ask about placements that have ended, to enable us to make a judgement about their 'success'. In this chapter the questions we ask and the issues we cover include:

- Whether the endings of the placements scrutinised in our survey were in line with the social work plan. Endings which are inconsistent with the plan are usually described as 'breakdowns' or 'disruptions'. However, the definitions of these concepts are problematic and will be dealt with later.
- Placements may also have lasted longer than planned. In these circumstances the plan can also be said, in a sense, to have broken down and we begin to be concerned about whether, and why, the child is drifting in the placement.
- We are also interested in whether, in the social worker's assessment, the placement lasted long enough in relation to the child's needs, irrespective of whether it lasted as long as planned or not.
- The circumstances which influenced the ending of the placement are also important. Events within the foster family (such as we saw in the Abbott family with whom Angela Collins lived) may affect the placement. The child's parents or other family members may also cause difficulties. And we want to know whether the child's behaviour was a significant factor.

We will address each of these issues in turn. Finally we will use a measure of success which is created by combining the results of two of our existing measures: the extent to which placement aims were achieved; and the degree to which placements, in retrospect, were thought to have met the child's needs.

The advantages of using a series of different measures of outcome are twofold. First, we can draw on a wider range of other research findings, which enables us to compare outcomes in Warwickshire with those in other authorities. And, second, we introduce internal checks. If our measures are giving us similar messages then we can be more confident of the results.

How and why placements ended

In our study we considered 256 placements in all, which were made for a total of 141 children and young people in care. Of the 256 placements, 178 came to an end during our monitoring period, either when the child left care or moved to another placement. Of the 141 children, 78 were still in care when we ceased monitoring. In this section we will examine the circumstances of the 178 placement endings, including:

- where the children moved to;
- the factors which played a part in the endings;
- the extent to which placements finished in a planned way or broke down; and
- the number of placements in which the child stayed longer than was intended when the placement was made.

Four out of ten of the placements which ended resulted in the child or young person leaving care. In Rowe's 1989 study, approximately half of the placements – a not dissimilar proportion – ended when the child left care. Two-thirds of our leavers returned to their families, a small number left care at the age of 18 or went to adoptive parents, but the rest of the leavers (about three in ten) moved to lodgings, flats or other types of accommodation.

We asked social workers to identify the kinds of problems which were associated with the way in which placements ended. From a list of seven typical problems they were asked to identify *all* of those which applied to the particular placement under consideration. Table 8.1 summarises the responses to these questions with the most frequent problems listed first. The numbers in this table do not total because social workers may have identified more than one issue for a particular placement ending.

Table 8.1 Problems in placements

Problem	Cases where applicable	
	Number	(% of endings)
Child's behaviour unmanageable by, or unacceptable to, carers	53	(32)
Child never really settled in placement	50	(30)
Placement satisfactory at first but problems later	50	(29)
Unexpected event in foster family caused disruption	18	(11)
Natural family caused difficulties	14	(8)
Parents withdrew child against advice	7	(4)
Court ordered change of placement	6	(4)

The most significant feature of this table is that the three factors associated with the largest number of placement endings were child-centred, and concerned either the behaviour of the child or the relationship between the child and the carers. This last point is an important one to bear in mind. The issue of whether a child's behaviour is manageable is not just a child-related issue but also involves:

- the type of placement made for the child (would some behaviour be considered more manageable in a residential setting compared with a foster setting?);

- the skills and experience of those providing the care (for example residential care staff compared with foster carers); and
- the level of external social work or other support provided for the carers (for example, foster carers with separate social work support services compared with those without).

The second and third issues above will be addressed later in this chapter and in Chapter 9.

The placements where the child's behaviour was problematic and those where the child was said not to have settled, concerned overlapping groups. The children in these placements were older. They were also identified as considerably less well integrated in their placements. However we measure outcomes, those placements where there were behavioural problems or where the child did not settle, came out very badly. Significantly fewer lasted as long as was planned or as long as was needed, and in significantly fewer was the placement aim said to have been achieved.

After what we have called the child-centred factors, the next most common events associated with placement endings were what might be described as purely placement-related factors – described in our questionnaire as an 'unexpected event' in the placement. Such an event would include, for example, the illness or death of a foster carer, but when the event was less dramatic than this we must be aware of the possibility of such an explanation being an excuse. As Rowe says, 'One cannot help wondering how often some event in the foster home was used as an easier reason for requesting the child's removal' (Rowe, 1989). Placement factors were associated with only a tenth of all the placements which ended, but in these placements the aims were much less likely to have been achieved (43 per cent of cases compared with nearly 80 per cent of those where placement factors were not identified).

The final factors we examined were those which can be called family-related. In a small number of cases (fewer than 10 per cent of endings) the child's family was said to have caused some difficulties in the placement. In even fewer cases (four per cent) the parents had withdrawn the child (who would have been in voluntary care) from the placement against the advice of social workers.

The children in the placements where family-related factors were identified as applying were all in foster placements, and were all relatively new admissions to care. In the judgement of social workers, these children were said to have been relatively poorly integrated in their placements, but from the survey data it is not possible to tell whether the families 'interfered' with the placements because their children were not integrated, or whether their interference was the cause of the low levels of integration. We only have social workers' accounts to depend on here and we should be cautious about relying solely on their assessments that, for the children concerned, these placements met the children's needs comparatively poorly. If we had answers to the same questions from parents and children, the overall impressions may be different.

If we compare these overall results with those produced by other researchers we find large areas of agreement.

- What we described as child-related or child/placement-related factors were identified as most commonly associated with placement endings (Berridge and Cleaver, 1987; Rowe and others, 1989). Behaviour problems were associated with placement breakdowns by Aldgate and Hawley (1986).
- Placement-related factors were identified by both Rowe (1989), and Berridge and Cleaver (1987) as much less common.
- These studies also agreed with ours that the proportion of placements in which action by parents brings about an ending is very small.

Planned and unplanned endings

In the introduction to this chapter we compared the placement endings for two of our case studies and described how placements which ended sooner than was planned created problems for the child or young person concerned, as well as for the existing and new carers, and for the social workers. The young person may feel guilty and will certainly feel unsettled by a precipitate move. The existing carers may also feel some degree of guilt and will frequently see themselves as having, to some extent, failed. The introduction to the new carers will be sudden and unplanned – not the best of beginnings for the child or carers. The case social worker will have to pick up the pieces from one arrangement and quickly organise another. She or he may feel responsible for having failed to foresee the events which took place and will certainly have to re-examine his or her plans for the case. In addition, the social workers in the Children's Services Team will be given the unexpected task of finding a new placement for the child at short notice.

For all of these reasons, unplanned endings to care placements are clearly undesirable. A number of studies have examined placement endings and have used what are sometimes called breakdown rates or disruption rates as a means of assessing outcomes in childcare. They have then compared these rates for different local authorities as one way of comparing practice.

Unfortunately, the various studies of placements which have been carried out have sometimes used a number of different definitions of what constitutes a breakdown or a disruption, and they have often used different methods for their calculations. The definition of a planned/unplanned placement change which we used was identified in our questionnaires where we stated, 'Planned/ unplanned refers to whether the move was in line with the case plan which applied prior to the move being made'. This definition allowed for changes in the case plans as placements progressed, assuming a plan existed.

In our survey we examined the details of all the placements which ended during our monitoring period and we calculated the rate of planned endings or breakdowns as a proportion of all endings. This definition and our methodology will enable us to make direct comparisons with Rowe's 1989 study.

Some investigations, such as that of the Audit Commission (1981), used a very different definition of what constituted a breakdown and so our results are not comparable with theirs. Other research projects, especially some earlier ones (such as George, 1970; Parker, 1966) concentrated on following up samples of long-term foster placements over a number of years. They asked why some placements lasted for five years or so when others ended prematurely. This methodology is very different from ours and we cannot sensibly make comparisons between their findings and ours. In addition, we would have reservations about the validity of such comparisons because, in the two decades or more since those studies were completed, attitudes towards foster care and the ways in which it is used have changed beyond recognition. Foster care is no longer an option mainly used for younger children and long-term placements. In authorities, including Warwickshire, it has become the main care resource, and is used to a much greater extent than in the 1960s for short-term placements and for older children.

This section will, first, provide an analysis of placement endings for all three groups in our study and for all types of placement. Where possible we will compare our results with those from other research. This exercise will then be repeated but for foster placements only. Some of the more recent research (Berridge and Cleaver, 1987 and Rowe, 1989) has focused on foster placements and, given the emphasis on fostering in Warwickshire, it will be important to draw on these key pieces of research.

Endings – all placement types

There were 184 placements which ended during our monitoring period and social workers identified nearly six out of ten endings as planned (using the definition given earlier). The actual breakdown rate, measured in this way, was 38 per cent. We can compare this figure directly with Rowe's placement outcomes study (1989) which examined nearly 6000 placement endings. For children aged five and over she found that a very similar proportion, 36 per cent of endings, could be classified as breakdowns. Her definition was compatible with ours but her sample differed slightly as we identified earlier. Rowe's monitoring period was slightly longer than ours but would not make any difference to the result given the method used to calculate the rates (that is the *proportion* of all endings). On this evidence then, Warwickshire does not seem to experience more placement breakdowns than do other authorities, which maintain a broader range of placement options.

What factors were associated with placements breakdowns?

Characteristics of the children

Table 8.2 shows clearly that older adolescents in Warwickshire were the most likely to experience placements which ended in a breakdown.

Table 8.2. Placement endings by age group

| | Age (years) No.(%) | | |
	5–13	14+	All
Planned ending	50 (71)	60 (53)	110 (60)
Unplanned ending	20 (29)	54 (47)	74 (40)
Total	70 (100)	114 (100)	184 (100)

Nearly half of the placement endings for young people aged 14 or over were breakdowns, compared with fewer than 30 per cent for the younger group. This difference was statistically significant. Rowe also found that older children experienced more unplanned endings; the 11 plus group in her study had a breakdown rate of nearly 40 per cent compared with 25 per cent for the five to ten age group. The Dartington Social Research Unit (1987) also identified older adolescents as one 'problem group' in terms of high breakdown rates, but their findings showed even higher breakdown rates for children aged five or under. This finding differed from Rowe's study. The under fives, it will be recalled, were not included in our research.

Apart from age (and possibly also the child's racial background – *see below*), nothing else in the characteristics of our cohort of children, including the reason for admission to care, was associated with the likelihood of placement breakdown. This finding was also reported by Thoburn and Rowe (1988) in a study of placements intended to be permanent – they found a dramatic rise in breakdown rates for children aged over eight.

In Chapter 7 we identified the difficulty we have in reaching firm conclusions about the experiences of Black children in care in the County because of the low numbers involved. Of all the placement endings which we examined, just 11 involved Black children, including children of mixed parentage. Bearing in mind these reservations, it is still important to highlight the issues as they relate to Black children in care. In general, as we found in Chapter 6, there appeared to be more similarities than differences in the experiences of Black and White children in care.

- In relation to placement endings, over six out of ten placements for White children ended with a planned move, compared with just over four in ten for Black and mixed parentage children. However, this difference was not statistically significant.
- The breakdown rate for Black children was 50 per cent compared with 30 per cent for White. Only one in five placements for Black children lasted as long as planned, compared with half those for White children. Three in ten placements for Black children lasted longer than planned, compared with one in ten for the White children. These differences achieved statistical significance but reservations are necessary because of the small numbers of cases in some of the sub-groups. Nevertheless these, albeit tentative, results give some cause for concern and merit more detailed investigation.

Returning to the sample overall, we had too few placements other than in foster care to be able to identify whether there were different breakdown rates associated with different types of placement. In any case, the findings from other studies provide a somewhat inconclusive picture. In their study, Millham and his colleagues (1986) found that for children who were still in care six months after admission, there were only small differences in the breakdown rates when comparing residential care, foster care and home on trial placements. When the researchers examined the placements for children who had remained in care for two years, some significant differences did appear. Twice as many foster placements had broken down compared with residential placements. Home on trial placements and independent living placements fell in between these two extremes. The difference between foster and residential care was thought to be more significant because the children who had experienced placement breakdowns were almost all subsequently placed in residential settings.

However, Millham and his colleagues added a note of caution. The residential placements made for the children in their study were, on average, of shorter duration than either foster or home on trial placements. This factor meant that, over a given period, fewer residential placements were likely to break down compared with foster or home on trial placements. Comparisons of breakdown rates require us to be aware of the *different ways* in which different types of placement are used.

Returning to our study, rather surprisingly we did not find that the circumstances surrounding the making of the placement were associated with whether the placement ended in a planned way or broke down. Whether the social worker was able to make the type of placement which was her first choice or whether the placement itself was planned or made in an emergency, did not seem to influence how the placement ended. Similarly, whether she or he originally had any choice between different placements had no measurable effect on the outcome. Moreover, we did not find any association between breakdown rates and either the location of the placement (the distance from the child's home) or the frequency of contact between the child and his or her parents.

We are not, however, saying that these factors are unimportant when placements are being made for children in care; other research has shown clearly that the opposite is true and that is why we addressed these issues in our research. Given the relatively small sample size in our study, the statistical tests we used required substantial numerical differences in order for us to claim significant associations between particular factors and outomes. What we will see below is that some characteristics of the children in care and some characteristics of their placements did demonstrate such statistically significant associations.

The *Lost in Care* study (Millham and others, 1986) identified a complicated relationship between the maintenance of links with parents and the likelihood of placement breakdown. They found that it was *changes* in the amount of contact (either decreasing or increasing) which were associated with break-downs, rather than the *level* of contact itself. Our data were not detailed enough to identify such changes and we detected no significant associations between: breakdown rates and the frequency of parental contact; social workers' views on whether the existing levels of contact were adequate; or the distance between the placement and the child's home (which could restrict parental visiting considerably).

In our study we did, however, find that the extent to which children in care were able to maintain their community links, including contact with friends, was associated with breakdown – but the association was the reverse of that we had anticipated. It was the placements of children who were best able to maintain these community links which were the more likely to break down! Breakdown was much less frequent for those for whom community links were more difficult to maintain.

Outcomes

What were the consequences of placements ending in a planned or an unplanned way? Our measures of outcome all gave the same finding – that outcomes were much less successful in placements which had ended in an unplanned way. In over eight out of ten placements which had ended in a *planned* way, placement aims were said to have been achieved fully or in most respects. For placements which broke down the proportion was just *four* out of ten. Additionally, nearly 60 per cent of placements which had planned endings were said to have lasted as long as needed by the child, while the figure for placements with unplanned endings was just 25 per cent – another statistically highly significant result.

Let us now move on to considering placement endings for children in *foster* care specifically. This is particularly relevant because of Warwickshire's reliance on foster care in the absence of its own residential facilities.

Foster placement endings

In our study, foster care accounted for over 82 per cent of all placements which ended during the monitoring period. The breakdown rate for all types of placement was, as we have seen, 38 per cent. The rate for foster placements was also 38 per cent.

The comparison we will again use here is with Rowe's 1989 study which, for children aged five and over, examined nearly 2000 foster placement endings. We have already identified that the definition used by Rowe and her colleagues was the same as ours and that the differences in methodology were not significant enough to make comparisons invalid.

The 38 per cent breakdown rate for the overall Warwickshire cohort, as we have seen, compares with a rate of 36 per cent in Rowe's study. As with the breakdown rate when we examined all types of placement, the differences between our study and Rowe's, just for foster placement endings, were not statistically significant. How should we interpret this? The boarding out rate for Warwickshire in 1979 was 67 per cent compared with 56 per cent on average for the six authorities in Rowe's study in 1985. The difference between these figures is of course accounted for by the fact that Warwickshire uses foster care to a greater extent than most, if not all, other authorities (see Chapter 3), in particular for groups of children including those who are older and those whose behaviour might be described as difficult. Given the consistent message from this and from other research studies, that age and difficult behaviour are both associated with poorer outcomes in foster care, then these comparative figures should be seen as a positive result for Warwickshire.

Let us now move on to compare and contrast factors which were associated with those foster placements which ended in a planned way and those which did not.

Characteristics of the children

When we looked at all types of placement we found that for our Warwickshire cohort only age was associated to a significant degree with the likelihood that a placement would end in a breakdown. This was also true of foster placements. A quarter of the placements for five to 13-year-olds broke down; for those over 13 the rate was more than double at 53 per cent. This association between age and increasing foster breakdown rates is, in general, reflected in other research. Rowe (1989) found increases in rates for older groups, except for the 16-plus group who experienced fewer breakdowns than children aged 11 to 15. Berridge and Cleaver (1987) also found the highest breakdown rates among older children, as did the Dartington researchers (Millham and others, 1986) and Thoburn and Rowe (1988).

Both Berridge and Cleaver (1987) and Millham (1986) found that more placements for girls than for boys ended in breakdown. Neither set of researchers ventured an explanation for this finding but the former noted that we know very little about the specific problems of girls in care, especially adolescent girls. For our Warwickshire cohort, we did identify different breakdown rates for girls (45 per cent) and boys (36 per cent) but these differences, given the size of our cohort, were not statistically significant.

Our findings concurred with those of Berridge and Cleaver (1987) in identifying no link between the reasons why children were admitted to care and how placements ended. In fact, these researchers found that little in children's care histories could be linked with placement breakdowns. The exception to this was the finding that children who had been in care for more than five years were three times as likely to experience intermediate placements which broke down, compared with children who had been in care for a shorter period.

These findings reveal the difficulty in providing placement stability for children with long care histories; a group whose problems seem to be remarkably resistant to social work intervention. (Berridge and Cleaver, 1987)

There were too few children in our study who had been in long-term care for us to be able to assess whether this finding was also applicable in Warwickshire.

Placement characteristics

As we found when we examined breakdown rates for all types of placements, the placement factors which were strongly associated with higher breakdown rates were concerned with the carers' failure or inability to meet some of the needs of the children placed with them, or their inability to cope with the demands placed on them by the children.

Again, as in our analysis of the data relating to all types of placement, we found that for the *foster* placements in our study, breakdowns were strongly associated with the degree to which children were integrated in their placement. A quarter of the placements in which children were said to be well integrated ended in an unplanned way; for placements where children were poorly integrated the figure was over 60 per cent.

The circumstances surrounding the making of the foster placement and those issues associated with the location of the placement, did not appear to affect the way in which the placements ended. The one exception to this, as before, was that placements which enabled the child to maintain his or her community links were *more* likely to break down compared with placements where these links could not easily be maintained. Berridge and Cleaver (1987) also failed to find any direct relationship between the distance between home and placements but they did find that placements where there was no contact between the child and his or her parents were much more likely to end in breakdown than placements where there was some contact, even if it was very limited.

Issues about the placing of siblings together or separately were also identified as having significant effect by the same researchers. The breakdown rate for children who were living completely separate from their brothers and sisters was twice that for children accommodated with at least one sibling. Again this is a finding which we cannot test in this present study; Warwickshire were, to their credit, successful in placing siblings together in a large majority of cases.

One further finding from the above researchers' work which we will address in detail in Chapter 9 is the role and effect of specialist fostering support teams on the success of foster placements and, in particular, on breakdown rates. They compared practices in two local authorities and in a voluntary agency, the last of which provided and supported 'specialist' foster placements. Their findings were that training for foster carers, increased levels of social work support, foster carers' length of experience and careful matching of children with appropriate foster carers were all associated with improved outcomes.

Placements which lasted longer than planned

Why should we consider, separately, the question of whether placements lasted longer than was planned? Some commentators argue that such placements should be considered as ones where a breakdown has occurred – but more as a breakdown in the social work plan than in the care arrangements. However, placements can last longer than planned for good reasons. A child might be placed in an emergency with foster carers and, though the social work plan envisages a relatively long stay in care, this initial placement may be a temporary one while a longer-term setting is identified. If, however, the child settles with this first set of foster carers and they are willing to care for a longer time and, crucially, have the necessary skills and experience, then it would seem to be good practice to revise the plan and to prepare the child for an extension of his or her stay. Such a placement would be judged to have lasted longer than initially planned, but for good reasons.

Our case studies give us examples of placements which lasted too long for other reasons, and which were not positive experiences either for the young people concerned or the foster carers. For instance, we left Becky Johnson living with her foster family, the Gardners. This placement had been intended as temporary while a long-term placement was found but, despite advertising specifically for a 'home' for Becky, nowhere had been found and she remained with the Gardners. Becky herself had obviously found this period difficult. The failure of the advertisements had done nothing for her (or indeed her social worker's) self-esteem and the uncertainty she was experiencing led to confusions about how to relate to the Gardners. The Gardners themselves had the difficult task of maintaining their relationship with Becky, while there was uncertainty about how long she would actually be staying. These problems were all caused by a shortage of resources; specifically, long-term foster placements for adolescents. The problems were not the fault of the young person herself although, to some extent, that was how she seemed to feel.

It is also a concern that the issue of what might be called 'placement drift' is connected with the wider problem of drift in care. Since Rowe and Lambert (1973) identified that large numbers of (younger) children were languishing in nominally temporary care placements while awaiting long-term family placements, concern about drift in care has regularly recurred. Rowe and Lambert identified the problem as the shortage of foster carers.

Our question to social workers about placements and plans, asked them to identify those which had, 'lasted longer than planned'. Since this question was asked only about placements which had ended, we can assume that the results are on the cautious side. A number of placements which we monitored, but which were continuing at the end of the monitoring period, would have lasted longer than intended, but in the results given below, these do not appear. The methodology we have used in the Warwickshire research means that the actual figures we produce for placement drift can be directly compared with some other research findings, but obviously not those which used different methods.

It is important to note that placement drift was a much less significant problem than placement breakdown. Overall just 12 per cent (of 146 placement endings) were said to have lasted longer than planned. Those at most risk of drift, interestingly, were the younger children – 18 per cent of the 5 to 13-year-olds compared with 12 per cent of the 14 and 15-year-olds, and just 6 per cent of those age 16 or more. This compares with those whose placements broke down who were a significantly older group.

All the children for whom placement drift was identified as a problem had, with one exception, entered care for reasons of neglect or abuse or because their parents were unable to care for them. These reasons for admissions were identified in Chapter 4 as being associated with younger age groups. Admission for reasons of behaviour was associated with older children and, as we have seen, their placements were less likely to drift and more likely to break down.

The 'drifters' seemed to be less of a worry to social workers. The same proportion of drifters and those whose placements lasted as long as planned were said to be well adapted to their placements. This compared with half the number of children whose placements didn't last as long as planned. In terms of placement aims, the drifters fell between the other two groups. In seven out of ten cases the aims were said to have been met fully. The figures for the other two groups were four out of ten (breakdown) and nearly nine out of ten (lasted as long as planned).

Given that on these measures the placements seem, to the social workers, to be satisfactory, is there any cause for worry? If we were able to follow our cases over a longer period we would be able to provide a more conclusive answer. As it is, we can draw upon other research findings.

Like us, Rowe (1989) and Millham (1986) identified the over five years of age but pre-adolescent group as most likely to experience placement drift. The Dartington Social Research Unit, with a more intensive study and a longer follow-up, also expressed serious concerns about children in this age group who were still in care two years after admission.

Long away from home, increasingly isolated, still experiencing transfer and breakdown in placements, often lingering in residential care and unable to fashion their own links with parents or wider family. (Millham and others, 1986)

Many in this group of children were heading towards long stays in care, more than usual difficulty in coping with the problems of adolescence and, at least in the authorities in the Dartington study, long periods in residential institutions.

Placement satisfaction and success

We have already looked at a number of different measures which are used to assess the outcomes of placements. One of our measures was the extent to which the aims for the placement had been achieved, and in this chapter so far we have considered how many placements lasted as long as planned, how many broke down and how many lasted longer than was planned. Each of these measures has its advantages and its limitations. Sometimes it is difficult to specify what the aims of a placement are, for example when an admission to care is made in an emergency. In other cases, the aims may not be achieved for reasons which have little to do with the placement itself. We have also seen that placements may not last as long as planned or may last longer than intended, but plans sometimes change for good reasons, and so this measure is not a comprehensive one.

The most adequate method of measuring outcomes would be the intensive approach we adopted in our case studies. In these studies, we were not just dependent on the views of the social workers but we could also see how information from different sources compared. Additionally, we were able to consider each case in its uniqueness and chart the changing plans, aims and circumstances which surrounded it. However, such an exercise is not possible for a large number of cases, and we also have a need for aggregated data to enable us to reach overall conclusions and thereby to make comparisons with other sources of similar data.

Recognising the shortcomings, as well as the strengths, of the various outcome measures, we have opted to use a range of different ones which look at different aspects of the cases. As we have already stated, this multiplicity of measures not only enables us to undertake a broader range of comparisons but it also provides internal checks – one measure against another.

We have already examined placements which broke down, that is did not last as long as planned, and those which lasted longer than planned. We will begin this section by looking at the numbers and types of placements which *did* last as planned. We will then move on to the new measures, the first of which addresses the question of whether each placement lasted as long as the child *needed* it – which may, of course, be different from whether it lasted as long as was *planned*. We will then use a combination of this measure and the measure of the extent to which aims were achieved to provide an estimate of what might be called success.

Placements which lasted as long as planned

Overall, exactly half of the placements which ended lasted for as long as was originally planned. The picture becomes complicated when age is taken into account because, as we have already seen, the older children had more premature endings (breakdowns) on average than did those under ten. However, the latter group experienced more placement drift than average and the oldest group least drift. The overall result when looking at placements which did last as planned was that the 14 to 15-year-olds had the highest proportion (56 per cent) and the youngest group, aged ten or under, the lowest proportion (44 per cent). However, given the number of cases we were dealing with, these differences were not statistically significant.

Numbers in our study were too few to assess whether placements in different settings were more or less likely to last as planned but there was a clear hierarchy of how placement aims were associated with whether placements lasted. Aims which involved the shortest stays in care and those which might be said to have the 'easiest' aims, as one might expect, had the highest proportion which lasted; nine out of ten placements where the aim was simply to provide short-term emergency care lasted as planned, compared with just three in ten where the aim was for long-term care and upbringing.

The interplay of factors such as the different types of aims and the length of placements combined to produce some unexpected results. Only just over a third of placements for children admitted for reasons of neglect or abuse lasted as long as planned; for the poor care cases it was 50 per cent and for the behaviour problems 60 per cent. These results can only be understood in the context of our previous findings. First, that the children admitted because of neglect or abuse experienced both high rates of placement breakdown and placement drift, whereas the behaviour group also had a high proportion of breakdowns but very few placements which drifted. And second that, typically, the placement aims for children differed according to the reason for admission.

Encouragingly for Warwickshire, our result which showed that 50 per cent of placements lasted, was slightly better than the overall result for children aged five or over in Rowe's six authorities.

Placements which lasted as long as needed

Once children have been placed with foster carers or elsewhere, plans may be formulated for the first time or may be changed as circumstances change. As we discovered with Becky Johnson, her social worker was beginning to consider the possibility of redefining her placement with the Gardners as long-term. It had originally been a short-term placement but, because of difficulties in finding any other suitable placement, changes in the plan were being considered. Our measure, based on whether or not the placement lasted as long as the child needed it, overcomes the possibility of changes in plans.

Table 8.3 gives the results broken down by age group.

Table 8.3 Placements which lasted as needed, by age

	5–10 (%)	11–13 (%)	14–15 (%)	16+ (%)	Total (%)
Lasted as long as needed	18 (64)	14 (44)	17 (49)	24 (39)	73 (47)
Did not last as long as needed	8 (29)	12 (37)	11 (31)	33 (54)	64 (41)
Lasted longer than needed	2 (7)	6 (19)	7 (20)	4 (7)	19 (12)
Total	28 (100)	32 (100)	35 (100)	61 (100)	156 (100)

The assessments by social workers after placements had ended were that, disconcertingly, fewer than half had lasted as long as needed by the child. Of the rest, four out of ten had not lasted as long as needed and some one in eight had lasted too long. This overall result compares unfavourably with Rowe's research. She found that 60 per cent of placements for children aged five or over lasted as long as they were needed.

When we look for factors which were associated with whether placements lasted as long as needed, we are not by now surprised to find that age was the most clearly associated child-related factor. If we compare the results for the Warwickshire cohort with Rowe's results for six other authorities (1989) what we find is that for children aged between five and ten, similar proportions of placements in the two studies lasted as long as they were needed. The overall difference between the two studies, which we have already identified, lies in the over-tens age group. The 43 per cent of placements lasting as long as needed for the over-tens in Warwickshire compares with a figure of 57 per cent in Rowe's study. Thus, in this respect, it would seem that Warwickshire's main difficulty is with adolescents, who elsewhere would experience residential care more frequently.

There was also an association between the reason for admission to care and whether the placement lasted as needed. Only a third of the behaviour cases lasted as long as needed compared with 45 per cent of the neglect or abuse and over half the poor care cases. There was no overall difference by ethnicity.

As with breakdown and drift, some placement-related characteristics were strongly associated with placements which lasted as long as needed, whereas other factors appeared not to be related at all. Significantly, measures of the skills and ability of the carers were statistically very strongly correlated with those placements which lasted as long as the children needed them. For example, we asked case workers how well the child's need for skilled and experienced carers was met. In placements where this need was met very well or quite well, 56 per cent of placements lasted as long as needed. Where the need was met not particularly well or badly, only 26 per cent of placements lasted as needed. Placement factors not related to this particular measure included the circumstances in which the placement was made and elements such as the location of the placement, distance from the child's home and the frequency of parental visiting.

As before, placements which enabled children to maintain close links with their friends and communities had negative results. Slightly fewer of these placements lasted as long as the child needed, but considerably more (50 per cent compared with 30 per cent) failed to last as long as needed. We have previously used details from our case studies to demonstrate how community links, and in particular peer group involvement, can put strains on foster placements.

Successful and unsuccessful placements

As a final outcome indicator, we have decided to follow Rowe and her colleagues (1989) by combining the results from two of these measures to give us an overall measure of success in relation to outcomes. Such a measure will, in Rowe's words, 'Give some sense of what proportion of placements turn out all right'. By adopting the same definition we have also ensured that we can use the comparative data on the six authorities in Rowe's study.

The overall measure of success we have adopted is a combination of the extent to which placement aims were achieved and the child's needs were met.

- A *successful placement* is one in which the aims were achieved either fully or in most respects and the placement lasted as long as the child needed it.
- An *unsuccessful placement* is one in which the aims were achieved only partially or not at all and the placement did not last as long as needed.
- A *mixed outcome placement* includes all of the remaining circumstances: where the response to either question was 'don't know'; where the placement lasted longer than the child needed; where aims were achieved but the placement did not last as long as needed; and where it lasted but the aims were not achieved.

Table 8.4 shows the results for the placement endings in our Warwickshire cohort compared with the results for children aged five and over in the six authorities studied by Rowe. (To ensure that the comparisons we are making are valid, here as elsewhere, we have used only those results from Rowe's study which referred to children aged five or over. We compared the age structure of both samples and found them to be broadly similar.)

Table 8.4 The success of placements (all types)

	Warwickshire cohort (No.=151)(%)	Rowe's six authorities Range (%)
Successful	39	47 to 58 (mean 54)
Unsuccessful	20	18 to 23 (mean 20)
Mixed outcome	41	24 to 32 (mean 26)
Total	100	100

The first point to notice here is that the results from the study by Rowe and her colleagues fell into very narrow ranges. These researchers expressed surprise at this result and more detailed examination showed that the overall results concealed differences in success rates especially between different types of placement.

The second major point to notice is that the findings for our Warwickshire cohort were markedly different from these other authorities. A mean success rate for Rowe's six authorities of 54 per cent compares with one of less than 40 per cent in Warwickshire. In Warwickshire, the figure for unsuccessful placements was about the same but there were more placements where the outcome was described as mixed. If we compare the raw data in the two studies we find that the differences in success rates identify Warwickshire as significantly less successful than Rowe's six authorities overall. This is a major finding from our study. Furthermore, on this measure, outcomes in the County are considerably worse than those in *any* of these six authorities.

More specifically, Table 8.5 compares the results for foster placement endings in the Warwickshire study with the results for Rowe's six authorities.

Table 8.5 Foster placement endings: success rates by age group

	Age 5–10		Age 11+		Total	
	War. (%)	Rowe (%)	War. (%)	Rowe (%)	War. (%)	Rowe (%)
Successful	46	62	37	46	39	53
Unsuccessful	12	14	24	25	21	20
Mixed outcome	42	24	39	31	40	28
Total	100	100	100	100	100	100

Overall and in both age groups, the success rate for the Warwickshire cohort was considerably lower than that for Rowe's authorities: again, this finding should cause the County some concern. Even though the proportions of outcomes which were successful were quite different, the proportions of unsuccessful placements were similar. The differences lay in the mixed outcome group. This means that there were more placements where either the aims were achieved or the placement lasted as long as needed, than there were placements where *neither* of these comments would apply.

One of the other factors which has an effect on outcomes in foster placements is the way in which fostering services are organised and foster carers supported. This is likely to be a particularly important issue for Warwickshire, given their much greater use of foster care for older and more 'difficult' children. This will be one main focus of Chapter 9.

Summary

This chapter has presented our analysis of how and why placements ended and how successful they had been. We adopted several different measures of outcome to evaluate success and the main findings were:

- Nearly 40 per cent of placements in Warwickshire broke down; about the same rate as in other authorities. Placements made for children aged over 13 were twice as likely to break down.
- Placements for Black children in care had a higher breakdown rate than those for White children and, using other outcome measures, Black children fared less well. This finding should be considered as tentative because of the small numbers of Black children in our study.
- One in ten placements lasted longer than originally planned, with younger children more likely to experience placement drift. Social workers were relatively unconcerned about this group despite research evidence which has shown such children to be at risk of long stays in care.
- Over half the placements lasted as long as planned – a slightly better result than in authorities with which comparison was possible.
- About half the placements lasted as long as needed – as assessed by social workers. This was found to have applied less often to older children and children admitted to care for behavioural reasons.
- A measure of success was used which considered the achievements of placement aims and whether placements lasted as long as need. Success was lowest for older children and in placements where the carers were identified as relatively unskilled or inexperienced.
- The overall success rate for our Warwickshire cohort was under 40 per cent. This compares with 54 per cent for six other authorities where directly comparable data was available. This result should cause concern for Warwickshire.

9. The Children's Services Teams – foster care involvement

Background

In earlier chapters we have seen that, compared with other authorities, Warwickshire places a much higher proportion of children with foster carers and that these numbers include older children, those with behavioural problems and young people who have experienced previous placement breakdowns. In other areas, these are the children who would predominantly inhabit children's homes and other residential settings.

Since the development of specialist fostering schemes in the mid 1970s, the impression has grown that, across the country, increasing numbers of children with these special needs have been placed with foster carers. However, as we saw in Chapter 4, the reality is that only a small proportion of these children are fostered; for most, residential care remains the main substitute care provision. (*See*, for example, Rowe and others, 1989; Millham and others, 1986; Berridge, 1985.)

In our survey data and case studies, we have identified the difficulties which can arise when children, such as those who are often described as 'hard to place', are fostered. The demands on those caring for the children are considerable, and additional social work support is required to enable the carers to cope. By the time Warwickshire reorganised children's services in 1986 there was a well recognised body of literature which documented the change, if not the extent, in the nature of fostering and the associated changes in the recruitment, training and support for foster carers who were taking on children from these 'hard to place' groups. Hazel (1981) wrote about the experiences of the pioneering Kent Family Placement Project in the 1970s and others reported on the experiences of later projects. (*See* Thoburn and others, 1986; DHSS, 1981; Thomas, 1988; Shaw and Hipgrave, 1983.) Many of the schemes described in these reports aimed to provide permanent, or at least long-term, family placements. They emphasised not only the importance of the recruitment, training and support for foster carers but also the matching of the child with the placement, and the careful preparation of all those concerned, including the child, the foster carers and parents.

From the information which is available, it appears that what were essentially permanent placement schemes were extended, in the 1980s, to provide shorter-term placements for hard to place children, especially teenagers, for purposes which included assessment, remand to care, emergency admissions and care for physically or sexually abused children (Shaw and Hipgrave, 1989). Apart from this extension of the purposes for which foster care was thought appropriate, many of the themes in the literature remained the same: the need for careful recruitment; the necessity of training and ongoing social work support for the carers, preferably from a worker other than the case worker; and the need for planned placements, where possible, with all those involved being well prepared. (*See* Wedge and Thoburn, 1986; Thoburn and Rowe, 1988; Aldgate and others, 1989; Pine and Jacobs, 1989; Rushton, 1989; Ferguson and Leighton, 1990.)

However, as the emphasis changed from providing permanent homes to providing shorter-term care placements with different sets of aims, so an additional focus developed and a different set of questions began to be raised. How were the needs of children in foster placements which were additional to simply requiring a short-term home to be met? Who was to meet those needs? And how much could the foster carers themselves be expected to do? This last question in particular also raised broader concerns about the nature of fostering. For example, as foster carers took on more professional roles (such as, assessment and involvement in reviews and planning meetings), they appeared more as social workers' colleagues than as unqualified volunteers.

Some of these changes were noted in Shaw and Hipgrave's 1989 survey of foster schemes. Interestingly, it was Hoghughi (1989) – who is usually associated with residential services – who stated very clearly that, when placing a child in foster care, ensuring that his or her basic physical and emotional needs are met are only the first elements in the process. For many children these preliminary steps need to be followed by an assessment of his or her condition and then treatment.

The basis of fostering is that [a child] is subjected to or presenting an unacceptable condition. Fostering is used as a means of reducing the extent and intensity of that ... condition and bringing it within our society's tolerance. (Hoghughi, 1989)

But the foster carers act as a part of a team in the treatment process.

Both the social worker and the foster parent become not only direct executive treatments agents ... but are part of an ecological approach where they also act as co-ordinators of a number of other people's efforts ... it makes enormous sense not to put the total burden for the treatment of the young person on the foster parents ... neither they nor anyone else by themselves can deal with the totality and complexity of all the problems that an adolescent presents and experiences. (Ibid.)

In 1986, Warwickshire Social Services Department not only made history by closing down its last residential childcare facilities, but it also moved to the forefront of fostering practice. Many of the developments in specialist fostering schemes in other parts of the country were applied to all foster carers in the County. The Department's aim was to expand and develop foster care provision so that the large majority of children in care could be accommodated in non-residential settings and appropriate support provided to maintain these placements in the community.

In Chapter 3 we described the structure which was established in 1986 to achieve the Department's aims. The main features of the new structure are noted below.

- A Children's Services Team (CST) was set up in each of the five divisions and each CST had a Direct Work Team and a Resources Team.
- The Direct Work Teams provided group work and intensive individual work with children whose living situation was at risk of breaking down.
- The Resources Teams were responsible for the recruitment, training and support of foster carers, and for the provision of foster placements.
- Contract foster parents were recruited and supported to provide short-term, task-centred placements for more demanding children and young people.
- The CSTs employed more than a quarter of the qualified social workers in each division.

For their placement outcomes study, Rowe and her colleagues (1989) selected six different authorities. One of the criteria on which the selection was based was the organisation of foster care services. The authorities ranged from one with no specialist fostering services (recruitment and placement were the responsibility of area teams) to those with some specialisation – either in areas or centrally – of recruitment, assessment and post-placement support. Two of the authorities also had centralised specialist schemes responsible for placing teenagers, or children with special needs, in permanent placements.

In only one of these six authorities did the scale of resources devoted to specialist fostering services approach the level of resourcing devoted to this work in Warwickshire. However, what does appear unique to Warwickshire is the 'direct work' aspect of the CSTs. The Direct Work Teams account for more than half the complement of the CSTs but their equivalent was not mentioned by Rowe in relation to any of her six authorities.

Rowe reached no firm conclusions about the advantages of one type of organisational structure over another but she pointed to the tension between centralising and dispersing services.

We are constantly reminded of the tension of, on the one hand, trying to disperse skills, knowledge and responsibility as widely as possible and as close to the community as possible, while, on the other hand, risking the neglect of highly complex, delicate and time consuming tasks which can be crowded out if there are no specialists with a specific brief and interest to ensure they are accomplished. (Rowe and others, 1989)

To some extent, Warwickshire's divisional base for specialisation should overcome some of these problems but not necessarily the further problem, identified by Rowe, of the potential for tension between area and specialist staff. In fact, in an inspection of boarding out arrangements in the County, this was a specific problem identified by the Social Services Inspectorate (1987). Berridge and Cleaver (1987) reached some tentative conclusions about the effects of 'agency-related factors' on childcare outcomes.

Our analysis revealed that differences in outcome ... are not wholly attributable to the ... age of children and parental and social worker involvement. Instead there are also unexplained, agency-related factors that are relevant... It was clear that there were differences between the three agencies with regard … to the selection of foster parents; case review; and the support offered to … foster parents… It would be surprising if such contrasting practices were not reflected to a degree in placement outcomes. (Berridge and Cleaver, 1987)

To the extent that Warwickshire's fostering services (including selection and support) were specialised, and comparatively well resourced, we can assume that these services were more widely available than in most other authorities. It is evident, therefore, that Warwickshire had considered carefully the resourcing of its services and realised that the County could only cope without residential provision if there was additional, community-based input.

In the rest of this and the following chapter we will describe the work of the CSTs in more detail and will also attempt to assess their impact. We deal with the Resources Teams of the CSTs – which had a specific role in relation to foster care – before looking at the Direct Work teams.

The Resources Team

Slightly fewer than half of the staff in each of the five divisional Children's Services Teams worked in the Resources Teams. The rationale for creating these teams and their brief was outlined in a report by the Director of Social Services to the Social Services Committee.

The cornerstone of the service to children in care is the provision of substitute family care… There is a continual need to recruit more foster parents and sheltered lodgings. In order to increase the skills of foster parents presently available and to ensure that they remain available a high level of training and support is required. The location of the responsibility for substitute family care within the Children's Services Teams will, I believe, considerably advance the training, recruitment, allocation and support of foster parents and sheltered lodgings. (Warwickshire Director of Social Services, 1986)

Prior to the creation of the CSTs there were serious concerns in the County about the ability to provide sufficient foster placements, and placements of good quality, given the increasing dependence on this form of substitute care. The problems, according to one senior manager, included:

- a static recruitment rate;
- excessive time taken for approving foster carers (up to 18 months);
- a bias in the social class of those recruited as foster carers (with too many middle-class foster carers);
- the lack of a standard approval system;
- patchy training;
- uneven support; and
- a high dropout rate.

(Interestingly, no mention is made of problems of recruitment from minority ethnic communities.) These general difficulties were not peculiar to Warwickshire. With the proportion of children living in foster homes increasing across the country, the DHSS inspected the boarding out practice of nearly a third of local authorities and they also found delays in recruitment and inadequacies in training (DHSS, 1981).

Recruitment

In Chapter 3 we identified that, in Warwickshire, the move away from residential care to foster care had been gradual and that the closure of the last of the Children's Centres had not resulted in a large, additional number of children requiring foster placements. The closures did not, therefore, lead to a great pressure on the newly established CSTs to recruit large numbers of new foster carers in a short space of time.

However pressure to recruit did exist and a Working Party, reporting prior to the reorganisation, identified the nature of the problems.

At present, purely in terms of numbers the Department seems to be recruiting a steady supply of foster carers. Most Divisions have a small surplus of foster home vacancies, probably enough to accommodate most of the youngsters now in residential care. However, the problem is not nearly solved because the vacancies invariably lie with inexperienced foster parents who want young children, while the need is homes for distressed and damaged teenagers. There is an acknowledged failure ... to meet the needs of too many foster parents under stress with difficult teenagers and drop-outs after one or two adolescent placements are common. There is strong evidence that the level of satisfaction among foster parents is highly correlated with recruitment success, so the Department's patchy reputation [for providing support] is problematic. Solutions lie in recruitment and support which are inextricably bound together. (Warwickshire Social Services Department, 1983)

So, although demographic factors and the gradual pace of the changes reduced the pressures, there was an explicit recognition that recruitment levels needed to be improved, along with support for foster carers.

Recruitment is mainly carried out on a divisional basis with each CST concentrating on finding carers in its own locality. Periodic campaigns using the press, broadcasting media, leaflets and pamphlets are timed to fit in with other responsibilities of the Resources Team. Recruitment campaigns need to be followed up by a lengthy assessment programme. In addition to general campaigns, one possibility, which we saw in the case of Becky Johnson, is advertising targeted at finding a placement for a specific child. Such an approach, however, was the exception rather than the rule, mainly because of the cost involved and because of doubts about the effectiveness of such an approach. Advertising for foster carers for Becky produced no enquiries at all.

People responding to campaigns are sent information packs and this is followed by an initial home visit by a CST Resources Team social worker. The aims of this visit are to provide further information about the Department and the role of foster carers and, if enquirers appear entirely unsuitable, to counsel them to withdraw. For those wishing to proceed, the next stages involve group meetings at which the role of foster carers and the implications for foster families of caring for a child are discussed. These group meetings involve staff from the CST and the Community Teams, plus, importantly, experienced foster carers. At the final group meeting prospective applicants are given an application form to complete.

Assessment and approval

As in many other authorities (*see* Shaw and Hipgrave, 1989) the process of assessment involves further interviews with the applicants and interviews with other members of the household, Police and other checks, and the taking up of references and interviews with the referees. Most of this work is carried out by CST social workers but there is also a role for social workers from the Community Teams. Again in common with many other authorities, Warwickshire uses the document known as Form F, developed by BAAF (British Agencies for Adoption and Fostering) as the main tool for assessment.

The timetable set down for completing these procedures is three months from the receipt of the application form from the prospective foster carers to the submission of Form F and supporting documentation to the Substitute Family Care Panel. This Panel is chaired by the Divisional Fieldwork Manager, and includes social workers and an approved foster carer. In addition to taking decisions about approvals, the Panel also monitors vacancy and waiting lists, receives end of placement reports and the annual reports on foster carer reviews.

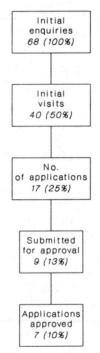

Figure 9.1 Recruiting foster carers in Warwickshire

Figure 9.1 presents a flow diagram for one division which shows clearly the amount of work involved in one year in the recruitment and approval process from the point at which initial enquiries are received. Interviews with staff in other CSTs suggested that the drop-out rates in this division were typical. Almost a half of those who made enquiries did not make further contact with the Department and presumably had second thoughts about becoming foster carers when they discovered, from the information sent out, what was involved. The drop-out rate between initial visits and approval was some six out of seven. This indicates a highly selective assessment process driven by CST social workers' commitment to ensuring that only suitable people are approved. This commitment is reinforced by the scrutinising role of the Substitute Family Care Panels, which are responsible for final approvals.

The County's experiences in recruiting foster carers are, in fact, typical of the experiences of other authorities in their attempts to recruit for specialist fostering schemes. The comments below are taken from Shaw and Hipgrave's (1989) survey of local authorities.

Initial enquiries are high but numbers of suitable foster parents remain low... Difficulty of finding families of the calibre required... Contract Scheme collapsed – not enough suitable families.

However, the way in which substitute care services in Warwickshire are organised is not typical of most other authorities. In the County, the CST in each division is responsible for providing substitute care for children of all ages. To this extent services are specialised but the form of specialisation in three-quarters of local authorities is different. In these authorities specialist fostering focuses on finding and supporting placements for children often described as 'hard to place', which usually means adolescents or children with severe physical or learning difficulties. In our interviews with social workers in the Resources Teams of the CSTs, it emerged that it was in fact these hard to place children, and especially young people with behavioural problems, for whom it was most difficult to find placements. In addition, it was these placements which required the most support. Nonetheless, the Resources Teams still had responsibility for *all* recruitment and training; for supporting *all* substitute care placements with foster carers or in supported lodgings; and for finding placements for *all* children. Despite this wide-ranging brief, other research suggests that specialisation increases the professionalism with which recruitment is undertaken and helps overcome what other research has described as, 'The selection of appropriate foster placements [which] is a somewhat haphazard process' (Berridge and Cleaver, 1987).

Why should Warwickshire have chosen their particular form of specialist fostering teams rather than one concentrating on hard to place children – especially as we have seen that in Warwickshire, as in other authorities, these children were recognised as the most problematic group? This question was raised in the report of a departmental working party.

One approach to recruitment is to advertise specifically for adolescents. This is successful by confronting recruits at the outset with the specific demands of adolescent fostering. (Warwickshire County Council, 1983)

But the report went on to pose an alternative, which was the recruitment of foster carers for more straightforward placements and then encouraging them to accept adolescents once they had gained experience. This method, the report said, has the advantage of not giving newly approved foster carers difficult placements early on, but it requires a stock of foster carers to be built up so that newly approved people can be introduced to the range of challenges which fostering presents, in a careful and systematic way.

To what extent have the CSTs been successful in recruiting and retaining foster carers and thereby building up the level of the resource? This question is difficult to answer because record-keeping systems across the County varied between divisions and some were not able easily to produce historical data. A summary of available evidence, relating to the period since the establishment of the CSTs in August 1986, follows.

- In the year up to June 1987, one CST reported recruiting 15 new foster families but set against this were 13 who had withdrawn.
- In the first five months of 1987, another division had approved three sets of foster carers but had lost seven who retired or withdrew.
- In a report to the Social Services Sub-Committee in March 1988, the Director noted that, 'The rate of foster care recruitment has exceeded the retirement or loss of foster carers by 54 during the period August 1986 to December 1987.' He identified the increased resources devoted to recruitment with the setting-up of the CSTs as one of the reasons for this increase, but he went on, 'There is still a shortfall in applications to foster older children, children with severe levels of disturbance and from families from the ethnic minority communities' (Warwickshire Director of Social Services, 1988).
- A review of services in one of the smaller divisions identified an overall decline in the stock of foster carers in two successive years. In 1987 five approvals were set against six withdrawals; in 1988 nine approvals were set against 12 sets of foster carers who ceased fostering.
- In the first six months of 1989, one divisional Substitute Family Care Panel approved 15 foster families while noting 13 withdrawals.

These rather patchy findings suggest that, with the possible exception of the period immediately following the reorganisation of childcare services, recruitment of new foster carers met with only limited success. The process of recruitment, assessment and approval is very demanding of staff time and this is compounded by the very high drop-out rate seen when comparing the numbers of initial enquiries and formal applications to foster with the numbers of eventual approvals.

The low numbers of approvals also need to be set against the numbers of foster carers withdrawing from fostering. The reasons why people withdraw are various, but we do have further evidence about the reasons why people, ostensibly, made this choice.

- In the year up to June 1987, 13 withdrawals in one division were made for the following alleged reasons: six withdrew because of changes in jobs, or a move from the area, or for other personal reasons; four left after difficult placements; one left fostering to adopt a baby from a neighbouring authority; one couple had been approved for a particular child who reached

18 years of age; and the final couple were counselled to retire because of overcrowding in their home.
- In the first five months of 1987 seven withdrawals in another division were accounted for by: two retirements on grounds of age; one leaving the area; one adopting a child; and three who were resting after stressful placements.
- In 1988, 12 withdrawals in a third division were stated to be because of: pregnancy, ill-health, or movement out of the area (5); following foster home disruption (2); child reached 18 but continued to live with family (1); adopted child (1); moved to foster for another authority (1); and the final two were 'counselled out' for unidentified reasons.

We have no way of knowing, of course, whether the reasons recorded are the true explanations for foster carers' withdrawal. However, the figures suggest that a large proportion of withdrawals are attributable to natural wastage, that is for reasons such as retirement because of age, for health reasons or because of movements out of the area. Many of these, therefore, may indeed be inevitable. However, a smaller, but also significant number, were identified as being the consequence of difficult placements. It is this last group which gives cause for concern, not least because as identified earlier, the Department has most difficulty in recruiting foster carers who are willing and able to look after the children who present the most challenging behaviour. This includes many young people who, elsewhere, would be placed residentially.

Graphic accounts of the reasons why some foster carers gave up fostering were provided in case studies described by Berridge and Cleaver (1987). They argued forcefully that the demands which difficult placements impose on foster families cannot be overestimated. Foster carers having nervous breakdowns, their own children moving out to live with grandparents, and overwhelming feelings of failure and guilt are all described. It is not surprising when we consider the details of cases that some foster carers withdraw. What is perhaps more surprising is that so many enlist in the first place and continue! Detailed case studies, such as the three we have presented in this report, demonstrate the need for extensive support to keep placements going, and also the need for support and counselling for foster carers when placements have ended – especially if this ending is unplanned.

The general problems in recruiting and retaining foster carers, which we have described above, also applied to contract foster parents. The roles of contract foster parents explicitly includes short-term placements for 'difficult' children and young people who may have experienced a family breakdown or placement breakdown in another foster home. As a part of the 1986 reorganisation package, funding for 11 sets of contract foster carers was earmarked. In the first 18 months of operation ten sets were approved but four subsequently withdrew. The recruitment of contract foster carers took longer than had been anticipated and, one and a half years after reorganisation, the establishment was only just over half the envisaged number. An internal review of the contract fostering scheme expressed concern about the heavy and almost continuous use which was being made of contract foster carers who had been approved – one couple had 12 different placements over a 15 month-period and their longest break without a child was just over five weeks. It was this pattern of use which the review associated with the four withdrawals from the scheme.

In 1990, in response to a report identifying these problems, approval was given to double the establishment of contract foster carers. It was anticipated that if sufficient people could be recruited, the demand on each set of carers would be reduced and at the same time, it would be possible to find a contract placement more quickly when the need was identified.

In summing up the evidence about the recruitment and assessment of foster carers in Warwickshire, we find ourselves in agreement with an internal review which was undertaken three years after reorganisation.

All CSTs reported problems in locating, supporting and maintaining a supply of placements, particularly for adolescents... In the upper age range, the availability of foster homes appears to be critical. (Mountford, 1989)

What we would add is that this is not a problem restricted to Warwickshire. Parker (1987) identified a number of demographic factors which were affecting the availability of people able and willing to take on the task of fostering. These factors included increasing numbers of women in paid employment. Other local authorities (*see* Shaw and Hipgrave, 1989) have also identified serious recruitment problems. What does make Warwickshire different is its high dependence on foster care and the fact, already identified in comparison with Rowe's recent research (1989), that the County expects a lot more of its foster carers, in that it places many more older children and difficult children with them than do other authorities.

In addition to problems in recruiting new foster carers, there is the problem of the loss of already approved families; a particular problem for Warwickshire as it recognises the need to increase overall numbers. The loss of experienced foster carers, which was identified in interviews, is particularly worrying. It is precisely these experienced families who would best be able to care for the more demanding children. That the level of experience is correlated with success has been shown in assessments of various schemes and in other research (*see* for example, Berridge and Cleaver, 1987; Thoburn, 1986; Aldgate and others, 1989; Shaw and Hipgrave, 1989).

Training

Warwickshire recognises the heavy demands on foster carers and the brief of the CSTs reflects this awareness. This brief includes not only recruitment and assessment but also training and individual, link worker support for foster carers. We will examine the role of link workers in the next section of this chapter; here the focus is on training.

Training is an essential part of the preparation of foster carers because, quite often, the job they are being asked to undertake is far outside the experiences of 'ordinary' parents. Very few parents know how to cope with the levels of anger or violence displayed by Becky Johnson or the highly promiscuous behaviour of sexually abused Angela. Across the country, the move away from the term foster parent to foster carer reflects a recognition of the changing task of fostering.

Nationally, training which recognises these demands has developed quite considerably in recent years and Shaw and Hipgrave (1989) identified some common approaches.

Training has had to take on additional areas, such as child abuse and sexual abuse and there is generally more emphasis on the specific expectations of the fostering 'task'. A variety of training modes are used ... Several respondents note that the 'specialist' approach to selection and training is now being applied 'generically' throughout the agency.

This last point is particularly relevant for the circumstances which apply in Warwickshire. With the exception of contract foster carers, the selection and training experience of all foster carers in the County is the same.

It is difficult to distinguish the contents of Warwickshire's assessment package from what might be called a training package for prospective fosterers. Certainly, one of the aims of the assessment is to give those attending a clear picture of what fostering involves:

- which children come into care and why;
- how they might behave;
- what other demands they might make; and
- what effect the presence of a foster child might have on other children in the family.

Existing, experienced foster carers in the County are included in these assessment programmes specifically so that they can pass on their experiences. The benefits of training have been identified elsewhere:

It was encouraging to discover that foster parents who had experienced rudimentary induction training were able to offer a greater degree of stability than those without preparation... Benefits might be expected not only in the quality but also continuity of the care experience. (Berridge and Cleaver, 1987)

Warwickshire's induction training is more than rudimentary and could, therefore, be expected to provide a good grounding for those approved as carers – as well as convincing some to withdraw their applications. There is also a Departmental commitment to provide foster carers with what might be called in-service training. However, it was clear from a number of interviews that such training was forced to take a relatively low priority when set against the demands of support for individual placements, placement finding and assessments. Workload monitoring in one division in 1989 identified foster carer training (excluding induction programmes) as accounting for only seven per cent of the Resources Team's time.

There is a wealth of material available about the training needs of foster carers and about how training might best be carried out. Staff in the CSTs are familiar with this literature – the problem they face is lack of time to make use of it. The inevitable consequences of this situation have been:

- inexperienced and relatively untrained foster carers finding themselves unable to care for, or cope with, some children;
- subsequent high levels of demand on both CST and Community Team social workers for crisis support;

- unsatisfactory placements, from the children's point of view;
- unplanned and possible unnecessary placement endings; and
- the early loss of some foster carers after difficult experiences.

Placement finding

Each of the Resources Teams in the CSTs runs an office-hours duty system to respond to requests for care placements from Community Team social workers. Out-of-hours, there is a county-wide emergency duty system and the officers who staff this have access to foster carer vacancy lists. In each division a foster care register is kept updated.

The CSTs also have a responsibility for identifying care placements when fostering is deemed unsuitable. The CSTs aim to recruit and provide supported lodgings placements and we have already identified that Departmental procedures give the CSTs a key role in applications for residential placements in the reserved beds with the National Children's Home facility at Sutton Coldfield. This role also exists in relation to other residential placements. The CSTs have developed a greater degree of knowledge and information about such placements than is available in Community Teams. It would only be in relation to placements home on trial, with relatives or friends, or in independent accommodation that the CST would have no formal responsibility.

Divisions have their own procedures for making placement requests but, typically, CSTs ask for as much notice as possible that a placement may be required. They also request that a referral form is completed and sent after the initial contact, which is usually made by phone. In its annual report one CST commented:

Our task would be greatly helped if we were to receive written home-finding referrals. Of the 247 referrals made [in the year] we have only received written information about 25. I recognise that many referrals are made in an emergency or potential emergency. However, written information would not only help in our attempt to match but would also enable us to pass on information to foster parents.

A study of fostering in the County, undertaken by a postgraduate student, also identified low levels of written placement referrals – a finding which the author criticised on several grounds, not the least of which was that telephoned referrals created a high risk of inadequate and inaccurate transmission of information, and thus potentially unsuitable placements being made (Verity, 1988).

The CSTs' request that the potential need for a placement should be notified as early as possible presents case workers with a dilemma. If there is a risk of a family or a care placement breakdown, how serious must that risk be before a referral is made? The evidence available suggests that where the need for a placement can be foreseen then case workers do make early referrals. However, the number of cases where planning is possible is limited because a large number of placements are required in crisis situations – a point we alluded to earlier. It bears repeating that other writers (for example Packman, 1986) have commented critically on the reactive and crisis-oriented nature of much childcare work.

A study of referrals during the first year of operation of the CSTs identified two-thirds of requests for placements as emergency, that is when there was an 'imminent threat of breakdown of the child's present placement'. A further quarter were said to be critical, that is where there was a 'serious threat of breakdown'. In fewer than one in ten cases was the referral non-critical. The consequences of these findings were said to be that the large majority of referrals:

Did not allow time for an adequate preparation of placement prior to the anticipated arrival of the child... The opportunity to effect an adequately planned/prepared and introduced placement of a child with a foster family is represented by those [ten per cent of] non-critical referrals received. (Verity, 1988)

One CST monitored the referrals it received over a year in a way which enables us to understand more clearly what emergency or critical might mean. Exactly one third of referrals to the CST were for placements needed *on the same day* as the referral. In such cases written referrals, proper matching, introductions – and preparation of the child, foster carers and parents would all be impossible.

We noted earlier that the organisation of specialist fostering services in Warwickshire differed from many other authorities. Specialism in other areas more often focuses on hard to place children, sometimes those with a disability but more frequently adolescents with or without behavioural problems. Some schemes are designed to provide permanent substitute care, others, focused, contract-based placements which are often time-limited (Shaw and Hipgrave, 1989). In Warwickshire, the specialist teams are responsible for finding placements (long-term, short-term and contract-based) for *all* children. The advantages of the more common organisation of specialism would appear to be the ability to protect staff resources committed to finding and supporting placements for the hard to place groups; and the possibility of gatekeeping these specialist resources so that placements are based on more adequate information, and are better prepared and planned. What we do not know about the consequences of this type of specialism concerns the quality of the service for children in need of placements who fall outside the brief of the specialist teams. How well are these ordinary foster carers assessed, trained and supported? And how well are new placements handled?

The availability of placements

The question of how effective the CSTs are in responding to requests for placements has been addressed in detail in previous chapters. There we saw that, by and large, when a placement was needed one was found, but there were problems in that often there was little choice of placement and, as a consequence, sometimes inappropriate and unsuitable placements were made.

One of the factors which contributes to lack of matching between the child's needs and what the placement can offer is the emergency nature of many of the placements. Another factor is the supply of placements. We have already identified that the County has had problems in recruiting sufficient numbers of foster carers, especially when we take into account the numbers who, for one reason or another, withdraw. However, what is crucial when a request for a placement is received, especially if the need is urgent, is the availability of foster carers with vacancies. Fifteen months after the creation of the CSTs, we undertook a census of foster placement vacancy lists. The results in Table 9.1 are from three of the County's five divisions (two of the largest and one of the smallest) and, according to CST Staff, the lists were typical of the numbers of placements and the types of placements usually available.

Table 9.1 Foster placement vacancies

Total foster carers with vacancies		43
Age of child:		
Proportion with places for children	up to 5	23%
	up to 12	56%
	12 or over	21%
Sex of child:		
Proportion offering places for	boys	91%
	girls	88%
Length of placement:		
Proportion offering	short-term only	95%
	long-term	14%
Period of time since approved:		
	Less than one year	29%
	1 to 2 years	18%
	Longer	53%

In 1989 an internal Departmental survey produced a figure of 54 foster carers without children *across the whole County*. The 54 families identified in the 1989 survey, amounted to a 'vacancy rate' of 17 per cent but the rate varied from 28 per cent or 19 placements in one division to as little as 4 per cent or just two placements, in another.

In our 1987 census (Table 9.1), the 43 foster carers were also spread unevenly across the divisions but between them offered 55 placements in total. However, discussions with CST Managers made it clear that a good proportion of these placements were 'not really available'. As many as a quarter of the carers were resting, perhaps after a previous placement, or temporarily unavailable, perhaps because of illness or holidays, or were not available because the CST was not happy about using the placement for one reason or another. However, the resting foster carers were not necessarily always seen as unavailable. One senior manager described the process of finding a placement:

In order to keep abreast of the current daily demand, the vacancy list is scoured and scoured again and either an existing foster parent is persuaded to accept a multiple placement – often outside their approved criteria – or a resting foster parent is press-ganged into 'active' service.

From the figures in Table 9.1 a number of positive features stand out. First, there was no particular imbalance of placements for boys or girls. In fact a large majority of the foster carers were listed as offering places for either sex. Second, over half of the vacancies were with carers who appeared to be quite experienced in that they had been approved for more than two years.

The problems which the figures make obvious are the lack of availability of placements for older children, and long-term placements. A quarter of the carers were interested only in babies or very young children. Over a half would take children aged up to 12 or so. But only one in five (approximately *eight* in number) would take children over 12. Children and young people in this age group account for more than a third of admissions to care and over a half of the total in care at any one time. However, the greatest shortfall was for long-term placements. Only six long-term vacancies existed on this list. We do not know how many of these foster carers would have been unavailable or how many were interested in babies or young children only, but the likelihood is that finding a long-term placement for an adolescent – even setting aside the idea of matching any other needs – would prove very difficult, even impossible. This was the case with Becky Johnson. No suitable long-term vacancies existed for her and sadly, when advertising was tried specifically for her, this also failed.

In our monitoring we also examined the ethnic origin of foster carers. From this vacancy list of 43, there were only three sets of foster carers where one or both of the partners was from a minority ethnic group; these were reported as Afro-Caribbean, East Asian and Muslim. Three vacancies from a list this size was approximately in proportion to the size of the Black population in Warwickshire. But this clearly represents an inadequate pool in terms of finding a placement for a Black child when the aim was to match not only on the basis of race, but also on factors including age, location, sex and length of placement, let alone language and religion.

Verity (1988) came to similar conclusions about the difficulties which social workers had in matching the needs of children of any minority ethnic group with what placements had to offer.

In reality, due to the lack of choice of foster families available, any comprehensive matching of child to foster family could only be claimed as occurring in a small number of placements.

He went on to say that:

The most urgent need [is] to bolster the numbers of foster families willing and able to care for teenagers.

In 1989 one division in the County experienced what was described as a crisis because of a level of demand for long-term placements for adolescents which the CST could not meet. As this chapter was being written, one solution being proposed was a separate, specialist fostering project to find and support long-term placements for young people aged 14-plus. The nature of the 'contract' between the Department and the foster carers was also being rethought. Interestingly, such an arrangement would, as we have already seen, be much more typical of that found in some other authorities.

Support for foster carers

In their study of foster placement breakdown, Berridge and Cleaver (1987) described the positive effects of involving foster carers more fully in the planning process and of providing them with good support. One couple who had transferred to a specialist fostering scheme from what might be called 'ordinary' fostering, commented:

It's better all round... We have our own special meetings where you can talk over the problems you're having. One of the biggest differences though is that you get treated better by the social workers.

However, these authors also identified experiences which were very different from this which included the isolation of foster carers, poor communication between social workers and fosterers, and poor social work support for carers. All of these were associated with placements which had broken down. Regular social work support to foster families was a low priority for social workers, who tended to respond to crises in placements. The authors went on to identify the effects of placement breakdowns on the children but also on the foster carers. They found that many foster carers held themselves to blame for the outcome of the placements and:

It was particularly disquieting to discover that, overall, little effort was invested in assisting foster parents to come to terms with their painful experience. Consequently, four couples [out of ten] have vowed that they will never again foster. (Berridge and Cleaver, 1987)

Berridge and Cleaver's evidence identifying the need for continuing support for foster carers, especially those caring for hard to place children, is also a theme in other studies (see for example: Thoburn, 1986; Wedge and Thoburn, 1986; Hazel, 1981; Thomas, 1982; Rushton, 1989).

In ordinary fostering arrangements, it is not uncommon that the only social work contact which foster carers have is with the worker responsible for the child. This worker will, not surprisingly, see her primary responsibility as being to the child and only secondarily will she feel responsible for the foster carers. When a child moves on, the contact between the social worker and the former foster carers will cease.

Shaw and Hipgrave (1989) discovered that, even in specialist fostering schemes, the amount of support offered to foster carers varied and the ways in which support was given also differed. Some schemes initiated training and support groups which would meet periodically but a number of these schemes were struggling with the notion of voluntary or compulsory attendance. If attendance was to be compulsory, should the groups be renamed supervision groups? In addition to these groups, where they existed, most foster carers had access to social work support from the specialist team. However, in many of the schemes, the level of resources and the need to choose priorities meant that there was, 'A general feeling that the support is not as good as it was or should be' (Shaw and Hipgrave, 1989).

The idea, common in specialist fostering schemes, that foster carers should have access to social work support in their own right, separate from the child's social worker, is extended in Warwickshire to all foster carers and to people providing supported lodgings. Each of these has their own named link worker in the CST Resources Team, and this social worker remains their contact point before, during and after placements and when they have no child in placement at all.

A system of link working had developed in some parts of the County prior to the reorganisation of childcare services in 1986. It was recognised that in areas where no such scheme existed, foster carers were being lost when no child was in placement (Warwickshire Social Services Department, 1987). There were also other reasons why the link working system in the County was extended to all carers. First, there was a recognition that, with the rundown and eventual closure of the Children's Centres, more was being required of foster carers. They were being asked, in many cases, to care for more difficult children and they were also being expected to perform a more skilled task. Second, it was seen as inevitable that the needs of foster carers would take a lower priority with the case-accountable social workers in the Community Teams, than the needs of the child in placement. In some circumstances, the best interests of the child and foster carers might even run counter to each other. An alternative to leaving the support of foster carers to the case workers was, therefore, seen as essential.

The different roles of the link worker and the child's social worker emerged clearly in our case studies. Angela's current set of foster carers had a close relationship with their link worker. She gave them general support in their role as foster carers but also supported them in relation to specific issues concerning Angela. The link worker maintained close contact with Angela's social worker and could thus pass information in both directions. When the placement became particularly difficult, the link worker was able to double the frequency of her visits. This was typical of other link workers too; visits would increase if there were problems in the placement. Not all of the placements we looked at in the case studies demonstrated working relationships which were as good as this. There were cases where there was confusion about exactly what role the CST link worker had in relation to the case. But overall, in the case studies, link working was seen as positive by all concerned.

Individual support for foster carers is very demanding of social work time and this is one of the reasons why some authorities run group support sessions as an alternative to at least some individual support (*see* Shaw and Hipgrave, 1989). Mountford (1989) identified that, in the Warwickshire divisions which had an organisational split between a Resources Team and a Direct Work Team, each social work post was responsible for providing link work support for between 14 and 22 foster families. One of the smaller teams itself reported that it had 56 foster families, support for which was spread throughout the whole Team but was in effect carried by the equivalent of less than *two* full-time social work posts.

The CST in one division in Warwickshire monitored its workload, and link working was identified as taking more staff time than any other single area of activity. A quarter of the Resource Team's social work hours were devoted to foster carer linking. One senior manager commented:

Workers are being currently faced with an ever growing need to provide individual link support to primary carers as the pressures faced by foster parents become greater through the nature and demands of the children placed with them and the manner in which they have been boarded out.

The last point refers to the high proportion of emergency placements being made which does not allow for adequate preparation for the child or carers.

The same manager also commented on the lack of group work support and training for foster carers. This, he said, took a relatively low priority because the demands from existing placements were more immediate and more urgent. Each of the CSTs does in fact support local branches of the National Foster Care Association. These groups are not attended by all foster carers – although they are open to all – and they run a mixture of informal social events and training sessions on general topics. Both the training and the social contact with people doing the same 'job' are undoubtedly valuable, but cannot substitute for flexible individual support available as and when required.

The roles of link workers

As we have seen, Departmental policy in Warwickshire is that all foster carers and people providing supported lodgings should have their own, named, link worker. Our survey of 215 childcare cases was undertaken more than two years after the implementation of the policy and we discovered that nearly nine out of ten of the children boarded out were placed with foster carers who did indeed have a link worker. Children who had been in care for more than 12 months were less likely to be in foster placements which had an attached link worker. In many of these cases the children had been in the particular placement since before the reorganisation of children's services and the introduction of the link worker system across the County.

In most divisions, nearly all of the link working was carried out by CST social work staff. Departmental policy documents define the role of link workers as:

To relate to the needs of foster parents in their general role of substitute carers. The need for contact is: to act as advocates on the foster parents behalf; ... to assist in the foster family's development of their role; to offer help and support to the family, regardless of any placement in progress. This role takes on greater importance during and after a difficult placement. (Warwickshire Social Services Department, 1987a)

In our interviews, Community Team social workers were asked to identify their roles and the link workers' roles in the process of making a placement, and then again once the placement had been made. Table 9.2 identifies the roles prior to the placement being made.

Overall, the responses suggested that many roles and responsibilities were not clear cut and that practice varied considerably from case to case. We did not examine how the roles were negotiated between individual case workers and link workers. In relation to approximately three-quarters of placements,

Table 9.2 Social work roles prior to placements being made

Role	Case worker only (%)	Link worker only (%)	Case worker and link worker (%)	Neither (%)
Discussions with parents about proposed placement	72	3	16	9
Discussions with child about proposed placement	79	1	12	8
Pre-placement discussions with foster carers	15	43	36	7
Visit to foster placement	16	36	21	26
Final decision about choice of placement	43	21	28	7

discussion about the proposed placement with the parents and the child were undertaken by the Community Team social worker (the case worker). What is surprising is that this figure was not higher and that in as many as one in six cases the CST link worker had any involvement. For reasons which are not clear, it was with older children and those in care for behavioural reasons, with whom the CST had most involvement. Parents were not consulted in more of the cases involving older children and the children themselves were less likely to be consulted if they were aged under 13.

Discussions with the foster carers and visits to assess the foster placement were taken on by the link worker alone much more often than by the case worker alone, but in a significant proportion of cases both workers took on this task. Whether the placement was planned or made in an emergency was the main constraining factor. The link worker alone took on these responsibilities much more often if the placement was made in an emergency. In all of the cases where there were no pre-placement discussions with the foster carers, the placement had been made in an emergency, and nearly nine out of ten cases where there were no placement visits were emergency placements. The Social Services Inspectorate (1987) was critical of some aspects of placement practice in Warwickshire. In many placements specific issues were not considered, including some of those required by regulation to be reported on in writing. However, elsewhere in their report, the SSI was positive about the support given to foster carers by the CST link workers and it was also complimentary about the annual review of all foster carers which is undertaken by the CSTs.

It was surprising that in fewer than half the cases, the case workers identified themselves as having sole responsibility for the final decision about the placement. As the case accountable worker, the responsibility is technically theirs but in one in five cases they identified the choice as being the link worker's. Presumably the CST were only able to offer one placement. The seven per cent of cases where neither worker took the final decision would also have been cases where only one placement was available and so, in one sense, there was no choice. Again, the way in which the placement was made affected the extent to which responsibility for making the decision was passed to the CST. The final choice about the placement was more often identified as the CST's decision when placements were made in an emergency.

Table 9.3 was produced in the same way as Table 9.2. The case accountable workers in the Community Teams were asked about their roles and the link workers' roles after a placement had been identified.

Table 9.3 Social work roles when placements were made and thereafter

Role	Case worker only	Link worker only	Case worker and link worker	Neither
	(%)	(%)	(%)	(%)
Accompanied child to placement	83	4	6	7
Accompanied parents to placement	42	0	2	57
Arranged meetings between parents and child	32	32	34	1
Met with child alone	88	0	4	9
Met with parents	90	1	5	4
Met with foster carers	93	0	4	3
Contact for foster carers in case of problems with child	29	3	65	4
Contact for foster carers for boarding out payments	6	69	23	2

From these results the obvious conclusion is that the Community Team social workers had the key role in relation to most aspects of placements with foster carers. Taking the child to the placement and direct contact with the child, parents and foster carers were identified as involving CST link workers in only very few cases. Link workers were identified as having primary responsibility for practical issues (such as boarding out payments), and equal responsibility with the case worker as the contact point if problems developed in the placement, and for arranging meetings between the child and his or her parents. This latter finding is somewhat puzzling but seems to be associated with cases where meetings were arranged away from the foster carers' and which often took place on the CST's premises.

Where neither the case worker nor the link worker took responsibility for particular tasks, either other workers were involved (for instance Becky Johnson was taken to one of her placements by a member of the CST Direct Work Team); or there was no need for social work staff to be involved (for instance many parents visited their children without social work accompaniment); or the placement lasted for too short a period for the particular task to be carried out.

The most curious result was that our respondents (the Community Team case workers) identified only a very limited role for link workers in contact with the foster carers. This finding does not correspond with the stated role of link workers nor with other evidence we have, for instance from our intensive case studies or from interviews with link workers themselves. As we saw earlier in this chapter, the large majority of foster carers have link workers and link workers spend a large proportion of their time in contact with their foster carers. We also have evidence that contact between link workers and foster carers increases when they have a child placed with them.

We would conclude that this discrepancy is based on inadequate communication between case worker and link worker. In too many cases the two social workers will both have been involved in the case but without sharing their knowledge and understanding with each other. In the case of Angela Collins, we heard from one link worker that she identified her role as providing general support to the foster carers and not as responding to the particular issues which arose while they were caring for Angela. Certainly, it was the practice of most of the link workers we interviewed to meet the foster carers when the foster child was not present and, while general issues would be on the agenda, in most of these meetings concerns about the particular placement would be raised. The link workers we interviewed recognised that, in responding to particular concerns, they had to remember that case accountability rested with the Community Team social worker and that any advice which they gave needed to be consistent with that given by the case worker. Communication between the two social workers would seem to be a prerequisite for ensuring a consistent approach, yet did not seem to be occurring.

To what extent did Community Team social workers value the input from CST link workers? Clear roles were identified for link workers at the pre-placement stage but, as we have just seen, only a limited input was recognised subsequently. We asked the case workers to evaluate the importance of the link worker input for all placements which had ended. 'Do you think that the involvement of the link worker meant that this placement was more or less successful?' The responses are summarised in the Table 9.4

Table 9.4 The impact of link work input

	Cases (%)
Much more successful	23 (23)
Slightly more successful	24 (24)
No difference	51 (52)
Slightly less successful	0 (0)
Much less successful	1 (1)
Total	99 (100)

In half the cases the link work was said to have made no difference to the outcome. This may of course have reflected the case workers' assessments that the link work input was ineffective. Alternatively, it might have been a recognition that some cases were not susceptible to social work input; for example, short, relatively uncomplicated stays in foster care. It was certainly true that in 80 per cent of our long-term in care group the link work input was said to have made outcomes more successful. This was also true for all children whose stay in care had lasted for more than six months.

In the other half of the cases the link work input was judged to have increased the level of success, sometimes by a quite considerable degree. There was just one case where the involvement of the link worker was said to be damaging. This was a case where there was a breakdown in communication between the case worker and the link worker; the two of them were giving the foster carers contradictory advice. Nonetheless, these findings are encouraging and provide some endorsement for Warwickshire's professional specialisation.

A large proportion of the staff of the CSTs came to their new posts from the previous Intermediate Treatment Teams or from the Children's Centres. We therefore anticipated that the link workers might have had more impact on placements for those children with whom they had most experience; that is older children and those presenting behavioural problems. In fact age was not correlated with perceived success at all. There was a correlation with the type of case, but the correlation was the opposite of that which we had anticipated.

Where the reason for admission to care was neglect or abuse, or poor care nearly six out of ten placements were said to have been more successful because of the link work involvement. Where admission was for behavioural reasons, only a third of placement outcomes were felt to have been improved through link working. Children and adolescents with behavioural problems have been identified as the group which were the most difficult to work with throughout our study.

Finally, we discovered that the overall degree of satisfaction disguised dramatic differences between the County's five divisions. In two, link work input was associated with more successful outcomes in approximately two-thirds of placements; in one, half the placements; but the extreme results were success rates of nearly 80 per cent in one division but only just over 20 per cent in another.

Summary

- The Resources Teams of the CSTs were responsible for: recruitment, assessment, training and support for all foster carers and providers of supportive lodgings; and for placement finding for all children. Specialist fostering teams in other local authorities typically focus on special needs or hard to place children.
- Recruitment of foster carers was time-consuming and labour-intensive. For every ten enquiries only one set of foster carers was approved.
- Problems of recruitment were increased by a steady rate of retirements of foster carers. A significant number of retirements followed demanding or stressful placements.
- The CSTs usually had very few foster placement vacancies, especially ones suitable for older children or long-term placements. Too few Black foster

carers made it very difficult to provide same-race placements for Black children in care.

- Two-thirds or more of requests to the CSTs for placements were for emergency placements. In these circumstances planning, preparation and matching were not possible.

- Warwickshire's policy was to provide all foster carers with their own named link worker. The link worker was attached to the carer and not the child. In many local authorities, social work support for carers is only available from the child's worker.

- There is strong evidence from research which associates positive placement outcome with the quality and quantity of support given to foster carers.

- Warwickshire's link worker system was initiated because foster carers were being asked to cope with more difficult children. There was also a recognition that the child's social worker is not in the best position to provide adequate support to foster carers.

- When making placements, case workers undertook most of the preparatory work with the children and parents. Discussions with the foster carers and pre-placement visits to the home were more often shared, as was the responsibility for making the final choice about the placement.

- If placements were made in an emergency, the link workers had a more significant role in dealing with the foster carers and in making the final decision about which placement was selected.

- The Community Team social workers identified themselves as having the key role in relation to most aspects of the work involved once placements were made. However, there was evidence that case workers underestimated the amount of time and support given to foster carers by the link workers.

- Community Team social workers associated the extent and quality of link work input with more successful outcomes for half the placements. In only one case did the case worker identify link work as resulting in a less successful outcome. The cases where link working was said to have made no difference more often involved short stays in care or in a placement.

10. Children's Services Teams – direct work with children and families

As we saw in Chapter 3, in each of the Children's Services Teams more than half of the staff resources were committed to what is called direct work. The aims of this direct work were described in a report to the Social Services Sub-Committee as being:

To reduce the need to receive children and young people into care; [and] to diminish the level of custodial sentencing of young people. (Warwickshire Director of Social Services, 1988)

The juvenile justice aim was already well established, and effective, before the introduction of the CSTs. The Intermediate Treatment Teams had successfully intervened in the justice system with the admirable result that the level of custodial sentencing of juveniles in the County was one of the lowest in the country.

There was an intention to extend the interventionist role of the IT Teams in the juvenile justice system to the care system.

Our understanding is that this [the Community Resources Team, a forerunner of the CSTs] is effectively an extension of Intermediate Treatment which provides an enhanced 'gatekeeper' role, the intention being to keep children out of care if at all possible. (Arthur Andersen and Co., 1985)

This reference is from a report for the Audit Commission, which was completed just before the reorganisation of children's services. This notion of 'care' as something to be avoided at all costs has been criticised in recent research (see for example Packman, 1986), and is addressed by the Children Act 1989. Care is not a unitary concept; children enter care for many different reasons and most stay only a short time. It can be argued that prevention should focus on the maintenance of children's living situations and relationships rather than narrowly on prevention of entry to care per se. No one would wish separation from parents to occur unnecessarily; however, the alternatives to admission to care can be very serious and, on some occasions, life-threatening.

How was the gatekeeping role of the CSTs implemented, how effective was it, and what was its relation to prevention? The main procedures for gatekeeping care resources were the Community Based Assessment of children (CBA) and divisional Children's Monitoring Groups. The CBA procedure was invoked when there was a strong likelihood of admission to care; or a severe threat of a disruption to a child's care placement; or when a substantial direct work input was requested from the CST.

The criteria for calling a CBA meeting do not in themselves reveal how 'prevention' should be interpreted. It was the experience of the researchers, based on observations and interviews, that no single notion of prevention dominated. At team level, there were those who held the view that care should be a last resort but others had a broader view and could see the value of planned admission to care when a wider set of circumstances applied. Fuller (1989) identified at least 11 different preventative goals which were applied in practice in one childcare project.

The initial CBA case conference in Warwickshire is chaired by the manager of the local CST and should be held within ten days of being requested. Emergency or urgent admissions to care are not held up by these procedures but, after such an admission, a case conference is required to be held within five days. The gatekeeping function of the CBA procedure was explicit in departmental documentation, but the CST's role in this process was only implicit in that the CST Manager chaired the first CBA case conference. An internal review in 1989 questioned whether the CBA process was being effective in its gatekeeping function. The number of CBAs was monitored over a period and was found to be fewer than the total number of admissions to care together with placement disruptions.

The other gatekeeping procedure involved divisional Children's Monitoring Groups. These met periodically, usually fortnightly, were chaired by the Fieldwork Manager, and had a membership made up of all Community Team Managers and the Manager of the CST. The brief of the Monitoring Groups included reviewing all new childcare referrals, and discussing whether cases should be allocated and what action, if any, should be taken. Observation of a number of meetings of different monitoring groups raised questions about their effectiveness in gatekeeping entry to care. First, many admissions were not anticipated and took place at very short notice. Most of these could not wait for the next meeting of the Monitoring Group. Second, the volume of cases to be discussed meant that most were given only limited consideration. And finally, in some meetings there appeared to be an unresolved tension about where the responsibility for decision making lay. Was it in the Community Teams, in discussion between the team manager and the social worker, or was it in the Monitoring Group?

When the CSTs were first established, the initial brief of the direct work teams covered the over-tens age group with the intention that eventually work would be undertaken with all those aged five and over; work with the under fives being the responsibility of Family Centres. The brief of the resources teams (fostering teams) covered the whole 0–18 age range from the time the CSTs were established. The reason for initially restricting direct work to the over-tens was a recognition that this would be the age group with which most of the workers in post would be familiar. Most of the workers came from the Intermediate Treatment Teams or from the Children's Centres. One CST did in fact work with the over-fives from the time it was established. The remaining

CSTs began to take referrals for work with younger children during the course of the research, as staff turnover and some training broadened the base of skills and experience. An earlier quotation identified two main aims for CST direct work. In practice two further aims were identified. The first was to prevent the breakdown of the placements of children and young people already in care. The second was to minimise the length of time children and young people spent in care.

Referrals for direct work were made by a variety of routes.

- Each CST had a referral form which Community Teams could complete and submit. The decision to make a referral was sometimes made at a Community Based Assessment (CBA) meeting.
- Referrals could be made by other agencies, such as the Education Department. As we saw in the case of Becky Johnson, an Education Department referral could lead to substantial CST involvement in cases not allocated to a Community Team social worker. Other education referrals might be made for a place in the education unit which some, but not all, of the CSTs operated.
- Juvenile justice referrals were handled separately and usually came from different sources.

The decision as to whether referrals to the CST for direct work should be allocated was based on the degree of concern about the child or young person's living situation. High risk situations and possible CST responses are described in the typical examples below:

- A young person appearing in court where a remand to custody was a possibility. If the CST could not prevent the case from coming to court by intervention at an earlier stage, it could offer an 'alternative to custody' package, which may include accommodation for the young person and possibly a package of day time support. Clearly this is very much in tune with the philosophy of the Children Act 1989.
- Where there was the possibility of a child being admitted to care because of the risk of family breakdown, the CST might offer assessment services or other work to complement the input by the Community Team case worker. Such services might also be offered to prevent the breakdown of a child's placement in care.
- If the referral was made after a child was admitted to care, the CST might again offer assessment work or other time-limited, task-centred work or services to enable rehabilitation to take place.
- An Education Department referral might be made after a child was excluded from school. Some CSTs had Education Units so that a child's education could be continued while other work was undertaken.

Some idea of the range of services offered by the CST Direct Work Teams can be gathered from the examples above, but there were other direct work services which at least some of the CSTs offered. These included:

- individual and group-based assessment programmes;

- task-centred work, for example, leaving care groups, grief counselling, individual work with abused children;
- intensive day care packages to prevent family or placement breakdown. Such involvements required heavy commitments of time and usually made use of sessional staff;
- befriending schemes for which sessional workers were recruited;
- sessional workers and full-time staff ran activity groups during some school holidays. Places on these schemes were offered to children living in fragile domestic situations;
- community development and community linking, especially with voluntary sector youth projects.

Although in essence the five CSTs provided broadly similar direct work services, there were some differences which were based on local circumstances and history. For instance, some CSTs inherited well-established holiday programmes and community development schemes from the Intermediate Treatment Teams which were incorporated into the CSTs at the time of reorganisation. Some CSTs acquired education units, others did not, and the brief of the units changed according to local circumstances, including the availability of other local educational resources. In some CSTs there was a much greater emphasis on group work approaches than in others. To some extent these differences were based on the inherited 'styles' of the IT Teams but those styles themselves reflected the widely differing geography of the County. As we saw in Angela Collin's case, in the more rural areas accessibility was a serious practical obstacle to the organisation of regular groups.

During the three-year period following the establishment of the CSTs, there were changes in the direct work services offered:

- One CST stopped offering group work altogether; a pragmatic decision based largely on problems created by the geography of the division.
- All of the CSTs were forced to prioritise their work because of the number of referrals. Prioritisation was based on the need to focus on the main aims set for the CSTs when they were created. The effect was that arguably more marginal activities were cut or given fewer resources. These activities included much of the community development work and the holiday activity groups.
- Educational provision made by the CSTs became more clearly targeted on young people near to school leaving age. In some cases education provision reduced when demand for places fell as a result of the Education Department decisions to introduce additional day placements in separate units for children with special educational needs.

In the rest of this section we will examine:

- the nature of the referrals made to the CST direct work teams;
- the type of direct work provided; and
- an assessment, based on responses from Community Team social workers, of the value of the direct work provided.

Who was referred to the CST?

During the period of our monitoring, the age group for whom the CSTs provided direct work services was extended to include the five to ten-year-olds. This extension was implemented at different times across the County, but the overall effect was that fewer of the children in the study who were aged ten or under were referred for direct work (14 per cent compared with nearly 50 per cent of those over ten). Looking at the over tens only, we found that those aged 14 or over were referred for direct work much more frequently than the 11 to 13-year-olds. In fact, more than half of these older children in our cohort were referred.

There were also significant differences in referral rates for the various groups in our sample. Fewest referrals were from the long-term in care group, that is those who had been in care for at least a year – only a quarter of these children were referred. The new admissions group had the highest referral rate at 54 per cent, which was significantly different from the other two groups.

The finding that fewest referrals were for the long-term in care group and the most for the new admissions is not a surprise. Research has repeatedly identified social work input as being at its most intense around the time of admission. However, for children who linger in care, social work input rapidly falls off and children can tend to drift. (*See*, for example, Rowe's summary of recent research findings in DHSS, 1985.)

Within Warwickshire, the low level of input to the long-term in care group is in line with the criteria identified earlier. Unless a placement was at risk of breaking down, a referral for direct work would not be expected. Exceptions to this included referrals for older children to leaving care groups. The third of our survey categories, the not admitted group, also had a significantly lower referral rate (just over 30 per cent) than the new admissions. This is despite the fact that this group had problems which were often as severe as the families whose children *were* admitted to care.

How are we to understand this difference in referral rates? The Manager of one CST identified two linked issues which also emerged as the key factors in other parts of the County:

We have problems in getting referrals until there's a crisis or until a CBA is called. But we [the CST] could not have taken on preventative work, non-crisis work, because we don't have the space.

We will see later that in a large majority of the cases in our study, Community Team social workers identified a 'crisis' as one of the conditions which applied in the cases which they referred for CST direct work. However, such a response was less of a procedural matter and more based on experience of the types of referrals to the CSTs for direct work which were and were not accepted. That is, the common perception was that referrals, for preventative work for example, would be less likely to be accepted for direct work input. This finding must put a question mark over the CST's role in the preventative strategy, which aimed to reduce admissions to care – one of the explicit aims for the CSTs when they were established.

The CBA system itself and the divisional Children's Monitoring Groups were the mechanisms by which gatekeeping of care was to be carried out. The success of these structures must be questioned in the light of the trends identified in Chapter 3, which showed that the proportion of children aged 18 or under in care in Warwickshire has remained steady, whereas the average figure for other authorities has declined markedly.

The process of referral was, of course, not just based on expectations that the service was more or less crisis-oriented. Community Team social workers would have seen the CST direct work teams as particularly experienced in working with adolescents presenting behavioural problems. This view would have been based on the history of the CSTs, with a large part of their staff drawn, first, from the old IT (Intermediate Treatment) teams, whose work would have been with exactly this group of children, and, in the second instance from the Children's Centres, whose staff would also have been most experienced in working with adolescents whose behaviour is often euphemistically called challenging. The Community Teams would also have based their referrals on past experience and we can, therefore, assume that they most valued the CSTs for work with adolescents and on behavioural issues.

These observations hold true for the period of our research, but we were aware that attitudes and expectations changed as new staff with different skills were appointed to the CSTs, and as existing staff grew more skilled and experienced in different ways of working and in work with different groups. If we repeated the survey of referrals now, we would expect a different, broader-based picture of CST direct work involvements to emerge, although we would still anticipate the majority of the work to be crisis-oriented.

Nearly 130 of our survey children were *not* referred for CST direct work services and we asked their case workers why not. We have excluded the children who were aged 10 or under who, for most of the period of the research, were not eligible for direct work services.

- In nearly half the cases the response was that the CST did not offer the services or skills which were required. These cases were largely children in long-term care who, presumably, were in stable placements; and children in the poor care group. Typically, children in this latter group had short stays in care as a result of their parent's temporary indisposition.
- One in seven were not referred because 'other professionals were involved'. These included the NSPCC Child Protection Team which had a role with children on the child protection register, and Education Department staff, including educational social workers and educational psychologists.
- Other explanations for non-referral included one in ten cases where the child or the family refused any CST involvement; and a small proportion of cases (four per cent only) where co-working took place within the Community Team – that is, where more than one social worker from the Team was involved in the case.

Requests for direct work

Referrals were made to the CSTs for a variety of different types of work to be undertaken. For some children referrals were made for more than one service. In fact for one in five children, three different services were requested, either at the same time or on separate occasions. Table 10.1 summarises the types of request which were made.

Table 10.1 Requests for CST direct work

Direct work services	Request	
	No.	(%)
Co-working with family or child (i.e. CST and Community Team social workers working jointly)	30	(23)
Individual work with child – assessment	30	(23)
Individual work with child – other	28	(22)
Group work with child – assessment	11	(8)
Group work with child – other	14	(11)
Work with family unit	7	(5)
Other work	10	(8)
Total	130	(100)

We examined these referrals in detail to see if any particular characteristics were associated with requests for particular services.

- Long-term in care cases were not referred for assessment. Slightly more of the not admitted group were referred for assessment compared with the new admissions.
- Group work of all kinds was strongly associated with the 14+ age group.
- Group work with the aim of assessment was mainly carried out with children referred or admitted to care for behavioural reasons.
- Where the referral was for work with the child and family, younger children and those not admitted to care were the most significant groups.

In response to two-thirds of these referrals the CST were said, encouragingly, to have offered the service 'in full'. For nearly a quarter, a partial provision was offered, but for one in ten cases the CST were unable to offer anything at all. There were problems in meeting requests for particular services:

- A disproportionate number of requests for assessment groups went unmet. From discussions with CST staff it was clear that the main problem was with getting enough referrals at the same time to create a viable group. This was especially difficult in smaller divisions and, as already noted, the CST in one of the smaller, but geographically disparate, divisions ceased offering group work options during the time the research was being carried out.
- One third of requests for work with family groups were not met. The reasons for this are unclear.

- Significantly, more than twice as many of the requests involving children not admitted to care were unmet compared with those in care. This supports our earlier contention that provision was to some extent rationed by giving priority to cases in crisis.

Direct work provided

Nearly nine out of ten requests resulted in some direct work input from the CST and Table 10.2 details the types of work which were carried out.

Table 10.2 Direct work provided by the CSTs

Service provided	No.	(%)
Co-working with family or child	27	(24)
Individual work with child – assessment	21	(19)
Individual work with child – other	28	(25)
Group work with child – assessment	7	(6)
Group work with child – other	9	(8)
Work with family unit	5	(4)
Other	15	(13)
Total	112	(100)

If we compare this table with the one detailing requests (*see* Table 10.1), we see that individual assessment and group work were the services where requests were least well met. Assessment usually requires involvement at short notice which may not have been possible. The prerequisite of group work is, as we have seen, enough children to make a group. However, overall, the types of service provided were broadly in line with those which were requested, with co-working and individual work accounting for over two-thirds of the work provided.

To provide some insight into what these categories actually entail, let us return to our case studies. Angela Collins was referred to the local CST at the time she was first referred to the Department and, within two weeks, she was involved in what was called a Girls' Assessment Group. In this, a variety of group work approaches were used to try to make an assessment of Angela's situation, both by observing her behaviour within the group, and by giving her the opportunity to talk to social work staff who were less intensively involved in the case and whom she was meeting in an informal setting. Angela was also involved in other groups during school holidays. These groups were mainly activity-based and Angela's involvement was intended to provide her foster carers with a break, as much as to provide a service to Angela directly. Other CSTs ran groups such as these during the holiday periods and the main criterion for referral was that the child's living situation – either with parents or substitute carers – was perceived to be in some jeopardy.

Another group which was common was one for young people in care, who were approaching the age at which they would no longer be the legal responsibility of the local authority. These leaving care groups focused on the young person's planned move to more independent living.

Becky Johnson had also been involved in groups run by the CST including an In care group – a support and activity group for children in care. But her contact with the CST had mainly been on an individual basis. The initial referral to the Department by Becky's school had been picked up by the CST. This initial involvement aimed to assess the reasons for her truanting and disruption in school through interviews with Becky, her mother and school staff. This assessment led to a package of work with Becky, which concentrated on her relationship with her mother and on her school attendance. This work was successful to the extent that the CST felt able to withdraw. Later on, after the relationship between Becky and her mother deteriorated and the case was allocated in the Community Team, the CST again became involved. The fact that Becky knew the CST social worker was valuable, and he and the Community Team social worker decided to divide the work to take account of this. The Community Team social worker described her relationship with the CST social worker as 'co-working'. In Becky's case one advantage, in addition to having a second worker in a complementary role, was the fact that the social worker from the CST provided a point of continuity during a period when three different social workers in the Community Team had been responsible for the case at different times.

In Chris Taylor's case we can find examples both of assessment work and of co-working. The advantages of this extra input were described earlier, but one of the issues which this example raised was whether the CST provided additional hours of social work at times when this was required or whether the services which they offered were of a different kind, possibly involving more specialised skills than were available within the Community Team. Chris's social worker held the view that an attempt to undertake 'family therapy' was not successful, because neither she nor the CST social worker were sufficiently skilled or experienced in such work; but, as we will see later on, there were also cases where the CST worker was identified as having a complementary set of skills.

In most cases where the CST offered a service to the Community Team social worker, it is heartening to observe that there was little or no delay between the time when the service was needed and when it was provided. In over seven out of ten referrals there was no delay at all, and in eight out of ten there was no wait or one of less than two weeks. In only six per cent of referrals was there a delay of more than a month, but this figure was higher when the referral was for group work – for reasons we identified earlier – and for children in the long-term in care group. Was this because referrals for this group were less crisis-oriented?

Input by the CST Direct Work Teams was, in a large proportion of cases, unexpectedly both substantial and long-term. Based on the estimates of Community Team social workers, in over half of the cases in which they were involved, CST direct work amounted to four hours or more a week. In 60 per cent of cases this involvement lasted for more than two months and in over 40 per cent it continued beyond six months. Even though the CSTs were comparatively generously staffed, these long-term involvements in a substantial proportion of cases would have been one factor accounting for the perceived shortage of direct work services and the consequent concentration on crisis work at the expense of preventative and other work.

There were also clear patterns of involvement with different groups and with different types of case:

- Where the reason for referral or admission was abuse or neglect, CST involvement tended to be more substantial and longer term. In two-thirds of cases the direct work input was for more than four hours a week and lasted more than six months.
- Least substantial involvement was with the long-term in care group. In nearly a half of these cases involvement lasted for less than four weeks, and in two-thirds of cases was for two hours or less per week. Even work with our not admitted to care survey group, where the referral was accepted, was longer term and for more hours per week.

Assessment of CST direct work services

In a series of questions we asked Community Team social workers to evaluate direct work input in relation to the cases in our survey of 215 Warwickshire children. The questions focused on three areas – referrals and coordination of provision, the nature of the direct work input and its perceived impact.

Referrals and coordination of provision

We asked a number of questions about the formal procedures for making referrals for direct work input. These questions were tightly worded and did not touch on the issue, discussed earlier, about which types of cases would be referred and under what circumstances. Overall, in response to our questions, there was a large measure of satisfaction with the referral procedures and the CST's responses to referrals. Fewer than a quarter of social workers agreed with a statement which suggested that the procedures were too slow or too bureaucratic. This is made more significant because, in six out of ten cases, the referral to the CST was made in a crisis when a rapid response was required. Each of our case studies gives examples of these crises, which often involved an actual or imminent breakdown in a young person's living situation.

We anticipated that there may be problems with the coordination of the work between the Community Team and CST social workers. The teams are both geographically and managerially separate but a system was introduced at the same time as the CSTs whereby, for individual cases, both social workers were supervised by one manager – either from the CST or from the Community Team. Case accountability remained with the Community Team social workers and so we asked them about feedback from the CST on their input. In over 80 per cent of cases detailed feedback was provided and it is interesting to note that in fewer than one in ten cases did Community Team social workers express dissatisfaction with the feedback from the CST.

The nature of CST direct work

There are a number of ways in which a specialist children's team could work. They could take over particular cases on a short-term or long-term basis; they could provide additional social work time for a fixed period in response to particular needs; or they could provide a range of skills and services which complemented those of the Community Team case worker.

In only a quarter of cases did Community Team social workers agree that they had spent less time on the case because the CST was involved. In a large majority of cases the CST involvement meant that more time in total was being spent on the case and, as we saw earlier, this often amounted to a substantial input of four or more hours a week on average.

There are obvious advantages in having additional social work resources outside Community Teams, which can be drawn on when necessary. Social workers in the Community Teams operate with more or less full case loads and there is a limit to the extent to which work on other cases can be dropped when a new case is allocated or a crisis develops in an existing case. Social workers in the Direct Work Teams of the CSTs do not 'hold' cases but take on *time-limited pieces* of work. This organisation means that response to referrals from Community Teams can be quite rapid. However, CST social workers were not just seen as additional hours at times of crisis; in over eight out of ten cases, Community Team social workers identified the CST worker as bringing additional skills or experience to the case, and these skills were valued. These findings are obviously encouraging.

The impact of CST direct work services

How valuable did the case workers assess the CST direct work input to be? Two separate questions gave similar answers. In six out of ten cases, Community Team social workers thought that objectives for the CST involvement had been achieved and that the involvement had resulted in better outcomes. In a few cases respondents were undecided or identified the direct work as having a neutral effect, which left about 15 per cent or so of cases where objectives were not achieved or the outcome was not enhanced. (Angela Collins' involvement in the girls' assessment group run by the CST would be an example which fell into this unsuccessful category.) Nonetheless, these findings overall are positive.

Summary

- More than half of the staff in each of the CSTs was involved in providing direct work services for children and families.
- The main aims of the CSTs' direct work were to reduce the need to receive children into care; to diminish the level of custodial sentencing of young people; and to prevent care placements from breaking down.
- Success in the juvenile justice field, which had been achieved prior to the setting up of the CSTs, was maintained. The County had one of the lowest levels of custodial sentencing for juveniles in the country.

- The effectiveness of the CSTs in reducing the need for admission to care was questionable. Admission rates did not decline, unlike the average for all English authorities. Much of the CSTs' direct work involvement was typified as crisis-oriented rather than preventative.
- Young people aged 14 and over were significantly more likely to be referred for direct work services. Children newly admitted to care were the most frequently referred group (54 per cent of cases); fewer children not in care were referred (32 per cent); and children in long-term care were referred least often (one quarter of cases). These referral rates were associated with the crisis-oriented nature of referrals to the Direct Work Teams.
- Nearly half of the referrals were for individual work with the child. A further quarter were for co-working (CST and Community Team workers together). Fewer than one in five referrals were for group work. The purpose of nearly a third of referrals was said to be assessment.
- In a large proportion of cases the CST provided the services requested with little delay.
- In a surprising number of cases the CST input was both substantial and long-term. In over half the cases the CST social worker was involved for more than four hours per week on average. Over 60 per cent of involvements lasted for more than two months; over 40 per cent went on beyond *six* months.
- In most cases, CST input was additional to, rather than a replacement for, Community Team input. Community Team social workers also valued the input from CST social workers for the additional skills and experience which they brought to the case. This positive view is reinforced by the fact that, in nearly two-thirds of cases the CST direct work involvement was identified, by the case worker, as leading to more successful outcomes.

196

11. The use of residential care

After the closure of its residential children's centres, Warwickshire Social Services Department was caricatured as the authority which did not make use of residential provision for children in care. However, the County does use residential placements for a small, but not insignificant, minority of children and young people.

As a consequence of this limited use of the residential option, very few cases involving residential placements were identified in the sample for our study. However, it seemed important to identify in detail exactly what kinds of residential provisions Warwickshire Social Services Department does use when residential placements are made and in what circumstances. We, therefore, decided to undertake a separate study of *all* residential placements made by the Department during a two and a half year period after the closure of the last of the Children's Centres. We examined files and also carried out brief interviews with the responsible case workers, although sometimes this was not possible because they had moved on to other posts. It is important to recognise that in this section we are discussing only residential placements made by Warwickshire Social Services Department. Placements in residential schools, for children *not* in care but having special educational needs, were also initiated by the Education Department but this group is not the concern here. This issue is discussed in Chapter 12.

We will begin this section by describing the formal departmental procedures which govern the making of residential placements, moving on to describe the children who went to residential placements; the types of placements which were made, and how long they lasted. Finally, we will consider social workers' assessments of the effectiveness of these residential placements.

Policies and procedures

Warwickshire Social Services Department's policy for the use of residential care is set down clearly in departmental documentation.

It is the policy of the Department to give children in care the right to family life by, whenever possible, placing them with foster parents rather than into residential care. (Warwickshire Social Services Department, 1987a)

For those children in care, living with a substitute family is infinitely preferable to being placed in residential care. For the very small number of children who need residential care, a special environment with a highly qualified staff group is essential. (Warwickshire Social Services Department, 1989)

It is the policy of the Department to use the four places retained at the National Children's Home (NCH) for those children whose needs cannot be met through other care resources or where other care resources were unavailable. (Warwickshire Social Services Department, 1987b)

The procedures for approval of residential placements with the NCH are set out separately:

A request for placement approval should be made by the Children's Services Team (CST) Manager ideally in writing but, in cases of emergency, by telephone to the Director... Placements at [NCH] should not extend beyond three months in duration. In the event of a placement being likely to extend beyond that period, authorisation should be sought from the Divisional Director from whose division the child originates. (Ibid.)

Later, we shall see what these procedures entailed but, in short, placements with the NCH which lasted more than the three months, or longer term placements in other establishments, were only approved on the basis of very detailed written submissions to the Director of Social Services.

These procedures and policies did not apply to some children in care who were placed residentially. These were children who were assessed under the provisions of the Education Act, 1981 as in need of special education, and for whom residential school placements were being considered. Recommendations for education in residential schools were made by Area Officers in written submissions to the responsible Assistant Education Officer. His decision was made after consultation with educational psychologists, educational social workers and the Social Services Department.

We were unable to identify exactly how decisions were made as to whether a child would best be served by following Social Services Department or Education Department assessments and procedures. From the information gathered from case files and from interviews, we developed the impression that one crucial factor was the *location* of an event or series of events which precipitated action by one department or the other. For example, a decision by a school to exclude a particular child would almost certainly be followed by a formal assessment of that child's special educational needs by the Education Department. However, that same child, while having problems at school, may also have difficulties at home or outside school, which might lead to involvement by the Social Services Department. If this child's relationship with his or her parents broke down to the extent that she or he could no longer live at home, then the Social Services Department might admit the child to care and the Community Based Assessment procedure would be brought into action.

Who was placed residentially?

As a completely separate exercise from our cohort study, therefore, we monitored all the residential placements made for children in care during a two and a half year period. A total of 42 children in care each had at least one residential placement but, as we will see, some had more than one. Some readers may feel this sounds rather a lot – perhaps 15 young people a year – but it is much lower than is usually discovered in local authorities. This number included 17 who were already in care but placed in the community prior to the start of the monitoring, and who were later placed in residential care or residential education. A small proportion of the 42 were also included in our cohort study. At any one time, as we have seen, the proportion of children in care who were placed residentially was about six per cent, that is some 33 or so young people.

Table 11.1 shows an analysis of the type of the first residential placements by age group. The majority of the residential schools in this survey were ones which provided for children whose needs, in educational terms, would be described as emotional and behavioural difficulties (EBD). Some of the residential school placements were for 52 weeks in the year. Others were term-time only and the Social Services Department made other arrangements (such as placement with foster carers) during the school holidays.

Table 11.1 First residential placements by age group

Age group	Residential care establishment(%)	Residential school (%)	Total (%)
8–10	0 (0)	2 (12)	2 (5)
11–13	5 (19)	7 (44)	12 (29)
14–15	11 (42)	6 (38)	17 (40)
16+	10 (38)	1 (6)	11 (26)
Total	26 (100)	16 (100)	42 (100)

Only two children were aged ten or under when they were placed and both went to residential special schools. Seven out of ten were young people aged 14 or over when they first went into a residential placement. This finding, that the majority of children in residential placements were adolescents, is not peculiar to Warwickshire. In Berridge's study (1985) nearly four out of five children were aged over ten and the figure in Rowe's study (1989) was similar.

The children who were placed in residential schools by Warwickshire were on average (mean) considerably younger, at 12 ½ years, than the group who went into residential care placements – their average age was nearly 15 years. One reason that schools were chosen for younger children was that with three, four or more years before they reached school leaving age, education was a more significant factor in the list of social work priorities. One way for these children to receive an education is for them to be placed in a school rather than a care establishment, where separate arrangements would have to be made for their education. Children aged 15 or so were nearer to the end of their compulsory education and, for them, education was seen as less of a priority when a placement was made. Our interviews with social workers confirmed that their considerations followed these lines. It will be interesting to observe whether residential special schools are used more routinely in future, in this way, by social workers. Indeed, other research currently in progress at the National Children's Bureau is examining whether this is the case.

Four out of every five of the young people placed residentially in this two and a half year period were male. There was no difference in the types of placements made for boys and girls but, compared with the girls, the boys tended to have fewer non-residential placements before their first residential placement. The girls were, on average, younger than the boys when they were first placed residentially (13 years compared with over 14). Department of Health figures and other research have also identified residential placements as more commonly made for boys than for girls, but not to the extent of the difference in Warwickshire. About six out of ten residential placements made for boys is the consistent result from these sources; fewer than the eight out of 10 in the County. When we come to examine the groups for whom residential care was used in the County and we compare this with other findings, we will be able to identify some of the reasons for this difference between the sexes.

The 'main' legal status of the 42 children placed residentially is shown in Table 11.2. By main legal status we mean that which applied for most of their time in care. Place of Safety Orders and Interim Care Orders are ignored in favour of more permanently applicable legal orders.

Table 11.2 Legal status and sex

	Male No.(%)	Female No.(%)	Total No.(%)
Voluntary care	11 (32)	2 (25)	13 (31)
Care orders	17 (50)	6 (75)	23 (55)
Remands to care	6 (18)	0 (0)	6 (14)
Total	34 (100)	8 (100)	42 (100)

There were just six remands to care and all of these were made for young men. If we exclude these remands then we find that considerably more boys than girls were in voluntary care rather than on care orders. The reason for this difference is not clear, but it could be a statistical quirk given the small number of girls in this residential population.

Among the 42 children in this sub-study there were three pairs of siblings – a lower figure than perhaps one might expect. Other studies (for example Berridge, 1985) have identified residential care as being used to keep siblings together. The use of residential placements was strongly associated with long periods in care. The average (mean) length of time spent in care prior to residential placements was nearly four years, and this figure included the 15 children who were already in care at the beginning of our monitoring. A number of these children had been in care for many years and were placed residentially after long-term community placements had broken down.

If we look at those children admitted to care during our monitoring period, we find that they had had between nought and seven placements before their first residential experience (average 2.4 placements). Most had been in care about three months before a residential placement was made, although some had been in care for over a year. Rather alarmingly, they had therefore moved rapidly between placements.

The total number of placements made for the children and young people in this part of the study, excluding those first admitted to care before August 1986 (when the last of the Children's Centres was closed), ranged from one to ten. The average number of placements per child was just over four, excluding short-term respite and holiday placements. Since three-quarters of these children were still in care at the end of the monitoring period, further placements and, therefore, higher total and average figures could be anticipated. Again, these are worrying statistics and demonstrate a high rate of instability for this particularly problematic small core of children.

Where were residential placements made?

Four children went straight into residential placements on admission; three into special schools and one into a secure unit following a remand to care by a court. Table 11.3 gives details of the types of residential placements which were made for the 42 children and young people in this part of the study. The first column lists their initial placements and the second any subsequent residential placements.

Table 11.3 Types of residential placement

Type of placement	First residential placement No.(%)	Subsequent placement No.(%)	Total placements No.(%)
Residential special school	19 (45)	5 (33)	24 (42)
National Children's Home	17 (40)	5 (33)	22 (39)
Secure unit	2 (5)	3 (20)	5 (9)
Other residential care	4 (10)	2 (13)	6 (11)
Total	42 (100)	15 (100)	57 (100)

School placements accounted for more than four out of ten of all the residential placements and four-fifths of these were the child's first residential placement. Those remaining were made after the young person had spent some time placed with the NCH. In most of these cases the first placement was used as a stop-gap, while the need for longer-term residential care was assessed and a placement was found.

The extent to which residential schools are used by social services departments to meet the social and emotional needs of children, rather than their educational needs, is a factor which has emerged during this research. However, this is an issue which has not been examined by other research and comparative data are not available. The majority (nearly three-quarters) of first placements in residential care establishments – as compared with schools – were with the National Children's Home which has an agreement with Warwickshire to provide four reserved beds. A much larger proportion of second residential care placements (50 per cent) were in establishments other than the NCH.

It is important to emphasise – as Table 11.3 confirms – that the policy in Warwickshire is *not* that residential should never be used. Rather the County feels that it should not run its own residential facilities. Furthermore, for the very small number of particularly problematic young people, specialist placements are purchased from elsewhere. Clearly, then, not every local authority or agency could emulate Warwickshire as there would be no one to provide specialist residential care.

We have already seen that the young people placed in residential schools were younger than those who went to residential care establishments. There were two further differences in the ways in which the two types of provision were used. First, children tended to have fewer placements on average before going to residential schools – fewer than three compared with nearly four for the placements in care establishments. Why this should have been so is not clear. One possibility might have been the involvement of the Education Department in the decision making procedures which applied to some of the children. The age of the children may also have been influential; there may have been a desire on the part of social workers to achieve at least a semi-permanent arrangement for these younger children once it was clear that a speedy return home was unlikely. A residential school would, to some extent, meet these requirements. Older children have the prospect of a shorter time in care even without returning home, and social workers would more often be looking towards a move to more independent living.

This takes us on to the second major difference in the ways in which the types of residential placements were used. NCH placements, on average, lasted for only two and a half months – the range was from two days to 11 months. Fewer than half of the school placements had ended when we ceased monitoring, but those which had, had lasted for nearly a year. Those continuing had already lasted for nearly one and a half years on average.

Overall, then, the picture we have is of residential care used for older children, who had had a considerable number of previous placements and who tended to stay in these residential settings for a comparatively short period – months not years. Residential schools were used sooner rather than later and for younger children who have much longer stays in these establishments. It is interesting to observe that the policies pursued in this respect by two departments within the same local authority appear inconsistent, a point we return to later.

Social workers' attitudes

In our interviews with the social workers responsible for these cases, we sought to identify why particular decisions were made, how departmental procedures were perceived, and how, in the workers' judgements, the policies affected the quality of care the children and young people received. From these interviews it was possible to identify some typical responses and below we address each of these issues in turn using quotations from the interviews. (In all quotations, names have been changed and identities disguised.)

Why was a residential placement made?

The commonest experience was of a series of foster placements which had been difficult and distressing experiences for all concerned and which may have ended in breakdown. In these cases the child was behaving in ways which were unmanageable by, or unacceptable to, the foster carers. In some of the cases a placement in a family setting was seen as inappropriate for the child. For example:

Dean was 15. His parents had always been too rigid and this ended with a violent family breakdown... The foster parents [three different sets] couldn't cope with his violent behaviour. [The placements] just broke down.

Eddie developed close relationships with his foster mothers but then [the relationships] broke down because he compared them with his natural mother. He couldn't come to terms with the nature of his mother's character. We tried to work on this issue but it failed while he was in the foster placements.

There were a number of cases where a part of the behaviour pattern was involvement in offending and the decision to make a residential placement was made, at least in part, as a way of placing him in a more controlled environment away from his peers:

After the first remand [to care] the offending continued. The contract foster parents asked for him to leave. We looked for alternative foster placements but none was available which we thought was suitable. We placed him in a secure unit on a short-term basis until he appeared in court.

In a small number of cases, a residential placement seems to have been the factor which enabled long-term care placements to survive:

After several years Gordon's behavioural problems got worse and the [foster] placement was on the verge of breaking down. There were problems at school too. We [the Social Services and Education Departments] agreed that residential school would address both the care and the educational issues... Now [the foster carers] find Gordon easily manageable at weekends and in the holidays.

The decision making process

Two quite distinct procedures applied to the making of residential placements. The first applied when the Social Services Department was wholly responsible for making decisions and meeting the costs. The second was used when the Education Department was the main instigator in the process, that is, had produced a statement of special educational needs and was considering a residential school placement.

Where the Social Services Department was the key department, the procedures followed were those described at the beginning of this section – that is, application was via the CST manager and then the Director or his nominee, but there were differences between applications for short-term and long-term placements. One team manager commented:

The CBA [Community Based Assessment] recommended a residential placement and the CST manager contacted [the Deputy Director] and got approval over the phone for a short-term placement. Reports followed identifying long-term options. It took two to three months to produce these and to get approval [for a longer-term residential placement]. These placed very heavy demands on the social worker.

There were cases where approval was not given for longer term residential placements. Unfortunately, we are unable to quantify how many there were. Where there was no Education Department involvement, the National Children's Home was, in most cases, the first and only available option.

There appeared to be three different sets of circumstances in which children were placed in residential schools:

- when the Social Services Department identified a school as the best long-term residential option with little or no Education Department involvement;
- when the child was assessed by the Education Department as having special educational needs and was then placed in a residential school;
- when there were discussions between the two departments about how best to meet a particular child's needs. Such discussions would usually involve negotiations over sharing the costs of a school placement.

Where there were no residential schooling costs falling on Social Services Department budgets, the procedures described earlier were not implemented. The approval of senior managements was not required.

Attitudes towards in-County children's centres

We asked if residential children's centres would have been used for these children and young people in this study if the facilities had continued to be available. We also asked whether children's centres would have been a better option for these children. Significantly, for about four in five children, social workers could see no advantages in having local children's centres. The exceptions were as follows.

Hugh was a boy of 13 who had been in a series of foster placements all of which had broken down because, the social worker felt, deep and unresolved issues existed between him and his mother:

A children's centre might have provided space for us to address Hugh's needs at an earlier stage rather than spending all our time arranging one placement after another.

For a few children, the distance to available residential facilities was a problem:

A local children's centre would have been a better option. The distance to the NCH was a real problem but it was the only option… The problems of travelling to [a later, more distant residential care placement] were even worse.

For other young people, particularly those involved in offending, social workers felt that a local placement would probably have resulted in a pattern of continued offending. For them, removal from their immediate environment, at least for a short period, was the priority.

But, for the majority of children, it is important to note that local children's centres were seen as inappropriate placements. For these children, specialist and sometimes long-term residential care was seen to be the requirement. Most of the staff who had worked in the department prior to the closure of the children's centres were clear that such specialist care was not available in the centres before they were closed, and most doubted whether they could have been reorganised to provide a service of this type:

If it was available, a children's centre would have been used but would almost certainly have failed because of Ian's behaviour and the effect he would have had on younger children... The National Children's Home is succeeding because it is different from the old style children's centre.

The success or failure of residential placements

We saw above that the small number of children who had residential placements were mostly very difficult to care for and many were emotionally quite damaged. What did their residential placements achieve? The comments below are based on our interviews with social workers. We will examine in turn:

- placements made following a remand to care or as an alternative to custody;
- placements in the four reserved beds with the National Children's Home;
- placements in other residential care establishments;
- placements in residential schools.

For eight young people, residential placements (nine in all) were made as a result of being remanded to care by the courts. Another four youngsters had eight placements between them, which were described by social work staff as a part of alternative to custody packages. By and large, the aim of the remands to care was to provide 'holding' placements for the young people prior to a court appearance. The placements were made mainly in the reserved NCH beds; one was in an Observation Assessment (O & A) Centre and two were in secure units. All of these placements were successful to the extent that the young people remained in care until their court appearance rather than being remanded to custodial placements.

The other placements, those which were described as a part of alternative to custody packages, were felt by social workers to have met with mixed success. Two of the four young people's moves were successful since their offending appeared to cease. However, the two others were unsatisfactory and the young people were transferred to secure units.

The next group of placements we will consider are those made with the National Children's Home in the four spaces reserved by Warwickshire. The NCH unit in which children from the County are placed is a small, purpose-built facility. Children placed there have their own rooms, and these and the communal rooms are pleasantly and comfortably furnished and decorated. This facility is in Sutton Coldfield, which is adjacent to the Warwickshire border but as much as an hour's drive from some parts of the County.

As we have seen, most of the non-educational residential placements were made with the NCH. Most were also of relatively short duration and were one-off placements. However, there were exceptions to this pattern of use.

- Several young people who were initially placed on a short-term basis had approval for the placements to be made long-term. One was our case study subject Chris Taylor, who stayed because an alternative placement could not be found. The other two placements were made long-term for geographical reasons. One young man was close to his father and was holding down a job locally. The other was from the nearest division to Sutton Coldfield and the regular contact with his family, which this made possible, was seen as important.
- Two children in residential schools had regular holiday placements with the NCH. In the views of the social workers, this was in their best interests but in both cases there was some disagreement with senior management about whether this was an appropriate use of the NCH reserved beds.

Together, these long-term placements and the regular holiday placements were a substantial commitment of a limited resource. There were times when six or more children were placed with the NCH but the problem was that only four places could be *guaranteed*. There were mixed feelings among placing social workers about the success of these NCH placements in meeting the needs of the children who were placed there on a shorter-term basis. The location of the establishment was one issue which was mentioned. For some children, mainly those involved in offending, removal from their immediate neighbourhood was seen as necessary; for others, the distance to the placement was problematic in terms of the continuity of the child's experience and of maintaining adequate social work input.

The other main issue which was mentioned, and about which there were different opinions, was the suitability of the regime, which appeared to suit some children but not others.

Eddie fitted in well ... there was no pressure on him [but] it was too far away.

It [the NCH] was really the only option but I didn't like that style of residential care [for Dean]... The boundaries weren't firm, it was too laid back.

It is possible to draw some conclusions about the provision made by the National Children's Home:

- For young people involved in offending it was usually an advantage to have a placement which was geographically distant, but for children in other circumstances the distances had only negative consequences.
- The regime – described as liberal, caring, 'laid back' – was felt by social workers to have suited some children but not all.
- Most placements were short-term and for these young people the main purpose of the placement was 'holding' not 'therapeutic'.

- A small number of young people spent longer periods placed at the NCH. Their placements had different aims which met with different degrees of success.

There were six placements made in residential care establishments (other than the NCH and not including schools) and the selection procedure for these placements was detailed, not least because this was required by the approval process. One consistent problem with these placements was their distance from the young people's homes. This was seen as acceptable in most cases if the main aim of finding a specialist resource, tailored to the child's needs, could be achieved. Each of these placements was made in small units which had clear philosophies and policies:

A specialist resource was what Dean needed at this time. They're into behaviour modification ... it works... They're committed, accepting but very firm.

Last summer a small, friendly residential environment would have helped ... for assessment. We had to use a contract foster placement because of the policy... A child like Julie needed the option of a residential placement... This is a 52-week one... The aim is for her to stay there until she's 16... It's enjoyable, she's already settled in and they've identified some of her problems. One of their aims will be to re-establish family links with her father and grandparents.

If we take long-term to mean placements which lasted for six months or more, then the majority of these (over 70 per cent) were in residential schools. Significantly, when these residential school placements were made as a result of Social Services Department procedures, they were not chosen primarily for their education input; their caring role was seen as equally, or even more, important. This is clearly a contentious issue. However, the impression from our interviews with the placing social workers was that the schools were, on the whole, less clear about their care philosophy than were the non-educational establishments.

The problem of how to find and choose a residential placement on the basis of very little first hand experience was another problem identified by a number of workers. The following are typical comments from social workers which address a number of issues including geographical location, care regimes, and the size of the schools:

The school was a joint choice [Education and Social Services Departments]. It's provided Eddie with structure and stability and they've done some individual work with him, but he's made only limited academic progress.

The Education Department recommended [the school]... It's worked out very well educationally and she's emotionally matured... It's a very stable and supportive placement.

It's not been very successful ... his behaviour and severe learning difficulties are still a problem. We've thought about changing schools but we need a balance between the need for a therapeutic community and regular contact with his [long-term] foster parents.

It was a bloody awful regime, too big. There was bullying... He refused to return, he was unhappy for all the time he was there.

It's a very good placement but they've had limited success in changing his behaviour. The distance is a real problem. What I'm very worried about is the future, when he's 16.

Summary

- The policy concerning the use of residential placements for children in care in Warwickshire together with the procedures surrounding the application of this policy ensure that very few children are placed residentially. Some children are placed in residential special schools after assessment by the Education Department.
- Forty-two residential placements were made in a two and a half year period. Although this may seem a lot – some 15 a year – it is far fewer than is found in other authorities. Forty per cent of residential placements were in schools. Three-quarters of the remainder were in reserved beds in a National Children's Home establishment.
- Most of the NCH placements were relatively short (less than three months was the average). Residential school placements lasted much longer (one and a half years on average).
- The average age of those placed in schools was 12^1/$_2$ and those placed in care establishments nearly 15 years.
- Eighty per cent of those placed were boys, which is a much higher proportion than in other authorities.
- Residential placements were strongly associated with long stays in care.
- Typically, the young people placed residentially had had several other non-residential placements, usually with foster carers, beforehand. Many of these earlier placements had broken down. Young people who were remanded to care were given residential placements much sooner after admission.
- The commonest experience leading to the use of a residential placement was a series of foster placements which had been unsuccessful or had even broken down. Many of these young people had unsatisfactory care experiences, involving rapid movements.
- Apart from school placements made following a decision by the Education Department, gatekeeping procedures for residential placements were very tight. Applications for longer term placements required detailed written submissions to be made to the Director.
- It is important to re-emphasise that Warwickshire's policy is *not* that there is no role for residential care; rather it feels that the County should not run its own residential facilities and specialist placements are best purchased from elsewhere. Clearly, not all authorities could operate with a policy such as this.
- In a few cases, an in-County children's centre place would have been preferred by a social worker but more often a more specialist provision was identified as needed. For most children the distance of the residential placement from their home was identified as a problem.

- Residential placements made after a remand to care were generally judged to have successfully achieved their aims.
- Short-term placements with the NCH were judged to have been suitable for some children but not others. For most, the distance was a problem. And the regime was felt to be appropriate for some but not all children.
- Overall, social workers were satisfied with other specialist, long-term care placements although distance was, in most cases, more problematic.
- There was less satisfaction with long-term placements made in residential schools. Some schools were seen as too big and there were doubts about the care regimes in others.

12. Special educational needs and the use of residential schools

From the outset, we were clear that a proper evaluation of the impact of Warwickshire's radical childcare policies should not be a narrow exercise. In particular, we were concerned that Social Services decisions might have broader implications beyond its own specific remit. One avenue that we explored in some detail, therefore, was the impact of the changes in Social Services policy on the Education Department. More specifically, we felt it important to examine whether the curtailment of Social Services residential care had led to increased demands for placements at residential schools funded by the Education Department in Warwickshire.

Indeed, throughout the 1980s, this was an issue of national concern. The numbers of pupils placed in residential special schools for children 'with emotional and behavioural difficulties' (termed before the 1981 Education Act 'maladjusted') rose markedly. It is unclear exactly why this happened. If one looks across the whole range of residential facilities for children – children's homes, community homes with education and custodial placements for young offenders – residential EBD schools would seem to be the only area where expansion occurred. This, therefore, is completely at odds with a broader move towards community care policies. The National Children's Bureau is engaged in other research which examines these issues in greater detail. It is focusing on the social and educational processes by which pupils are defined as having emotional and behavioural difficulties and being in need of a residential placement. The research is also examining the quality of education, and social and emotional care provided by a sample of schools.

We do not know, then, the reasons why this expansion in the use of residential EBD provision took place. Some have commented that this set of institutions is operating a parallel welfare system to that provided by Social Services care and accommodation. The Children Act 1989 should provide better integration than hitherto. However – and although we look to our detailed research to provide some of the answers – it would seem that the way in which children enter one system rather than the other is, to at least some degree, still a matter of chance. This will depend on where the child's problems are first highlighted. If the main concern is expressed initially within school, referral to educational psychologists may lead to a statementing process under the 1981 Educational Act. Some children may then end up at residential special schools.

Alternatively, if difficulties are first picked up by social workers at home or in the local neighbourhood, a different set of solutions may come into play. If separation from family is deemed necessary, placement with foster carers is likely or placement within some form of children's home. It is not evident that the overall system for dealing with children with problems is a rational one, and individual children with similar problems may receive different professional responses depending on, for example, where they live and who first takes action.

It has also been suggested that the Social Services care system and the residential EBD system are not unrelated, and that changes in one may have reverberations in the other. Indeed, it has been reported anecdotally that the increase in residential EBD placements can at least partly be attributed to the closure of many children's homes. According to this view, certain children require residential care and, if Social Services options are unavailable, they may receive it by default at the hands of education departments or independent schools. Prior to our undertaking this evaluation in Warwickshire, this view was expressed by some observers. It is also important to report that in 1986 this opinion was held by Warwickshire Education Department. Indeed, a memorandum from the County Education Officer to the Director of Social Services in April 1986 included the following passage:

I think you know that it is the view of my colleagues that the Social Services Committee's recent new policy of phasing out all residential care facilities in the county is leading to an increase in the number of children referred to the Education Department for placement at residential special schools.

This view, however, was disputed by Social Services. It undertook a detailed exercise examining the situation of children from every social work team in the County placed in residential special schools. Overall, it was concluded from this exercise that those children placed in out-of-County schools would not necessarily be located within the authority if Social Services policies were different.

Because of these different views, and because it was also evident to us that our evaluation would be incomplete without scrutinising this subject, we decided to gather detailed information. This consisted of two main exercises. First, we contrasted the use of residential EBD placements with the number of Social Services home placements available within the County. Secondly, we undertook a survey of all County Council local educational authorities in England in order to gather comparative data with which Warwickshire's position could be compared.

Warwickshire – residential placements

Figure 12.1 summarises the information gathered for the first of these two exercises. The horizontal axis of the graph consists of the years from 1977/8 to 1986/7. The vertical axis represents placements per thousand of the estimated 0 to 18 population in the County in each of the relevant years. The graph has four lines. The top line represents the number of pupils supported in residential

EBD placements by the Education Department in each of the school years indicated. Up to 1983/4 the figures are for children identified as 'maladjusted' and needing special educational provision under the 1944 Education Act. After 1983/4 the figures are for children assessed under the 1981 Education Act as having special educational needs identified as 'emotional and behavioural difficulties'. The figures have been corrected to take into account the school population in Warwickshire in each of these years. The stepped line shows the actual number of places available in the Social Services Department's residential homes.

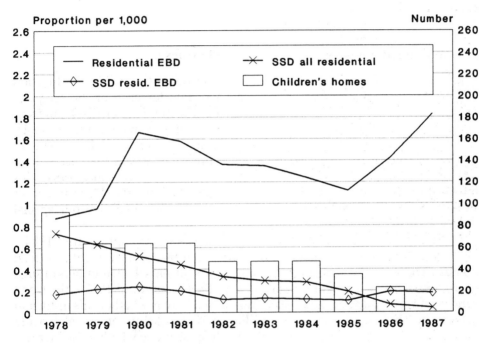

Figure 12.1 Warwickshire: Residential placements and children's home beds

Moving downwards, the next line represents children in the care of War-wickshire Social Services Department who were placed residentially in all types of placement, excluding penal establishments and residential schools. The bottom line represents children in care in Warwickshire who were placed in residential schools.

If the period from 1984 is considered, it can be seen that the Social Services Department closed 47 places in its own residential establishments in less than two years and was left with four reserved beds in a National Children's Home establishment in Sutton Coldfield. Since 1984, the proportion of children identified as EBD by the Education Department and placed residentially has increased markedly from some 1.1 per 1000 of the school age population to over 1.8. Given the coincidence in these trends it is not unreasonable to ask whether there is a link between them. One can also understand the Education Department's cause for concern, particularly as it was footing the bill.

However, it would be wrong to assume there is a cause or link between these two trends. If the graph is considered over a longer period, it is clear that the steady decline in Social Services residential places for children has *not* always been associated with increases in EBD (or maladjusted) residential school placements. The period 1977–1979 saw parallel trends but, from 1979–1984, residential EBD school placements *fell* at the same time as Social Services Children's Centres continued to be closed. There is, therefore, no direct long-term link. In order to examine this issue further, we need to put these matters in a broader context and look at what was happening in other county education authorities.

Trends in other county local education authorities

This section presents the results of a survey of County Council local education authorities in England. The survey collected data for each of the six years between 1981/2 and 1986/7 and, in addition to the numbers of EBD children, also recorded whether they received education in day or in residential schools. Details of school-age populations were also collected from the LEAs surveyed so that standardised results could be presented that would take account of differential and falling school populations. Unfortunately, since 1984, this information has not been gathered and published by the Department of Education and Science, which meant that we had to undertake our special survey.

As described earlier, in Warwickshire there was a sharp upturn after 1984/5 in the numbers of EBD children who were being placed in residential special schools. This upturn occurred after several years during which numbers of such placements had been steadily falling. Since 1984/5 and until 1987/8 the trend continued steeply upwards. The question posed here is whether this upturn in residential EBD placements was peculiar to Warwickshire or was also being experienced by other LEAs. This will then help us judge whether the increase in Warwickshire can be linked to the closure of children's homes.

In all there are 39 Shire (Non-Metropolitan) County local education authorities in England. Data from Warwickshire LEA was available directly to the researchers and postal questionnaires were sent to the Directors of Education in the other 38 LEAs. The questionnaire was short and asked a limited range of questions (total school population; total number of children identified as EBD/maladjusted prior to 1984; and the numbers of these EBD children placed in day and in boarding schools) for each of the years 1981/2 to 1986/7. A covering letter explained the purpose of the survey.

Overall, 30 of the 38 authorities (79 per cent) responded to our enquiry, but only just over half of these were able to provide complete sets of data. Some authorities had problems collecting the data we requested, either because they were held at an area rather than a county level or because it would have been too time consuming a job to extract the data from their particular manual or computerised system. Another could not provide the data because their computerised record-keeping system constantly updated individual records.

However, for most of the LEAs which returned incomplete questionnaires the problem arose in providing data for the period since 1984, which of course is the period in which we are particularly interested. The main reasons why data from 1984 were not available from these authorities is that when, in 1984, the Department of Education and Science ceased requiring LEAs to provide information broken down by particular categories of special educational need, the authorities stopped gathering this information. In the light of the trends discovered by Warwickshire LEA, which did continue monitoring, and considering the Warnock Committee Report's (1978) recommendations that such statistical monitoring should not cease, the decision by some authorities not to collect data about trends in EBD (or other categories of special need) is disquieting. One wonders how they are able to identify trends and plan services.

Results of the survey

Total EBD numbers

Figure 12.2 shows the results for the 12 LEAs that were able to provide complete data sets for the total number of children identified as EBD. The results are given in the form of numbers of children per 1000 school age population to correct for the different sizes of the LEAs.

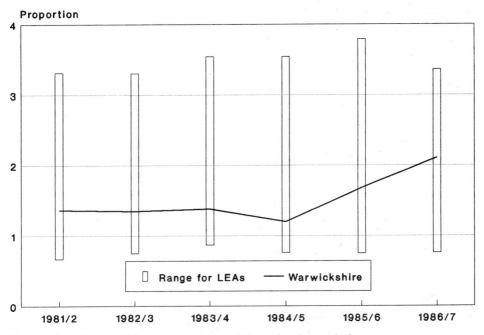

Figure 12.2 Total EBD placements per 1000 school population

Each of the vertical lines represents the range of values for each year for the 12 authorities; for example for 1981/2 one authority identified approximately 0.7 children per 1000 as EBD, whereas another identified as many as 3.3 per 1000.

The main point to note from this figure is the very wide variations in the numbers of children identified as having emotional and behavioural difficulties in each year. Remarkably, four or five times as many children were identified as EBD in some authorities compared with others. This of course could have major implications. On the one hand it may mean pupils receiving a more appropriate and rewarding educational experience. Alternatively, it may mean children being labelled unnecessarily and being stigmatised. This variation between LEAs has long been noted. The Warnock Report commented that, 'In one London Borough ten times as many children were ascertained as maladjusted as in another' (Warnock, 1978). The Report went on to note, however, that a series of research projects had demonstrated that the incidence of special needs when objectively assessed using consistent criteria did not vary greatly from one LEA to another. The Report continued,

Some of the variations between authorities may reflect variations in local policy and the strength of assessment services, but they also suggest a relationship between the rate of ascertainment and the availability of special provision. (Warnock, 1978)

The solid line running across Figure 12.2 presents the figures for Warwickshire and shows that from 1981/2 to 1985/6 it lay in the bottom third of the range, but that by 1986/7 it was at the mid-point for the 12 LEAs.

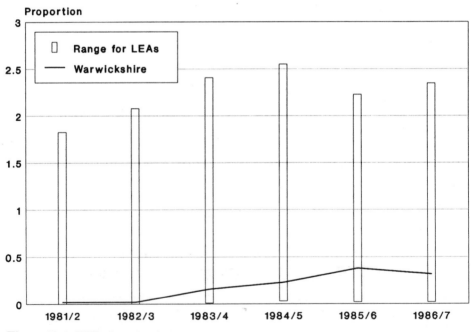

Figure 12.3 EBD day placements per 1000 school population

Total day EBD placements

Figure 12.3 shows the results from the 13 LEAs which provided complete sets of data relating to the number of children identified as EBD who were placed in *day* provision of one kind or another. Again the most significant result is the very large variation in the range of the results. Some LEAs placed as few as 0.1 or 0.2 children per 1000 school population in EBD day provision, compared with as many as 2.5 children per 1000 in others – the lowest and highest figures, therefore, varied by more than a factor of ten.

Total residential EBD placements

The results from 17 LEAs are displayed in Figure 12.4. The main point about these results is the one we have come to expect – that some LEAs place proportionately more than *ten* times as many children in residential placements as some others. However, there are two additional features apparent from this figure. First, between 1983/4 and 1986/7 the lower end of the range increased from about .02 children per 1000 to nearly 0.3 children per 1000 – that is, from that year *all* the LEAs were placing a significant number of EBD children in residential provision. Secondly, since 1984/5 the top end of the range fell from around 3 children per 1000 to fewer than 2.5 children per 1000.

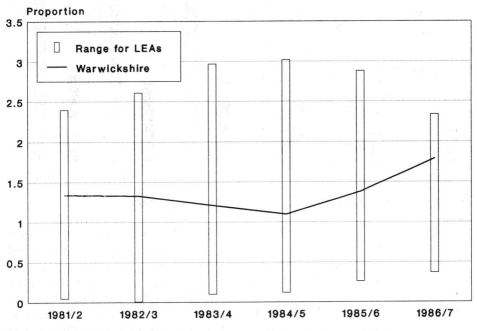

Figure 12.4 **EBD residential placements per 1000 school population**

Warwickshire LEA remained in the top third of the cases throughout the period we are examining.

Trends in EBD numbers and placements

We have given above details of the number of children identified as EBD, the placements which were made for them, and the different results in the various LEAs. What we are also interested in are the trends in these numbers during the periods 1981/2 to 1986/7 and, in particular, 1984/5 and 1986/7. How did the overall numbers of children identified as EBD change during these periods and were there changes in the types of placements which were made?

Figure 12.5 shows how, in a selection of LEAs, the number of children per 1000 school population identified as EBD changed over the period 1981/2 to 1986/7. For reasons of clarity, just seven sets of returns are included, but the range covered by the data and the type of trends found in all the returns are well represented in the selection.

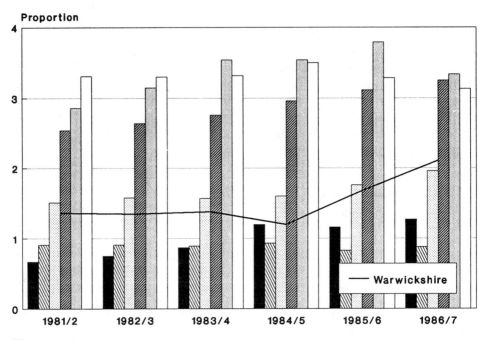

Figure 12.5 Trends in total EBD per 1000 school population

We have already commented on the wide range of figures found in any one year but from Figure 12.5 we can see that individual LEAs more or less maintained their position in the 'league table' of numbers of children per 1000 identified as EBD. There were small changes up or down from year to year and also longer term trends, but these were gradual. In none of the authorities did the figures jump from the bottom to the top of the range (for example, from fewer than one to over three children per 1000) from year to year, or even over the six-year period we are examining.

It is also interesting to examine the *overall* trends in the LEAs we are considering. Figure 12.6 has three lines which represent the average (mean) trends in total EBD figures, day EBD placements, and residential EBD placements. What we have are more or less steadily increasing trends for each of the three sets of data. In 1986/87 an additional 0.29 children per 1000 on average were being identified as EBD compared with the 1981/2 figures. Most of this increase appeared to be accommodated in day provision, which accounted for an additional 0.21 children per 1000 on average. The increase in the use of residential provision was much smaller; an average increase over the period of just 0.07 per 1000.

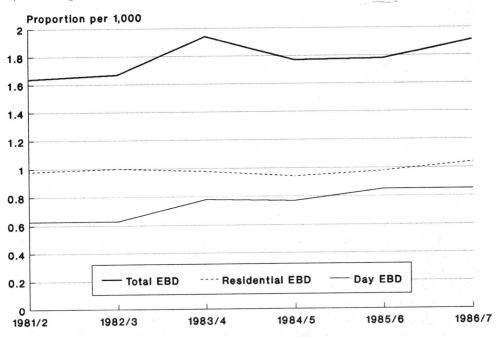

Figure 12.6 Mean EBD figures for all surveyed LEAs

As well as being concerned with the trends over the whole of this period, we are also interested more specifically in the years since the implementation of the 1981 Education Act, that is the period since 1984/5. Table 12.1 shows these changes more clearly.

Table 12.1 Average (mean) increases in EBD figures (children per 1000 school population)

	Total EBD	*Day EBD*	*Residential EBD*
1981/2–1986/7	0.06	0.04	0.01
1984/5–1986/7	0.07	0.06	0.02

The figures in this table show the average increases *per year* for the seven LEAs during the periods 1981/2 to 1986/7 and 1984/5 to 1986/7. They show that total EBD figures, and day and residential placements increased more rapidly for the LEAs in our survey during the later period.

Returning to Figure 12.5, we can see that the mean data we have been considering above disguises marked differences between LEAs. Let us move on to consider those differences.

Total EBD assessments

Table 12.2 provides details of the changing figures in total EBD assessments for those 12 LEAs that responded to our questionnaire.

Table 12.2: Total EBD assessments: Average increase/decrease per year (children per 1000 school population)

	Mean	*Minimum*	*Maximum*	*Range*
1981/2–1986/7	0.06	−0.10	0.15	0.25
1984/5–1986/7	0.07	−0.19	0.46	0.64

How are these figures to be interpreted? Taking the period 1981/2 to 1986/7 the mean increase per year in children identified as EBD was 0.06. However, this average is calculated from a set of data which represented on one extreme an LEA with an average annual *decrease* in EBD assessments of 0.1 per 1000 per year, and at the other extreme an LEA with an average annual *increase* of 0.15 per 1000 per year. In all, one quarter of the LEAs experienced a fall in total EBD assessments per 1000 over the period, and the remaining three-quarters experienced an increase.

The comparison with the period 1984/5 to 1986/7 is revealing. Not only was the mean rate of increase in total EBD assessment slightly higher but the differences between the LEAs were also more marked. One LEA experienced a *decrease* in assessments of nearly 0.2 per 1000 per year, while another experienced an *increase* of 0.64 per 1000 per year. Over this period a quarter of the LEAs saw an average yearly decrease, 17 per cent no change and 58 per cent an increase.

Returning to the particular question which stimulated this part of the research, we find that Warwickshire was the LEA which experienced the highest rate of increase in EBD assessments per year over the whole 1981/2 to 1986/7 period and also over the 1984/5 to 1986/7 period. The rate of increase in the later period was much more rapid compared with the whole period (0.46 per 1000 per year compared with 0.15). This will have to be taken into account in explaining the increased use of residential EBD placements.

Day EBD placements

We repeated the above calculations in relation to *day* EBD placements and the results are shown in Table 12.3. These results show trends similar to those for the total EBD assessments. The average (mean) rate of increase was greater during the later period than over the whole of the survey period, but these averages disguise wider disparities between the LEAs. During 1981/2 to 1986/7 only 15 per cent of LEAs experienced a decline in EBD day placements, with the maximum rate of decline being 0.02 children per 1000 per year. The remaining 85 per cent of LEAs saw increases, the maximum being 0.11 per 1000 per year.

Table 12.3: Day EBD placements: Average increase/decrease per year (children per 1000 school population)

	Mean	Minimum	Maximum	Range
1981/2–1986/7	0.04	−0.02	0.11	0.13
1984/5–1986/7	0.06	−0.10	0.24	0.34

From 1984/5 to 1986/7 nearly a quarter of the LEAs saw a decline in day placements with a maximum rate of decline of 0.1 per 1000 per year. The remaining three-quarters experienced increasing figures with a maximum of 0.24 per 1000 per year. Again, during the later period differences between the LEAs were much more marked. If we identify which LEA was experiencing the most rapid rate of increase in day placements, we find that it was the same one for the whole of the monitoring period and for 1984/5 to 1986/7, but this time the authority was not Warwickshire. In fact the changes in Warwickshire were close to the average both for the whole period and for the later period.

Residential EBD placements
Table 12.4 gives the results for residential EBD placements. The average (mean) rate of increase for the whole of the monitoring period and for 1984/5 to 1986/7 is low. Between 1981/2 and 1986/7 approximately 40 per cent of the LEAs experienced a decrease in residential placements per 1000 population per year. One LEA saw its figures fall by an average of 0.14 per 1000 per year over the period. The highest rate of increase was 0.09.

Table 12.4 Residential EBD placements: Average increase/decrease per year (children per 1000 school population)

	Mean	Minimum	Maximum	Range
1981/2–1986/7	0.01	−0.14	0.09	0.23
1984/5–1986/7	0.02	−0.34	0.35	0.69

Between 1984/5 and 1986/7 half the LEAs experienced a decline and half an increase. The average yearly changes ranged from −0.34 to +0.35 per 1000 per year. Again we discover that during the post 1984/5 period the experiences of the LEAs differed much more widely. We also discovered that *Warwickshire* was the LEA which experienced the highest average yearly increase in residential placements, both over the 1981/2 to 1986/7 period and between 1984/5 and 1986/7.

Interpretation of the findings
It was clear from earlier *Statistics of Education* produced by the Department of Education and Science that although rates of ascertainment of 'maladjustment'

varied between LEAs quite considerably, there has been a long-term national trend upwards (*see* Ford and others, 1982 for a summary). With the implementation of the 1981 Education Act the DES discontinued references to educational 'handicaps' and instead focused on 'special educational needs'. It also changed the way in which it collected data on the numbers of children requiring special educational provision. The new method of data collection made it impossible to identify the *principal* special educational need of children despite the fact (as noted earlier) that the Warnock Report, to which the 1981 Act was a response, had recommended the use of a monitoring form which would make such differentiations possible. In our survey and the letters which accompanied some of the returns, we were given no indication by LEAs (including those not able to provide complete data sets) that there was anything other than a broad continuity between the application of the 1944 Education Act terminology 'maladjusted' and the 1981 Education Act identification of 'emotional and behavioural difficulties' as one type of special educational need.

Our evidence reveals that the numbers of pupils defined as having emotional and behavioural difficulties has continued to increase since 1984. That this trend should have continued is not surprising if we consider the broader context in which maladjustment and special educational needs such as EBD occur. Tomlinson argues for the importance of examining:

The development of special education in the light of prevailing social, economic and professional interests rather than in terms of an ideology of humanitarian progress. (Tomlinson, 1982)

In the particular case of maladjusted children, she argues that the extension and development of mass education after the war imposed particular requirements:

To develop a workable system it was essential to exclude as many children as possible who might obstruct or inconvenience the smooth running of the normal schools, hence the need for careful categorisation. (*Ibid.*)

She goes on also to identify particular professional interests.

Maladjusted children have broadly become important clients, enhancing the prestige of psychologists and the developing child guidance movement.... (*Ibid.*)

Ford and others comment on the growth in numbers of maladjusted children throughout the 1950s, 1960s and 1970s:

The notion of maladjustment depends ultimately upon the context of any piece of behaviour... Economic expansion provided the wherewithal to create extra places [which] were quickly filled by schools which, under pressure to meet the ambiguous and sometimes contradictory expectations of being the primary socialising agent and disseminators of academic knowledge, found that the biggest drain on their resources were the pupils who could not or would not subscribe to the academic and behavioural norms. (Ford and others, 1982)

At a different level of analysis other writers (such as Galloway, 1985) have shown that structures within schools, such as flexibility in adapting the curriculum and teaching methods, and the quality of support and pastoral care systems, have a marked impact on the numbers of pupils identified as disruptive or maladjusted.

However, the implementation of policies and practices such as those identified as positive by Galloway not only requires a clear vision on the part of the staff of schools, it also requires additional resources. Were these forthcoming? Despite the financial implications of the 1981 Education Act no new central government money was made available. In their detailed study of the implementation of the 1981 Act, Evans and colleagues state that:

The majority of LEAs surveyed had increased their spending on services for children with special educational needs in real terms... However, the wider definition of special educational needs and the increased awareness of special needs have meant that demand has increased also.... (Evans and others, 1987)

They conclude:

Resource limitations have undoubtedly led to frustration and cynicism... Movement to reallocate resources has been against a background of increasing constraints on public spending.

Given the financial context outlined by Evans and her colleagues, and the continuity of social, political and professional interests throughout the period of the implementation of the 1981 Education Act, it is not surprising that the Act apparently did not bring about a reversal in the trend of identifying increasing numbers of children as maladjusted or EBD. Thus, legislation intended to bring about better integration for children with a variety of learning problems seems, for disruptive and disaffected pupils, to have had the reverse effect.

When we examined the trends in day and residential EBD placements separately we saw that, on average, both types of placement in our sample of authorities were increasing throughout the whole period but that the use of day placements rose much more quickly than residential placements. How are we to understand the differences in the changing use of day and residential provision?

Let us consider first the implications for resources and look at the actual numbers involved rather than the proportions of the annual school age population. In the LEAs we surveyed the average fall in the school population between 1981/2 and 1986/7 was of the order of 9.1 per cent. When we look at the total *numbers* of children identified as EBD this *increased* by 4.8 per cent over the period. Day placements actually increased in number by nearly 15 per cent but residential placements *fell* by 1.3 per cent. Relating these figures to placements, by the end of this period each LEA on average provided an extra 13 day placements but two, or slightly fewer, residential placements. Overall then, over this five-year period we were seeing a slight growth in day provision (or purchase of day places) for EBD children and a small decline (or fewer purchases) of residential places. However, as we saw, these average trends disguised marked differences between LEAs.

In some LEAs, day and residential placements increased (or decreased) together but in other authorities there appeared to be a steady transfer from one sector to another, with either a growing proportion of residential placements or a growing proportion of day placements. Why might these changes happen? Resource limitations and attempts to control expenditure, together with very different responses from LEA to LEA to providing for special educational needs are all factors which could have played a part. We do not have the detailed information about the LEAs we surveyed to explain the changes, but for Warwickshire we do have access to that information and, as an example, the case of Warwickshire is enlightening.

If we return to look at Figure 12.3, where the solid line represents the changes in EBD placements made by Warwickshire, we see that after making very few day placements in 1981/2 and 1982/3 the County began to make considerably more day placements. The explanation for this is a purely local one. From 1983/4 onwards day placements became newly available to the Education Department from two sources – one a Social Services Department CHE (community home with education) and the other a special school run by an adjacent LEA. Presumably, when this CHE was closed in 1984, some day pupils were at greater risk of residential special school placements!

There is a further, local explanation for the upsurge in residential EBD placements from 1984/5. A paper to the Education (Schools) Sub-Committee in 1986 reminds us that the Education Act 1981 was implemented on 1 April 1983. It was reported that one of its initial effects was a slowing down of the referral and assessment rate of pupils with special educational needs. It was felt that this was due partly to the emphasis on mainstream schools to maintain on their rolls pupils with special educational needs; but perhaps more importantly, the new assessment procedures the Act introduced led to long delays in the placement of children. The paper adds that additional educational psychologists and administrative staff were appointed, which led to the delay being substantially reduced. It concludes that the rise in the number of children placed out-County in 1985/6 and 1986/7 can be attributed to this clearing of the backlog.

To what extent can trends also be linked to policy decisions as suggested in the Warnock Report? Again we have insufficient information about the LEAs we surveyed but we can use Warwickshire as an illustrative example. Figure 12.7 shows trends in residential EBD placements in Warwickshire over the period 1977/8 to 1986/7. The feature we are particularly interested in is, of course, the upturn in residential placements in 1984/5. However, the other dramatic turnaround in residential placements occurred in 1979/80, when a rising trend in residential placements peaked and, in subsequent years, turned sharply downwards.

Let us first consider whether the availability of resources had any effect on placement numbers. From 1979/80 (the earliest year for which figures could be traced) to 1986/7 the numbers of children in in-County residential EBD provision varied little. No new facilities within the County were opened (or closed) and the beds available for County use were more or less constantly filled. The increases and decreases in the numbers of residential EBD placements were, therefore, occurring in *out-County* placements.

The Education Committee was under pressure to find areas in which to make cuts in its budget in the late 1970s and early 1980s and turned its attention, amongst other things, to out-County residential special school placements. In September 1979 Warwickshire's County Education Officer reported to the Education Committee on the need to make immediate cuts in the current year's budget (April 1979 to March 1980) of over one per cent. The spending

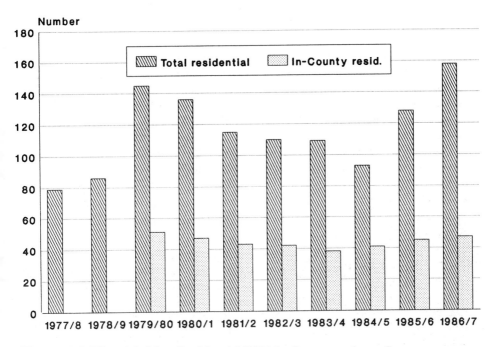

Figure 12.7 Warwickshire: Residential EBD in-County and out-County

committees were told by the Policy and Resources Committee that government restrictions on spending, 'Mean a new lower base for Council services which will not be achieved by expenditure cuts of a one-off nature' (Warwickshire Director of Education, 1979a). Among the cuts identified by the Chief Education Officer was a, 'Reduction in the number of children at independent and non-maintained special schools' (Warwickshire Director of Education, 1979b). These cuts would total approximately £60,000 for a full year or approximately 12 places at costs then current.

A year later the Chief Officer was again reporting to his Committee in an atmosphere of continued cuts.

Reduction in placement of pupils at independent special schools: A reduction has already been made in the numbers of pupils admitted to out-County residential special schools... Further savings should accrue from more detailed scrutiny of each case in consultation with the Social Services Department, though reductions in placements will necessitate alternative provision being made in our own special or primary and secondary schools. (Warwickshire Director of Education, 1980)

His report went on to describe the need for a detailed study of the whole provision of special education which was later begun and has since led to some new resources being provided within the County. However, before the first of these new provisions was established the numbers of out-County residential placements had fallen considerably.

Summary

This survey of local education authorities was undertaken so that trends in the numbers and placements of children identified as EBD (maladjusted) in Warwickshire could be compared with trends in other authorities. The reason for wanting to make the comparisons was to identify whether what was happening in Warwickshire was peculiar to the County or was in line with national trends – in particular, the upsurge in residential EBD placements that coincided with the Social Services Department's closure of its children's homes. What conclusions, therefore, can we draw?

- Throughout the whole of the period 1981/2 to 1986/7, Warwickshire was the LEA which experienced the largest increase in total EBD (maladjusted) assessments, however, the increases in the County were not very far out of line with a number of other LEAs.

- From 1984/5 to 1986/7 Warwickshire again experienced the largest increase in total EBD ascertainments *but* this time the County appeared to be out of step with the other LEAs in the survey. Warwickshire's increase was over six times the average increase but, given the fact that some authorities experienced a decrease, it is more significant that Warwickshire's rate of increase was over 2.5 times that of the LEA experiencing the next highest increase. The Education Department attributes this to delays associated with the implementation of the Education Act 1981, although it is unclear why this should affect Warwickshire much more significantly than other local authorities.

- Warwickshire experienced increases in day and residential EBD placements throughout the period. Day placements grew mainly in response to the availability of non-departmental resources – such as at a local community home with education. In-County residential placements remained more or less steady throughout the period in line with the number of places available; out-County residential placements grew throughout the period. Over the whole period the growth was not far out of line with a number of other LEAs, but from 1984/5 to 1986/7 the increases were nearly three times those of the LEA with the next highest increase.

- Over the whole period 1981/2 to 1986/7, increases in total EBD and residential EBD numbers in Warwickshire were the highest among a number of comparable LEAs, but the increases were not far out of line with some of those other authorities. From 1984/5 to 1986/7 Warwickshire experienced increases in total EBD and residential EBD numbers which were considerably higher than those other LEAs. The conclusion to be drawn from this is that between 1984/5 and 1986/7 local factors were operating which resulted in significantly different trends in Warwickshire. The primary difference was in *total* EBD ascertainments. Provision for these extra numbers was primarily made in out-County residential placements.

- To return to the original question of whether the Social Services closure policy led to the simultaneous upsurge in residential EBD placements, our results must remain inconclusive. It is clear that in important respects developments in Warwickshire were unlike any other County we surveyed and we are unsure why this should be. It is possible that there could be a connection between Social Services policy and the impact on special educational services, but it would need a different research approach from ours to prove the case one way or the other.

13. Conclusion

We now come to the end of our detailed examination of childcare policies in Warwickshire. In this final chapter, we shall give a brief account of what we feel are the major implications arising from this research. More specifically, we shall address five key questions which, in our view, have been commonly posed about childcare in the County since it closed the last of its remaining children's homes in 1986. It is particularly important in these five areas that policy makers – both nationally and locally – managers and practitioners are clear about the implications of our evidence. Especially on such a controversial subject as this, which impinges on deep-seated ideologies and vested professional interests, many will draw inaccurate conclusions given the slightest chance. No doubt this will still occur but, hopefully, it will be less likely to happen if we make our position clear on these key issues.

This final chapter, therefore, will not attempt to summarise all of our main findings – readers can breath a sigh of relief. We have provided regular summaries throughout the preceding text that serve this function. We make no excuse that our report is a detailed one. The State's care of our most vulnerable children is a subject that deserves the closest scrutiny. Developments in Warwickshire were also complex, and needed careful documentation and analysis. In addition, the evaluation of childcare policies is far from straightforward and needs to be approached from a number of angles. Equally importantly, there was widespread misunderstanding about what occurred in Warwickshire and more than a fair amount of disinformation. Given that some other authorities in Britain and abroad may be poised to follow the County and have told us that our research will have some influence on their decisions, we have felt it important to undertake a rigorous investigation.

We did this, readers will recall, by combing the relevant literature; following over a 15-month period the progress of 215 children and young people who would be strong contenders for residential care elsewhere; undertaking a small number of detailed case studies in which we spoke at length with young people, their carers and others; interviewing key managers and others in the County; and conducting separate examinations of the use of residential care by Warwickshire and the implications for the Education Department. Let us now turn to what we feel are the key questions. These are:

- Does Warwickshire have a non-residential policy?

- Was the closure of children's homes a cost saving measure?
- Was Warwickshire able to find foster placements for all children who needed them?
- Did the closure of the children's homes divert children into the residential special school sector?
- What were the effects of Warwickshire's placement policies on the quality of placements and on outcomes?

We shall consider each in turn.

Does Warwickshire have a non-residential policy?

The answer to this question is 'no', but this needs some elaboration. Warwickshire representatives have never claimed that there is no role for children's homes or that other local authorities should necessarily do what they did. As we saw in Chapter 3, historically the County has always had very few children in residential care and in the past has been relatively well-off for foster carers. Warwickshire would argue, therefore, that what it feels is appropriate for itself would not necessarily work for others in different circumstances.

Indeed, we revealed in our brief review of the recent history of developments in childcare in Warwickshire (*see* Chapter 3), that the County had never deliberately planned to be left with no residential facilities of its own. The final push to close the last of the Children's Centres appears to have come from residential staff rather than managers. This, its seems, may have been encouraged by a number of factors:

- the very negative view in the County towards residential childcare;
- a lack of clarity about the aims of residential facilities and the specific roles of their staff; and
- the fact that, paradoxically, many residential workers – the majority of whom were professionally qualified as fieldworkers – were opposed to residential care.

Some observers may conclude from all this that residential childcare in Warwickshire, therefore, withered partly by default as well as by design.

The County never disguised the fact that, when the last of its children's homes was closed, some young people would continue to need residential placements. Therefore, it entered into an arrangement whereby it had immediate access to four places in a small residential unit, just over the County border, run by a voluntary organisation (NCH). Some others go to specialist residential centres elsewhere.

To put this into some perspective, in the period since 1986, Warwickshire has had at any one time only one or two per cent of children in care placed residentially – that is some ten or so children. The average national figure is nearer 20 per cent. Clearly this is a major difference. However, it is important to appreciate that, in addition, between three and four per cent of children in care in Warwickshire were placed in residential special schools – mostly for pupils with emotional and behavioural difficulties – approximately 20 children. This is close to national average figures.

Although the number placed residentially was small, an aspect of concern to us has been the experiences of these children prior to being placed in residential care. Obviously we can be wise with hindsight and it may not be easy to anticipate exactly which children will fail repeatedly in foster care as they embark on their care careers; nonetheless, it seemed to us that the degree of instability experienced by these 15 or so young people a year was, frankly, unacceptable. It had to be demonstrated repeatedly that foster care had failed before a residential placement could be countenanced. One young man passed through ten different placements in under two and a half years. A less rigid view may be more appropriate.

Although we said above that the County does not have a totally non-residential policy, there is one qualification to this which should be mentioned, which can give rise to confusion. While concurring with what is said in the previous sentence, senior managers of Warwickshire frequently assert nonetheless that 'Every child has a right to a family life'. This does seem to us somewhat contradictory. We would also take issue with this latter point; not because we wish to deprive children of loving homes but because we believe the statement to be rather a simplistic one. As we saw from our earlier evidence, it is not easy for Social Service Departments to provide older children in particular with stable, rewarding, substitute family experiences. A rapid succession of foster placements, which are either planned to be short-term or which breakdown, are not, to us, synonymous with 'family life'. Unfortunately, this was the experience of a significant number of adolescents in Warwickshire. Moreover, certain benefits of family life can be derived without physically living within it. Indeed, many young people living in children's homes felt this was the best way of preserving family life for them, when their care was *shared* between parents and residential workers (Berridge, 1985). The Children Act 1989 also takes this view.

In sum, then, Warwickshire does *not* have a position that there is no role for residential care. However, at times, their message is a confusing one.

Was the closure of children's homes a cost saving measure?

Let us now turn to what, in our view, is the second key question. This is a relevant one to ask, especially since one of the reasons for the national, post-war shift from residential to foster care was explicitly financial. There has always been a cost differential between a residential and a foster placement even if, for similar groups of young people and if the services provided are costed fully, the difference is much narrower than many observers would have thought (Knapp and Fenyo, 1989).

As we reported earlier, in 1982 the Short Committee (House of Commons, 1989) visited Warwickshire, and members of the Social Services Committee and officers were asked whether residential homes were being closed as a cost saving measure. This was denied: one councillor admitted that the authority was 'low spending' but the Chair of Social Services stated that any savings made in the closure of residential facilities were channelled back into services for children and families.

We examined Committee papers and budget details for the 1980s and found that revenue savings made when residential centres were closed were not lost but were, indeed, redirected to other areas of childcare work. Recommendations to Committee were always composed so that suggested savings balanced against recommendations for new policies and provisions. All of these were accepted.

Clearly, then, Warwickshire did *not* embark on its policies in order to save money, nor did these policies cost less once implemented. The Children's Services Teams, for example, were as we saw in Chapters 9 and 10 a major investment, and one of their primary roles was to strengthen foster care services in the absence of a local residential option.

Was Warwickshire able to find foster placements for all children who needed them?

We now come to the heart of our evaluation of Warwickshire's childcare policies. Many managers and practitioners outside the County, in both Britain and abroad, on being informed that such a radical policy had been pursued, received the news with disbelief. Despite many closures, residential care continues to be used extensively for adolescents in most authorities and it is seen as virtually inconceivable that you could do without it. Furthermore, some observers felt that large numbers of young people would live not in foster homes but would return home on trial, or be placed in custody, lodgings, bed and breakfast accommodation or other marginal placements.

Our evidence revealed that Warwickshire was, in fact, successful in placing the vast majority of its young people in foster homes. In this respect, it is dramatically different from other authorities. Eight out of ten of the placements made for our survey group were with foster carers, which is about double the figure for other local authorities. Furthermore, the County used foster care for adolescents *five times* more often than other agencies. Even more startlingly, other research has discovered that nationally almost half of all placements experienced by children as they pass through care are in residential settings. This compares with only *three per cent* for our survey group.

We can see, therefore, that Warwickshire is very successful in placing young people in foster care. All but a very small number of new admissions to care are placed with foster carers. Most assessments are also carried out while children are fostered. But unlike most other authorities, Warwickshire also uses foster care for the majority of teenagers. In addition, a child whose placement has broken down will also usually be found new foster carers. On the whole, social workers did not decry the lack of local residential resources. Warwickshire's achievement, therefore, is not just in making *more* foster placements but in *extending* the use of foster care.

Before we become too euphoric, however, there were two major problems with these placement policies. First, the needs of children from minority ethnic groups were inadequately met. Although there were relatively few Black children in our survey group, the overwhelming majority were placed with White foster carers – this was particularly the case for Afro-Caribbean children and those of mixed parentage. As we know, and as Department of Health guidance reiterates, children's needs are generally best met in same-race placements. This was not an option for most Warwickshire children. The County is not alone in its shortage of foster carers from minority ethnic groups but in other authorities there is the option of using a children's home for a brief period if a same-race foster placement is not immediately available. Warwickshire's revised policy, therefore, is not appropriate for all sections of the population.

The second major problem with Warwickshire's placement patterns concerns the availability – or more accurately *non-availability* – of foster carers. As we have shown above, the County is successful in achieving its objective of placing the vast majority of its children and young people in foster care; but this, of course, is only the first step. What matters ultimately is the quality of fostering experience that is encountered. Later in this Chapter, we review the evidence on the outcomes of foster placements. However, here we take an intermediate step and address the choice of foster homes available. Social work text books contain laudable statements about carefully assessing children's needs and then matching them with the attributes of, say, individual foster homes. Factors to be taken into account might include the location of the placement, its proximity to the child's school, experience of foster carers, their ethnicity, numbers and ages of own children, their particular strengths and weaknesses, and their leisure interests. One would then seek to locate the child with the foster home that best met the child's needs.

Unfortunately, the text books in this respect are of limited relevance to *practice* in Warwickshire as in well over *half* the cases where a placement was needed, there was only *one* placement available, and that was sometimes with carers who were not felt to be wholly suitable. This problem of course is not restricted to Warwickshire (Rowe, 1989; Berridge and Cleaver, 1987) but the implications for the County are particularly serious as it has consciously narrowed its range of options. Assessment and matching, therefore, are to a large extent rhetorical. There is also the very important issue of the degree of choice that young people themselves are able to exercise over what happens to them and where they live.

Did the closure of the children's homes divert children into the residential school sector?

Readers will recall that we discussed this issue in Chapter 12 so here there is only need to reiterate the main findings. We expressed concern in particular about the national situation of children defined as having emotional and behavioural difficulties (EBD). Overall, though reliable statistics are difficult to come by, it seems that the numbers of these pupils living and being educated in *residential* schools continues to grow. There are significant – and quite worrying – disparities between local education authorities on this subject, yet this overall increase seems to be completely at odds with trends affecting residential care for children more generally. As far as we are aware, no one seems to know how or why this is happening. Indeed, so far there has been no overall view as to whether or not it is a desirable development. The National Children's Bureau intends to help fill this knowledge gap with future and current research.

As far as Warwickshire is concerned, we revealed that the closure of the children's homes coincided with a significant increase in the number of pupils placed away from home in residential EBD schools. The Education Department in 1986 was strongly of the view that the two events *were* connected, but Social Services, having investigated the issue on a case by case basis, disagreed. Our evidence showed that the picture was a complex one and it was not possible to demonstrate a direct causal link.

We saw that between 1984/7 and 1986/7 Warwickshire had a major increase in the *total* number of EBD pupils and that this was unparalleled in any of the other Counties we surveyed. Local, day educational resources were limited and out of County residential schools were therefore sought. The Education Department attributed this upsurge to the backlog that was created once the 1981 Education Act was implemented in the County. It is unclear why Warwickshire should have been so idiosyncratic in this respect.

In conclusion, then, our evidence does *not* confirm that the upsurge in residential EBD numbers can be attributed to the closure policy. It is possible that there was some link but the way in which our research was designed has not disclosed one. Our results, therefore, are inconclusive.

What were the effects of Warwickshire's placement policies on the quality of placements and on outcomes?

This, of course, is the litmus test of whether Warwickshire was correct to do what it did – did it lead to better experiences for children? To be fair to the County, this question has also been of paramount concern to it, as reflected in the fact that Warwickshire has itself funded this three-year, independent, detailed research study. If the results were to be uncomplimentary, the County would be exposed to considerable public and professional embarrassment.

We discussed in Chapter 8 that evaluating outcomes is a complex research task. For example, the placement may be positive in some respects but not others; and, in any case, who exactly is going to evaluate what is or is not successful? In ascertaining the extent to which Warwickshire's policies could be deemed to have successful outcomes for children, we gathered a wide range of data that enabled us to draw comparisons with what research has shown to happen in other local authorities. In this, we were particularly fortunate to be able to draw on Jane Rowe and her colleagues' recent (1989) authoritative and nationally representative study. In undertaking these comparisons, we were careful to make sure that our respective populations matched.

We can summarise our results as follows. Encouragingly, a majority of placements in Warwickshire – using a variety of measures – would be said to be satisfactory or better than satisfactory: in about seven out of ten placements, social workers reported that their aims for the placement had been achieved either fully or in most respects. This figure is about the same as the national picture revealed in Rowe's study. In addition, the overall placement breakdown rate in Warwickshire was also about the same as reported elsewhere. We should remind ourselves, however, that there was some evidence that Black children were more likely to experience failed placements. We also showed earlier that same-race placements were generally not available.

On two further criteria, the County also emerges unfavourably. Social workers' assessments of the integration of children in placements compared adversely with another national study. Moreover, although placements did not breakdown more frequently, children in our sample moved between placements more often than one would expect. Just 40 per cent of our sample experienced only one placement in the 15 months; the figure in Rowe's study was 57 per cent. A third of our Warwickshire children experienced three or more placements. Despite monitoring for a slightly longer period, significantly fewer children in Rowe's nationally representative study had this number of moves – her figure was only one in five.

We know that children entering care frequently come from highly unstable and unrewarding backgrounds and that the care system sets out to provide, often for the first time, a period of predictability and of being looked after by consistent, concerned adults. Frequent placement changes are incompatible with this aim. We should point out that residential experiences are by no means always stable and predictable, and there can be an array of adults coming and going. Nonetheless, in this area, Warwickshire clearly compares unfavourably with other authorities and these findings should give grounds for concern.

Finally, we again followed Rowe's research in trying to establish a composite measure of success: this was based on both the extent to which social workers felt placement aims had been met, and also whether placements lasted as long as children were thought to have needed them (*see* Chapter 8). For placements generally, Warwickshire again compares unfavourably with Rowe's six authorities; in fact, the County comes out considerably worse than any of the six. The same applies when we look at foster care specifically – this applies to pre-adolescents as well as older children. Again, these results are disconcerting and should lead to the County examining carefully aspects of its practices.

Final thoughts

We conclude with some final observations. Our investigation has been a detailed one and we have been fortunate in approaching our task in being able to draw on the work of other childcare researchers. This has enabled us both to understand what we discovered and also to set Warwickshire in a broader context. For the first time, perhaps, we are fortunate in the UK to have such a strong knowledge base. However, during the course of our work we have encountered areas about which insufficient information is available, and we would urge other colleagues and research funders to pursue them. For example, we still know very little about the experiences of older adolescents in care and which interventions are the most fruitful. It was clear that the major problems for Warwickshire came from adolescents posing behavioural difficulties – in other authorities many, if not most, of these would be placed in residential settings. Further work in this area would certainly be welcomed by service-providers.

Another major problem that we highlighted concerned the supply of foster carers in Warwickshire. Despite the very substantial resources invested in the Children's Services Teams, which had specific responsibilities for this area of work, the County clearly had major difficulties with the recruitment and retention of foster carers. Foster care is the cornerstone of our community care policies for children yet it has attracted remarkably little research interest. The pressures on foster carers identified in our study are unlikely to recede in the foreseeable future and a research contribution would be welcome.

A further area of concern of our work in Warwickshire concerned the experiences of children from minority ethnic groups, which we concluded were unsatisfactory. This is a complex and controversial area of investigation, which so far has attracted minimal interest from (predominantly White) researchers and funders alike. Not only should specific research address particular issues, but every study should consider the implications of its subject matter for our diverse society. The National Children's Bureau has mounted initial work on this subject, which it plans to develop.

A final area in which further research would be timely concerns children with emotional and behavioural difficulties. Though part of a separate system, there is clearly much overlap with young people who come to the attention of Social Services. Again, work at the Bureau is addressing some relevant issues but broader efforts are required.

Throughout the course of our research and our writing we have often been asked whether we felt Warwickshire was right to develop its policies as it did. The evidence we have provided shows that the outcomes were mixed and readers will have to come to their own conclusions on reading this book. In any case, there is no indication that the County is considering reversing its policies and so the question may be of historical interest only. However, we have urged other authorities to think long and hard if they have contemplated repeating what Warwickshire did. The County always had very little residential care and its increased use of fostering in the last decade is no different to what has happened nationally – the key point is that it *started from a different position*. Other authorities will not be beginning from the same point and the implications are likely to be quite different, especially when the demographic trends governing the size of the 0–17 population are taken into account (*see* Parker, 1987).

Another pertinent question for others considering imitating Warwickshire is to ask from where significantly larger numbers of foster carers are to emerge? As we have seen, the County made a major investment in foster care support services, yet found recruitment and retention highly problematic. Furthermore, because of other demographic changes, there will be greater competition in future for women's labour, which will quite likely have an adverse effect on the supply of foster families. We should also remind ourselves that Warwickshire has few more foster carers today than it did a decade ago; the increase in the *proportion* of children in care who are fostered has been achieved largely because of a decline in the child population. Others contemplating similar action to Warwickshire, therefore, should be extremely cautious and consider the negative aspects of the policy as well as its positives.

Finally, we would again like to remark on the commitment and forethought demonstrated by Warwickshire County Council in its approach to this research. In executing the policies and laying itself open to independent scrutiny, the County has been both confident and enterprising. We trust that it will be equally determined to review its services in the light of our evidence, and to take appropriate steps. We hope also that a wider audience will have found our work helpful in reflecting on appropriate services for severely disadvantaged children and families.

Bibliography

ABSWAP, *Black Children in Care*. ABSWAP: 1983.

Adcock, M., *Terminating Parental Contact*. BAAF: 1980.

Ahmed, S., Cheetham, J., and Small, J. (eds), *Social Work with Black Children and Families*. Batsford: 1986.

Aldgate, J., 'Identification of factors influencing children's length of staying in care', in Triseliotis, J. (ed.), *New Developments in Foster Care and Adoption*. Routledge and Kegan Paul: 1980.

Aldgate, J., 'Foster children at school: success or failure?' *Adoption and Fostering* Volume 14, No. 4, pp 38–49: 1990.

Aldgate, J., Colton, M., and Heath, A., 'The educational attainment of children in care'. *Adoption and Fostering*, Volume 11, No. 1: 1987.

Aldgate, J., and Hawley, D., *Recollections of Disruption – a Study of Foster Care Breakdown*. NFCA: 1986.

Aldgate, J., Maluccio, A., and Reeves, C., 'Adolescents in foster families – an overview', in Aldgate, J., Maluccio, A., and Reeves, C. (eds) *Adolescents in Foster Families*. Batsford: 1989.

Arthur Anderson, *Child Care Report: Warwickshire Social Services Department*. Arthur Anderson: 1985.

Audit Commission, *The Provision of Child Care: Final Report*. HMSO: 1981.

Baldwin, N., *Planning to Care*. Department of Applied Social Studies, University of Warwick: 1986.

Barclay, P., *Social Workers: Their Role and Tasks*. Bedford Square Press: 1982.

Barton, R., *Institutional Neurosis*. John Wright: 1959.

Berridge, D., *Children's Homes*. Basil Blackwell: 1985.

Berridge, D., and Cleaver, H., *Foster Home Breakdown*. Basil Blackwell: 1987.

Bowen, L., *Why Close Children's Homes?* Unpublished MA Dissertation, Department of Applied Social Studies, University of Warwick: 1986.

Bowlby, J., *Maternal Care and Mental Health*. World Health Organisation: 1951.

Bowlby, J., *Child Care and the Growth of Love*. Penguin: 1953.

Bunyan, A., and Sinclair, R., 'Gatekeepers to care'. *Practice*, Volume 1, No. 2, pp 116–28: 1987.

Cheetham, J., *Social Work Services for Ethnic Minorities in Britain and the USA*. DHSS: 1981.

Colton, M. J., *Dimensions of Substitute Child Care*. Avebury: 1988.

Coombe, V., and Little, A., *Race and Social Work*. Tavistock: 1986.

Curtis Report, *Report of the Care of Children Committee*. HMSO: 1946.

Dartington Social Research Unit, *Outcomes in Context*, Unpublished seminar report: 1987.

Department of Health and Social Security, *Boarding-out of Children Regulations*. HMSO: 1955.

Department of Health and Social Security, *A Study of the Boarding Out of Children*. DHSS: 1981.

Department of Health and Social Services, *Social Work Decisions in Child Care*. HMSO: 1985.

Department of Health and Social Security, *Inspection of Community Homes, 1985*. DHSS: 1986.

Dingwall, R., Eekelaar, J., and Murray, T., *The Protection of Children: State Intervention and Family Life*. Blackwell: 1983.

Essen, J., Lambert, L., and Head, J., 'School attainment of children who have been in care'. *Child Care, Health and Development*, Volume 2, No. 6: 1976.

Evans, J., *Report to Education (Schools) Sub-committee*. Warwickshire County Education Officer. December 1986.

Evans, J., *Decision Making for Special Needs*. Institute of Education, University of London: 1987.

Fanshel, D., and Shinn, E., *Children in Foster Care*. Columbia University Press: 1978.

Fanshel, D., 'Parental visiting of children in foster care: key to discharge'. *Social Services Review*, Volume 49, No. 4: 1975.

Farmer, E. and Parker, R., *Trials and Tribulations: Returning Children from Local Authority Care to their Families*. HMSO: 1991.

Ferguson, S. and Leighton, M., 'Fostering Understanding'. *Community Care*, No 799: 1990.

Fisher, M., Marsh, P., and Phillips, D., *In and Out of Care*. Batsford: 1986.

Ford, J., Morgan, D., and Whelan, M., *Special Education and Social Control.* Routledge and Kegan Paul: 1982.

Frost, N., and Stein, M., *The Politics of Child Welfare.* Harvester Wheatsheaf: 1989.

Fuller, R., *Researching Prevention.* Social Work Research Centre, University of Stirling: 1989.

Fuller, R., and Stevenson, O., *Policies, Programmes and Disadvantage: A Review of the Literature.* Heinemann: 1983.

Galloway, D., *Schools, Pupils and Special Educational Needs.* Croom Helm: 1985.

George, V., *Foster Care: Theory and Practice.* Routledge and Kegan Paul: 1970.

Goffman, E., *Asylums: Essays on the Social Situation of Mental Patients and Other Inmates.* Penguin: 1961.

Goldstein, J., Freud, A., and Solnit, A., *Beyond the Best Interests of the Child.* Free Press: 1973.

Hardingham, S., 'The right to family life: how one County sees it'. *Social Services Insight,* 6 March 1987.

Hazel, N., *A Bridge to Independence.* Blackwell: 1981.

Hill, M., Lambert, L., and Triseliotis, J., *Achieving Adoption for Love or Money.* National Children's Bureau: 1989.

Hoghughi, M., 'Direct work with adolescents, an integrating conceptual map', in Aldgate, J., Maluccio, A., and Reeves, C. (eds) *Adolescents in Foster Families.* Batsford: 1989.

Holman, R., *Trading in Children.* Routledge and Kegan Paul: 1973.

Holman, R. 'The place of fostering in social work'. *British Journal of Social Work:* 1975.

Holman, R., *Inequality in Child Care.* CPAG: 1980.

House of Commons, Social Services Committee. *Children in Care.* HMSO: 1984.

Hutchinson-Reis, M., 'And for those of us who are Black? Black politics in social work' in Langan, M., and Lee, P., *Radical Social Work Today.* Unwin Hyman: 1989.

Jackson, S., *The Education of Children in Care.* School of Applied Social Studies, University of Bristol: 1987.

Kahan, B., *Growing up in Care.* Basil Blackwell: 1979.

King, M., 'The role and content of residential care', in Wilkinson, J. and O'Hara, G. (eds), *Our Children: Residential and Community Care.* National Children's Bureau: 1988.

Knapp, M., and Fenyo, A., 'Economic perspectives on foster care', in Carter, P. and others (eds), *Social Work and Social Welfare Year Book 1*. OUP: 1989.

Knox, B., Published letter, *Social Services Insight*: 24 April 1987.

Maluccio, A., Fein, D., Hamilton, J., Klein, J., and Ward, D., 'Beyond permanency planning'. *Child Welfare*, Volume 59: 1980.

Melotte, C., 'The placement decisions'. *Adoption and Fostering*, Volume 95, No. 1: 1979.

Millham, S. and others, *Give and Take: a Study of CSV's Project for Young People in Care*. Dartington Social Research Unit: 1980.

Millham, S., Bullock, R., Hosie, K., and Haak, M., *Lost in Care*. Gower: 1986.

Mountford, C.S., *A Selected Review of Fostering Services*. Paper submitted to Director's Management Team, Warwickshire Social Services Department: 1989.

Packman, J., *The Child's Generation*. Blackwell and Robertson: 1975.

Packman, J., *The Child's Generation*. Blackwell and Robertson: 1981 (2nd edition).

Packman, J. and others, *Who Needs Care? Social Work Decisions About Children*. Basil Blackwell: 1986.

Parker, R., *Decisions in Child Care*. Allen and Unwin: 1966.

Parker, R., *Caring for Separated Children*. Macmillan: 1980.

Parker, R., *A Forward look at Research and Child Care*. School of Applied Social Studies, University of Bristol: 1987.

Parker, R., 'Residential care for children', in Sinclair, I. (ed.), *Residential Care: the Research Reviewed*. HMSO: 1988.

Parton, N., *The Politics of Child Abuse*. Macmillan: 1985.

Payne, C., 'Images of care'. *Social Work Today*: 3 October 1978.

Payne, C., 'Contradictions in care of children'. *Social Work Today*, 27 April 1987.

Pine, B., and Jacobs, M., 'The training of foster parents for work with adolescents', in Aldgate, J., Maluccio, A., and Reeves, C., (eds), *Adolescents in Foster Families*. Batsford: 1989.

Rowe, J., Caine, H., Hundleby, M., and Keane, A., *Long Term Foster Care*. Batsford: 1984.

Rowe, J., Hundleby, M., and Garnett, L., *Child Care Now*. BAAF: 1989.

Rowe, J., and Lambert, L., *Children Who Wait*. ABAA: 1973.

Rushton, A., 'Post-placement services for foster and adoptive parents – support, counselling and therapy?' *Journal of Child Psychology and Psychiatry*, Volume 30, No. 2: 1989.

Russell, P., 'Handicapped children', in Kahan, B. (ed.), *Child Care Research, Policy and Practice*. Hodder and Stoughton: 1989.

Rutter, M., *Maternal Deprivation Reassessed*. Penguin: 1981.

Shaw, M., and Hipgrave, T., *Specialist Fostering*. Batsford: 1983.

Shaw, M., and Hipgrave, T., 'Specialist fostering 1988 – a research study'. *Adoption and Fostering*, Volume 13, No. 3: 1989.

Small, J., 'Transracial placements, conflicts and contradictions', in Ahmed, J., Cheetham, J., and Small, J. (eds), *Social Work with Black Children and Their Families*. Batsford: 1986.

Smallridge, P., *The Warwickshire Direction*. Social Services Department, Warwickshire County Council: 1988.

Social Services Inspectorate, *Report of an Inspection of Boarding-Out Arrangements for Children in Warwickshire*. DHSS: 1987.

Social Services Inspectorate, *Social Services in a Multiracial Society*. HMSO: 1988.

Stein, M., and Carey, K., *Leaving Care*. Blackwell: 1986.

Strathclyde Regional Council, *Room to Grow*: 1979.

Stubbs, P., 'Professionalism and the adoption of Black children'. *British Journal of Social Work*, Volume 17, No. 5: 1987.

Thoburn, J., Murdoch, A., and O'Brien, A., *Permanence in Child Care*. Basil Blackwell: 1986.

Thoburn, J., and Rowe, J., 'A snapshot of permanent family placement'. *Adoption and Fostering*, Volume 12, No. 3: 1988.

Thomas, M., 'Fostering agreements, taking positive steps', in Aldgate, J. (ed.), *Using Written Agreements with Children and Families*. Family Rights Group: 1988.

Thorpe, D. and Bilson, A., 'The leaving care curve'. *Community Care*, No. 683: 1987.

Thorpe, D., Paley, S., and Green, C., *Out of Care*. George Allen and Unwin: 1980.

Tizard, B., and Phoenix, A., 'Black identity and transracial adoption'. *New Community*, April 1989.

Tomlinson, S., *A Sociology of Special Education*. Routledge and Kegan Paul: 1982

Trasler, G., *In Place of Parents*. Routledge and Kegan Paul: 1976.

Triseliotis, J., 'Growing up in foster care and after', in Triseliotis, J. (ed.), *New Developments in Foster Care and Adoption*. Routledge and Kegan Paul: 1980.

Triseliotis, J., 'Residential care from a historical perspective', in Wilkinson, J., and O'Hara, G. (eds), *Our Children: Residential and Community Care*. National Children's Bureau: 1988.

Triseliotis, J., 'Foster care outcomes: a review of key research findings. *Adoption and Fostering*, Volume 1, No. 3: 1989.

Utting, Sir William, *Children in the Public Care: a Review of Residential Child Care*. HMSO: 1991.

Verity, P., *Fostering in Warwickshire: Ability to Provide*. Unpublished report: 1988.

Vernon, J., and Fruin, D., *In Care: A Study of Social Work Decision Making*. National Children's Bureau: 1986.

Warnock Report, *Special Educational Needs*. Report of the Committee of Enquiry: 1978.

Warwickshire Director of Education, *Report to the Education (Finance and General Purposes) Sub Committee*: 3 July 1979(b).

Warwickshire Director of Education, *Report to the Education (Policy and Resources) Sub Committee*: 21 August 1979(a).

Warwickshire Director of Education, *Report to Education Committee*: 1980.

Warwickshire Director of Social Services, *Annual Report of Chief Officers, 1975/6*. Warwickshire County Council: 1976.

Warwickshire Director of Social Services, *Reorganisation of Children's Services*. Report to the Social Services Sub-Committee: March 1986.

Warwickshire Director of Social Services. *Report to the Social Services Committee*: April 1986.

Warwickshire Director of Social Services, *Transracial Placements, Report to Working Party on Services to Ethnic Minorities*: 1987.

Warwickshire Director of Social Services, *Report to Social Services Sub-Committee*: March 1988.

Warwickshire Social Services Department, *Report of the Working Party on Services to Adolescents*: 1983.

Warwickshire Social Services Department, *From Home to Family: the Warwickshire Direction*: 1987.

Warwickshire Social Services Department, *Services for Children: Substitute Family Care, Foster Parents*: 1987a.

Warwickshire Social Services Department, *Establishments, Operational Practice: NCH Retained Places*: 1987b.

Warwickshire Social Services Department, *Community Services, Operational Practice: Admission of Children into Care*: 1989.

Warwickshire Social Services Department, *Report of the Ethnic Minorities Working Party*: 1988.

Wedge, P. and Phelan, J., 'Moving towards a wider range of foster homes'. *Social Work Today*, 2 June 1988.

Wedge, P., and Thoburn, J., *Finding Families for 'Hard-to-Place' Children.* BAAF: 1986.

Weise, J., *Transracial Adoption.* Social Work Monograph 60, University of East Anglia: 1986.

Whittaker, D., Cook, J., Dunne, C., and Rockliffe, S., *The Experience of Residential Care from the Perspective of Children, Parents and Caregivers.* University of York: 1985.

Wolkind, S. and Rutter, M., 'Children who have been in care – an epidemiological study. *Journal of Child Psychology and Psychiatry*, Volume 14: 1973.

Index

References in the index are to childcare practice in Warwickshire unless otherwise stated.